More praise for *In the Shadow of the Epidemic:*

"In the second decade of AIDS, the short-term emergency solutions of the 8os are no longer enough; we need a way of living and staying uninfected for an indefinite future, about which many gay men are at best ambivalent. No one has risen to this new challenge more articulately than Walt Odets. *In the Shadow of the Epidemic,* already controversial, is essential reading for anyone who cares about AIDS prevention or about gay men. It is a moving, courageous, and profoundly humane book. And I believe it no exaggeration to say that it will save many lives."—Michael Warner, editor of *Fear of a Queer Planet*

"Dr. Odets's work is extraordinarily insightful, provocative, and courageous."—Benjamin Schatz, Executive Director, Gay and Lesbian Medical Association

"This will be *the* literature on the subject. *In the Shadow of the Epidemic* is a remarkable work. Odets's practice, his clarity of thought and introspection have provided us with a true gift."—Alvin Novick, Yale University and editor-in-chief of *AIDS & Public Policy Journal*

A series edited by Michèle Aina Barale, Jonathan Goldberg,

Michael Moon, and Eve Kosofsky Sedgwick

In the Shadow
of the Epidemic

BEING HIV-NEGATIVE IN THE AGE OF AIDS

Walt Odets

DUKE UNIVERSITY PRESS Durham 1995

© 1995 Duke University Press
All rights reserved
Printed in the United States of America on acid-free paper ∞
Typeset in Berkeley Medium by Tseng Information Systems, Inc.
Library of Congress Cataloging-in-Publication Data appear
on the last printed page of this book.
Second printing, 1995

for Robb

What will life do to us, if it did that to *him?*

Contents

Acknowledgments

There are so many who have contributed so much to the fight against AIDS, to the lives of so many in the gay communities, and to my life and work. These people have helped my patients die and survive, have helped me to survive, and have helped me to begin to understand the meanings of the epidemic, what survival might mean, and how survival might be lived. Thus, in an important sense, I might be considered editor of this work and they coauthors. I hope this note will stand as a small expression of gratitude for all they have contributed.

Ed Wolf, George Simmons, and Eric Rofes of Shanti Project; Catherine Maier at The San Francisco AIDS Foundation; Woody Castrodale, who is devoted to the understanding of HIV-negative issues and has contributed immensely to my understanding; Michael Isbell, Richard Elovich, and Daniel Wolfe of Gay Men's Health Crisis; Dana Van Gorder; Mark Cloutier; David Zuckerman; Tom Moon; Ken Pinhero, Rob Hopke, Jim Fishman, and Michael Crosby of Operation Concern; Irma Liberty, Carol Brosgart, Gary Feldman, Muriel Rose, and Suzanne Heininger of the Alta Bates-Herrick East Bay AIDS Center; Les Solomon; Bob Scott; Keith Barton; David Greenberg of Summit Adult Immunology; Einar Sunde; Linda Zaretsky of San Francisco's Tenderloin Clinic; Gary Lomax of Pacific Medical Center; Jane Beurger, Elena Moser, Scott Halem, and Scott Walton of the Pacific Center for Human Growth; Steve Graham, Lahr Bryer, and Joe DeMilia at Kaiser Permanente; Paul Preston; Rabbi Yoel Kahn; Rachel Schochet, who has made important research contributions to the understanding of HIV-negative gay men; Charles Dithrich; Robert Stern; Ron Henderson; Rob Marks and Jim Dilley at the University of California at San Francisco (UCSF) AIDS Health Project; Sam Blazer; Stephen Follansbee of Davies Medical Center; Jill and Tom Delbanco and Steve Cadwell, all of Boston, and all of whom have helped in the clarification of ideas; Tom Merrifield in Student Health Services at the University of California at Berkeley; Zalman Rosenfeld of the Marin AIDS Network; and Robert Hays at the Center for AIDS Prevention Studies.

There are also ten who have helped me by reading the manuscript as I have finished drafts, making suggestions and contributions that have been invaluable. They are Donald Abrams, Tim Teeter, Alvin Novick, Charles Dithrich, Dan DiVittorio, Katharine Muir, Eric Rofes, Will Johnston, Ben Schatz, and Ralph Dickinson.

Next, there are those who have had a personal hand in my survival, in itself no small contribution to the work. They are Ella Baff, John Badanes, Stephen Zollman, Leslie Sobelson, Linda Zaretsky, Justin Simon, and Robert Caramico. Donald, Tim, Al, and Dan, among my ten readers, have done double duty, and they belong here too.

Finally, there are my psychotherapy patients to thank. They have provided me not only with insight, but with an immense richness of experience, and I thank them for allowing me to be part of so many extraordinary lives.

In the Shadow of the Epidemic:
Being HIV-Negative in the Age of Aids

Introduction

A book about being HIV-negative and about issues of survival needs roots. A decade ago the most informed among us could have had no clue about the meaning of the title, and even now, though the literal meaning may be intelligible, the human meaning is perhaps still obscure—even for many of us living in the mainstream of the AIDS epidemic in the United States. I trace the personal roots of this book and its meaning back to the summer of 1985. On the north side of town, near the Golden Gate Bridge, I sat in the Silver Cloud Bar and Grill on Lombard Street. I was with a friend from graduate school, Joe Brewer, a man who suffered a terrible loss early in the epidemic and who, with a friend, Martin Delaney, had founded an organization to investigate and inform people about treatments for HIV, an organization now well known as Project Inform.

That night Joe was trying to enlist my volunteer help with a simple drug study—things were done quite informally in those days—and we also spoke about the relationship between the psychology and the politics of being gay. I had a lifelong aversion to political and sociological explanations. As an undergraduate in the sixties, I abandoned any hope of finding meaning in political activity and joined the departments of philosophy and religion. I studied Schopenhauer, Wittgenstein, Mahayana Buddhism, and Zen, and found what seemed genuine insight about the human plight and relative happiness in an absolutely apolitical solitude.

Like human life as a whole, homosexuality seemed to me understandable without resorting to politics or sociology. They elucidated nothing, I was sure, about a purely personal and psychological issue. That night Joe was simultaneously sonorous and relentless in a way that only Southerners can be (he is from Atlanta), and *he* was talking politics. Although his effort was characteristically intelligent and articulate, I was resistant.

I would not have my feelings politicized. What he said, more or less, was that AIDS had changed whatever used to be true about my position, and these days if you were not politically active, you were not gay: You were just a *homosexual,* and he lingered on that last word with a kind of unholy marriage of smile and snarl that left no doubt that that was not what you wanted to be. The government, and particularly the Food and Drug Administration, was killing gay men wholesale by their neglect of the AIDS epidemic, and homosexuals who were not part of the solution were, if not *exactly* part of the problem, at least colluding with it. After dinner Joe walked me across the street to my car. We talked another moment, I kissed him good night, and we hugged.

Had I looked over his shoulder at that moment, I would have seen the summer fog churning above the Golden Gate and advancing up Lombard Street. On such nights, it would tumble like a monstrous, slow-motion tidal wave, a sight that sometimes reminded me of my childhood terror at black-and-white movies in which a dam broke in the hills above a small town, and a wall of water washed children, their pets, and their mother's furniture into oblivion. Still unaware of tonight's foggy advance, I got into my car, made an illegal U-turn at Webster Street, and headed west on Lombard. In three blocks I was suddenly in it—summer's gray, saturated wall of fog that was sluggishly, silently burying San Francisco. A bit startled, I turned on the windshield wipers and the radio. Bob Dylan sang from *Highway 61 Revisited,* and I laughed at myself for being surprised that, in June, the fog should be taking the town. I had, I thought to myself, too many assumptions and expectations about the world and about how things were supposed to be in it. But I still did not know of the feelings I would come to have about the AIDS epidemic, which at that moment was also crawling across San Francisco, leaving behind not the quiet of fog, but tracks of desperation, grief, and anger that might never be eradicated.

Two years later, in the summer months of 1987, I found myself three days a week at a dilapidated desk volunteering as housing coordinator for the Committee for the March on Washington for Lesbian and Gay Rights. The event was to take place in October of that year. The committee shared a storefront on Market Street, a block from the center of the Castro District, with the Names Project quilt people. Sitting at my desk, which was up against one wall and facing out across the large room, I had a constant view of the cutters, sewers, and riveters. All were working to produce, catalogue, and assemble memorial panels for those who had died of AIDS.

My job for the march committee involved coordinating with the Washington, D.C., committee to provide free housing for people who wished to attend but had financial limitations. It was exciting and energizing as these things are with their human contact, camaraderie, and common purpose. But in contrast to this success, there was something else very powerful going on in the storefront room on Market Street that summer, and it was on the walls and floors, in the faces of men and women working on the quilts, and, finally, I realized, deep inside of me. It was the overwhelming experience of AIDS and the toll it was taking, and it was the dawning realization that we were half a decade into the epidemic and it was *not* supposed to have gone on this long. Each panel of that quilt was about a person, and one could read into each a childhood, an adolescence, aspirations, successes, disappointments, family, lovers, and friends. Each panel, however simple, seemed the story of a full human life, but each had also ended in the awful stranglehold of AIDS. Though I don't think that in three months I actually heard "AIDS," "epidemic," or "death" spoken out loud, they were a palpable presence in the room. It was often unbearable to look hour after hour at the thousands of panels that hung and lay on every surface. And, as if that were not enough, every afternoon, the U.S. Postal Service and United Parcel Service arrived with hand truck after hand truck stacked with boxes of new panels, sent from around the world by surviving lovers, family, or friends for addition to the quilt.

Although the panels are intended to memorialize and celebrate the lives of those who have died, the stacks of unopened boxes, awaiting attention from overworked staff, began to make me think less and less of celebration, and more and more of newly arrived corpses. Handcarts bounced and rattled their way inexorably past my desk every afternoon, and stacked on them were not boxes, but coffins, mostly filled with gay men. These arriving panels were piled wherever they would fit, waiting to be unwrapped, catalogued, edged with canvas, and installed in their designated positions in the quilt. If the panels seemed corpses, those who worked on them seemed more and more like morticians, readying man after man for a mass funeral of absolutely staggering and unexpected proportions. Our room felt tinier and tinier with every delivery, and I thought to myself, "It is 1987, these deliveries are not going to stop, and we are in terrible, terrible trouble."

It was 3:30 in the afternoon, late in August, and time for more deliveries. In their daily ritual procession, the corpses bounced and rattled past the dilapidated desk of the Coordinator for Free Housing. Throughout those months I had thought repeatedly about the conversation with Joe two years ago in the Silver Cloud. I had been slowly realizing it was not Joe's effort to politicize that I resisted that night; nor was I avoiding volunteer work for Project Inform. It was his *grief* that I could not accept and did not want. Though Joe had already lost his closest friend to HIV, I had not yet lost anyone important. I read about the epidemic, heard about it from friends who had friends, and watched the truncated, simplistic reports on television. But I wasn't living it. I did not want to, and I was not going to let Joe make me. In 1985, I was still among those who were not "personally" affected by HIV, and I could still resist acknowledging the incredible size, horror, and unmanageability of what was going on. In the Silver Cloud with Joe I had unconsciously entertained the fantasy that I would never feel his grief as my own. I already had enough grief for my own reasons: I had lost both of my parents by age sixteen, and, between 1981 and 1985, had lived through another five major deaths, all unrelated to AIDS (which, from the retrospective perch of 1993 is a peculiar irony). I *would not* take on more grief from the epidemic. I wanted to deny it was possible, and for the time being my stance had the seamless plausibility that only denial can bestow to protect us from life's most awful facts.

As it happened, only a few months after my meeting with Joe, a man with whom I was in love suddenly seroconverted. I had told Joe about him—and his good health—in the Silver Cloud. That he was only HIV-positive and not yet ill made no difference. I knew enough death to feel the loss long before it made itself literal, and I was stunned with grief. A half decade later, over dinner in the Castro, I told Joe about this, and I apologized to him for my rejection of his grief that night in the Silver Cloud.

Though still allergic to organized politics, by 1987 I had become very gay in Joe's sense of things, and that is one reason that I found myself sitting day after day in the colorful morgue on Market Street. By August, the job of the Coordinator for Free Housing had become too big for one, and I took on a co-coordinator. David lived in a transient hotel at Market and Fifth streets, and had just moved from Boston. His lover had died there two months before, after a last year of awful illness. The lover's parents had thrown David out of the house the two had shared for seven years, and taken everything. He had to get out of town, he told me. And he was a painter, he was HIV-positive, and his health was just now beginning to fail. He was a huge help on the job, he was a good companion, and we shared a sense of the irony of our work—of a triumphant march committee buried hip-deep in corpses.

In the cool evenings after "work," David and I would walk up Market to The Zuni, where we sat by the fire if we could. They roast chickens in that fire. David and I both liked white Burgundies and often split a bottle with dinner. After one glass, a bewilderment would begin to smear the intelligence of his face, and I could suddenly see what he disguised during the day: the toll of the last years in Boston, and of what he anticipated for himself over the next one, or two, or maybe three years.

After dinner we would often try to walk off the food and wine, as happy to be out in the chilly air and on our own as we had been, two hours before, to come into the warmth and sociability of the restaurant. These nights too, here on the south side of town, the fog often tumbled in and encircled the base of Sutro Tower perched on the top of Twin Peaks. The tower's flashing red tips poked out above the fog, seeming to call silently for help, like the beacons of a life raft, becalmed and stranded in mid-Pacific. Fog, second only to a heavy snow in muffling the rattles and roars of urban life, would on rare nights drop all the way down the east slopes of the Peaks and into the Castro, and on those nights it would bring silence to this troubled part of town too. One night it was very wet and quiet, and the saturated air around us hung as if ready to fall to the ground with the thud of a wet blanket big enough to cover the city. David and I walked past a row of elegant Victorian houses, and I thought to myself that the interior light no longer brought images to my mind of happy, gay domesticity living itself out in the warmth implied by the orange glow. It seemed to me that now there was surely only despair and pain in these houses, and that it was only the mercy of the soft, muffling fog that kept some audible evidence of that truth from us. As I had these thoughts, David startled me by suddenly waving his hand grandly around the neighborhood as if perhaps he owned it and breaking the silence with an interrogation: "Do you think life for these people is still as it was supposed to have been?"

"Supposed to have been?" I asked.

"I meant before everyone got sick," he said with annoyance at my stupidity. I had no idea how to answer him.

During the day, I protected myself from being overwhelmed by not really looking at the quilt panels. I don't know exactly what David did, but I could not look, unless I was willing to cry. I treated the panels as mosaics—allowing in color, surface, and pattern, but no information. I avoided actually reading anything. The simplest words—*Robert I Miss You,* or *May 17, 1958–June 3, 1987*—would sometimes sweep me down rivers of grief, mostly personal, and these episodes, now more and more frequent, cut deeply into my usefulness for the march, and into every corner of my sense of well-being.

It all got in anyway. I sat there for three months and absorbed almost every detail of everything in front of me, though I repressed much of it at the time, and have to this day. Often a panel would burst through my vagueness with undeniable clarity about what it was and what it meant, and the experience gave clear meaning to the idea that something might sear itself into one's mind. One day a new arrival hung across from me— it was for "Paul," and there was a last name too, but I do not remember it. Rendered in cloth and thread, a too thin, androgynous figure stood cloaked in black, holding an umbrella, and a raven stood beside him on the ground. The embroidered inscription in front of them read, "Last night it did not seem as if today it would be raining." My grief suddenly flooded out, as if having reached some critical limit of pressure, and I knew at that moment that it *was* raining, and that I still was not able to bear letting all of that in—or out.

I was continuing to deny what the epidemic meant and would in-creasingly mean to me, and in that moment I knew that I had to think very hard about AIDS and my feelings about it, or eventually I would be lost. I cannot say in exactly what sense I thought that might happen, but the danger was clear and palpable. As a psychologist, in psycho-therapy myself for many years, I knew that I came to the epidemic with too many serious losses stretching back to early childhood, and that I was easy prey for an event like this one. In that moment, staring at the black figure and the bird and their lament, it suddenly felt as if I were being sucked helplessly into a churning wake of devastation and grief that AIDS trailed behind itself like a marauding, outlaw ship in no big hurry to leave the scene of the crime.

Those are the personal roots. It was then that I started to work on this book, in contemplation at least, for I knew that my personal survival de-pended on the best possible clarification of my feelings. I had determined with reasonable certainty by this time that I was still HIV-negative, a fact the significance of which I did not yet understand. But I was aware of the peculiarity of not feeling more consistently fortunate about that. Thus my first piece was a 20-page paper on the subject of HIV-negative men. It was about being HIV-negative, feeling ambivalent about that, about grief, loss and survival, and about the conflict and confusions of an HIV-negative "identity." I sent the paper to a handful of friends, feeling that I had clarified only the tiniest corners of these murky issues, but I was overwhelmed by the enthusiastic response. People felt that for the first time they had a voice for similar feelings, and were immensely appreciative.

As I understood new issues, or old ones better, the paper expanded, the mailing list grew, and I began a busy schedule of speaking engagements on the subject. By early 1990, I had, by word of mouth, received about 600 requests for copies of what was by then an 80-page paper. One speaking engagement was at the monthly meeting of Bay Area Physicians for Human Rights, a gay physicians' organization in San Francisco. A member of the audience, Donald Abrams, assistant director of the AIDS program at San Francisco General Hospital, approached me. Although I had submitted an abstract on the subject of "HIV-Negative Psychological Issues" for the 1990 International AIDS Conference in San Francisco, it was rejected for presentation. Donald felt it was an important subject, and was chairman of the conference "Track D Committee," concerned with topics about "Social Impact and Response." Through his intervention, I did make a presentation at the conference, to a group of about 2,400, and from this event came another 600 requests for copies of the paper. By the end of 1991 I had printed and mailed more than 3,000, responding to requests from people in Australia, New Zealand, several African countries, every country of Western Europe (except Spain, for reasons I do not know), and virtually every state in the union.

Paralleling this enthusiasm and interest was much criticism about the impropriety—or sheer effrontery—of my addressing the issues of HIV-negative men while men with AIDS were dying. Surely, the feelings went, those lucky enough to have escaped AIDS could keep their whimpering down so the truly sick could be attended to. A fellow psychotherapist in San Francisco, Tom Moon, related a similar response to his proposal for offering HIV-negative workshops at a mental health conference for gay men. He was told by a member of the steering committee, "This is like Germans wanting to get together after the war to congratulate themselves on not being Jewish." *Out/Look,* the presumably progressive (and now defunct) lesbian and gay quarterly, rejected two manuscript submissions from me on the subject of HIV-negative issues. The first, in 1989, described my paper as "moot" without further explanation; and in 1990 the editorial board felt the subject was "too controversial." Under new editorship, they did finally publish a piece about "survivor guilt" in 1991.

In 1990, however, Eric Rofes, then executive director of San Francisco's Shanti Project, read a copy of my paper and wanted to discuss the possibility of my consulting on HIV-negative issues for Shanti staff and volunteers. I was surprised. A longtime Shanti staff member, Ed Wolf, was *the* pioneer in such work in San Francisco. But this was something he did personally and not as Shanti staff. For this powerful AIDS service agency to place its prestige, personnel, and funding behind HIV-negative concerns seemed quite radical at the time. Eric invited me to meet for breakfast early on a weekday morning at what I later learned was his customary window table in Castro Street's Cove Cafe.

"How will I know you?" he asked.

"I will be the one looking for someone," I offered.

"That will never work," Eric objected. "Everyone there is looking for someone. That is the whole milieu of the Castro."

We did find each other, and though I had barely managed to struggle out of bed at this hour, Eric had already been to the gym and was full of oxygen and energy. We had an extended discussion, and he wondered aloud to me if Shanti's backing a project on HIV-negative issues would not open "a political Pandora's box."

"Oh, I'm sure it will," I said.

"Let's do it anyway and see what happens," he responded, to my surprise.

I think Eric's courage on this matter, and Donald Abrams's at about the same time, marked a watershed for the politics, if not the substance, of attention to HIV-negatives in San Francisco. In the past few years there has been a greater and greater acceptance of the importance of these problems, both in terms of human suffering and in terms of ongoing new HIV infections. Over the past two years, Shanti has done a number of workshops and retreats on HIV-negative issues. Other important mental health agencies, including the University of California at San Francisco's AIDS Health Project and California Pacific Medical Center's Operation Concern are now providing similar, although very limited, services.

At this point, there is one intolerable simplification that I must confront, lest it obscure too much truth. That is the idea that attention to the problems and concerns of negatives is an abandonment of those who are HIV-positive or ill with AIDS and *necessarily* fuels divisiveness in gay communities. To deny that there are differences on some issues and concerns between those who are HIV-positive and those who are not is a denial of the obvious. In my psychotherapy practice I work with both (though more with those who have HIV), and I have come to feel that uninfected men are significantly underrepresented in the psychological literature and in the concerns and understanding of psychotherapists working with them. This is particularly true with regard to psychosocial issues such as the HIV-negative gay "identity," disenfranchisement of negative men in larger gay communities, and survivor guilt. Neglect of these issues can only bear destructively on the psychological well-being of these individuals and the future of gay communities as a whole.

Just as there are differences between HIV-positives and HIV-negatives, there are important commonalities. *All* gay men now live with the epidemic. On survival, loss, and grief, negatives certainly hold no exclusive contract. Many men have suffered more loss and survived more death than any one man could be expected to endure, and my book is written for all who have survived and who have lost, regardless of whether or not they must also deal with HIV or AIDS within their own bodies. My effort is to bear witness to what we are living and dying through, to try to describe it in useful ways, and to clarify some of its meanings. There is only one possible approach for this task: to try to comprehend the AIDS disaster and human life as a whole, undivided by fear, prejudice, and politics. Being "HIV-negative"—which is to say ordinary and uninfected—has meaning only because others are positive. If uninfected men, in loathing or in fear, abandon those who are HIV-positive, they must eventually see that they feel only self-loathing and flee only themselves. Just as negatives have no exclusive on survival, positives have no exclusive on illness, suffering, and death—although their timetable is often much more pressing. Any human sense and meaning I am able to make of the HIV-negative experience must also make sense of the lives of those who are positive, who are dying, and who are dead.

I have just said that this book is written for survivors who live with and without HIV in their own bodies. My concern with survival has another meaning too, and one especially important for uninfected men, so many of whom now live in loneliness, denial, or fear. The notion of *other kinds of survival,* the subject of chapter 9, is meant to open up for discussion the meaning of survival itself. In the most important senses of survival, being uninfected with HIV is only a small beginning. We must find paths that allow survival not only as human organisms, but as communities of *human beings,* regardless of serostatus, who are able to live passionately and intimately, to love, and to make lives in other regards worth living. Survival, in this sense, has nothing to do with our antibody status, and nothing to do with how much time we have on the planet—it has only to do with how much *heart* we are able to discover within ourselves and bring to our daily lives.

I dedicate my work to all of us who have tried to be who we are by living from our hearts, and have tried to live with passion. Robb did that until he died on a Monday night in the early winter of 1992, and this work is especially for him, that he might understand why I did not die with him.

A Word about the Writer and the Reader

I am a clinical psychologist, a gay man, and a member of the gay community in San Francisco. I am writing here as a psychotherapist who has worked individually and in groups with many gay men over the past years, and who has lost more than three dozen psychotherapy patients to AIDS. As a gay man, I have also lost a number of close friends, and as a member of the gay community, I have seen the awful toll this epidemic has taken on those who have so far survived. My work here is largely for the general, nonprofessional reader who is concerned with AIDS and the issues that now face gay men and the future of the gay communities. But it is, I fear, also a work about the sad future of this country as a whole. If we continue to respond to AIDS along the paths of ignorance, hatred, and neglect that we have tried for the past twelve years, the gay communities will no longer be alone in the tragedy explored here, but merely a harbinger.

Because I believe psychological clarification is a useful approach to the issues of the AIDS epidemic—both within gay communities and society at large—I also write in part for the psychologist and psychotherapist. However, I have tried throughout to keep specialized psychological language to a minimum, and have made every effort to explain it when I could not find better words with which to express my ideas.

The text contains much first-hand clinical material, and it comes from several sources. When the material is from other than my own clinical work, the footnoted reference identifies the source. Material that is unreferenced is from my clinical work, from notes made immediately after psychotherapy sessions. Though I rarely take notes during sessions, notes made after sessions help record what has happened, my thoughts on the material, and thoughts about where the therapy is going. I am then able to refer to these notes before the next session. Because I use a word processor, I can search for particular topics or issues, and this has been useful for both the clinical work and my writing. Obviously, every effort has been made to conceal the identity of the individuals quoted in these passages, and all names, as well as specific biographical material that might allow identification is falsified. I have made a careful attempt, however, to avoid distortions of meaning resulting from this process. Where absolute concealment of identity seemed difficult or impossible without distorting meaning, or when the material quoted was extensive, I described to the psychotherapy patient the nature of the project and received permission to use the material.

I write as a clinical psychologist and an observer of people in everyday life. I am not interested in "scientific" psychology that "objectifies" and quantifies data, and I have found little of such work useful in understanding the epidemic, our feelings about it, or what to do about it. Rather, I write from personal observation, understanding, and opinion. It is my impression that psychology and human life are a subjective experience (from both sides of the "therapeutic couch") and that most of what we can know of importance about them necessarily rests in feelings, impressions, opinions, and human (not statistical) probabilities. I state here for the record: Anything in this book that is not a quotation from others or presented as an objective fact, is my opinion, impression, or personal understanding.

Many early readers of the manuscript asked me to stop repeatedly referring to *HIV-negative gay men* or *uninfected gay men,* the cumbersome phrases I had used in earlier drafts because they are mostly what the book is about. Hereafter, I refer to them as *negative men, negatives,* or *uninfected men,* and the reader is to understand that they are also gay, and if their sex is not specified, men; I do the same for *positives.* The use of these monikers, however, should not be construed as a suggestion that the serostatus of an individual is an adequate characterization of anyone in toto. Robb, to whom this book is dedicated, once said to me that "gay rights" were a hopelessly shallow but necessary waypoint on the road to human rights. I would say the same regarding our current distinctions in many gay communities between positives and negatives or the infected and the uninfected. If we within the gay communities are not able to emerge on the far side of this epidemic as relatively whole human beings, we will have lost both the battle and our war. If distinctions of serostatus were not necessary to clarify my thoughts, I would have preferred to speak simply of *humans.*

Chapter 1
Why We Need a Book about
Being HIV-Negative

Look at me! Orange icing no longer tastes the way it used to, the ride to the plaza is no fun, nothing satisfies, except sometimes the apricots which blaze reminiscently of your hair & now I have put hundreds of copies of your photograph up on my wall (I make myself look at each one although they are all the same), the word "betrothed" appears in my silliest dreams, and my hands no longer strike me as a very ordinary man's hands. How peculiar that such a dangerous thing might happen in love. When my hands no longer strike me as ordinary, it seems inconceivable what might next occur.—Ippy Gizzi, from Letters to Pauline [1]

During the past decade, the gay communities in the United States have made a sad and lonely expedition into deep space, a perilous undertaking against an apparently indomitable enemy that seems not even close to finishing its destructive work. Long before this expedition began, astronomers had hypothesized a theory about *dark companions:* invisible planets that travel unseen beside visible planets, and explain observed gravitational phenomena that cannot otherwise be understood. Today there are many dark companions following gay men on their journey through the AIDS epidemic, lurking in the complex shadows of our perceptions, our denied perceptions, and other corners of our inner space.

One dark companion—still only poorly perceived—is the complex social and psychological epidemic among those gay men who are still uninfected with HIV and might survive the AIDS epidemic itself. We in the gay communities have not *completely* ignored this issue. But we have denied and underestimated virtually every aspect of the AIDS epidemic: how long it would last, how many it would take, how awful the process would be, and what legacy it would leave for survivors. Our attention to the needs of survivors—who are mostly HIV-negative and are the primary subject of my book—has been based on a huge underestimation of the nature and severity of the problems facing these people. As a result, we now have in the gay male and bisexual communities of uninfected men a second, completely uncontrolled epidemic—a psychological one—that threatens the health and welfare of millions of Americans.

This psychological epidemic most severely affects an unknown number of bisexual and gay men who are not (or reasonably believe they are not) infected with HIV. This is potentially a huge population. Although levels of HIV infection seem to be increasing, current figures from the San Francisco Department of Health continue to suggest that about 50 percent of San Francisco's gay men are still uninfected with HIV. Nationally, the percentages of uninfected gay men must be much higher, especially in nonurban areas, and it may be reasonably conjectured that in the United States there are as many as five to ten uninfected gay men for every gay man who is infected. Such figures are shocking—because of their imprecision, and because they remind us how many men *are* infected. But they also shock because, at a time when many within gay communities feel—if not actually *think*—that everyone is dead, dying, or at risk of dying of AIDS, we are also reminded how many men are still uninfected.

These uninfected gay men with psychological issues comprise the group often described as the "worried well." But more than a decade into the AIDS epidemic itself, there are many among these worried well who have a huge part of their lives and feelings wrapped up in the tragedy of AIDS. In many cases, negatives have a psychological experience—a personal and social identity—that is more like that of a sick or dying man than many who are HIV-positive. There is, however, an anomaly here: a "worried well" in the grips of its own epidemic. The very term is a collusion with many gay men's own denial about the effects of the AIDS epidemic. The San Francisco mayor's office has said that by 1990 more San Franciscans had died of AIDS than all the San Franciscans who died in the four great wars of the twentieth century, *combined and quadrupled.*[2] And most of these deaths are from within the gay communities. Is it conceivable, in a social event of this magnitude, that survivors in these communities might be merely "worried" or that they could be "well"?

All gay men live with HIV and AIDS, whether the virus now exists in their own bodies or in the bodies of those they love, live and work with, identify with, and sometimes fear. Being gay means being profoundly affected by the epidemic, and for those who feel they are not, I can only again mention denial. Denial not only exists within the individual, but within society at large. Broad social denial colludes powerfully with the denial of those who live in the middle of the epidemic and who must protect themselves from seemingly unbearable psychic pain. Denied or not, being gay and being uninfected is now *a condition*, not the absence of one. Being uninfected is a personal and social identity, like being gay, and it must be similarly clarified, consolidated, and acknowledged in the world. Being uninfected thus involves precisely the kind of "coming out" process that being gay does. Ed Wolf, longtime San Francisco AIDS worker, was the first to explicitly describe this idea to me:

> Early on in the epidemic we all were all running around trying to take care of people with AIDS: we were running our heads off. And one day sitting in a hot tub with four other guys who were all talking about their medication—they all had AIDS, except for me—I started thinking, that I'd never discussed my serostatus with any of them. I'm really in the closet about this—about being HIV-negative. I'm ashamed to admit this to them. It's really like coming out of the closet all over again: Hey, I'm HIV-negative, this is who I am, this is me, and we can't be friends unless you know about that. I thought when I *came out* the first time—as gay—that this was the big thing. But now I realize that I've got to come out all over again, and I've just been denying to myself the real importance of doing that.[3]

Personal denial like Ed's has been almost universally supported within the gay communities, which needed to direct their resources to infected men. But we within gay communities have also lacked an explicit understanding of HIV-negative issues, and, in many cases, the individuals in charge of public policy and AIDS education programs have been exercising personal denial about AIDS and what it has meant to them. One unexamined assumption underlying much of our denial is that AIDS is simply another medical issue, like cancer. Those without the disease are not part of the "affected population." But the AIDS epidemic is now an event—despite its inequitable concentration in relatively discrete communities—that keeps company with the two World Wars and the Great Depression as a psychosocial event of twentieth-century world history. In such events it is not only those on the front lines, but the entire society, that is ultimately involved in important human ways.

Why We Have Denied the "HIV-Negative" Condition

On & on as if hell were never ending (and it is, by legend, and I'm in it) or more never ending even than heaven, its obese rival. Standing here in hell I have recounted my purposes for life over and over with as much rhapsodic anguish as a little candle, blessing myself as I touch my forehead with the back of my hand, that I at least am not a child of this house, these ridiculous half-men who have only the anus half left and that is what they show me.—Ippy Gizzi, from Letters to Pauline [4]

In the first decade of the epidemic, a period characterized by shock, despair, and emergency, it has often seemed selfish, inappropriate, or simply ridiculous for the uninfected to have any important feelings *about themselves*. Feelings about oneself seemed the exclusive right of those who were infected, sick, or dying, particularly if the feelings were going to demand time or resources. In 1988, before virtually any public recognition of an HIV-negative identity—although even then it was a well established reality—I participated in a panel discussion titled "AIDS and Seronegative Gay Men." It was astonishing to see the evening devoted to a discussion of those with HIV and AIDS. Virtually the entire panel and participating audience drifted irresistibly into an authentically concerned, but programmatically inappropriate, analysis of the problems of those dealing with AIDS itself. Those without HIV could not experience their feelings about their own lives as worthy of discussion or worthy of the concern and attention of others. This is an attitude widely felt in the gay communities of uninfected men—and is *sometimes* supported by the resentment or anger of HIV-positives—and it has contributed to the broadly based denial of HIV-negative issues.

In many ways, uninfected men have accepted a structure like that of families in which one child is treated as healthy, "good," and unproblematic. The parents, absorbed by their own problems—including another child, who is perceived as sick or needy—come to take the good child and his apparent needlessness for granted. The entire family's organization—the distribution of responsibilities and structuring of relationships—comes to rely on the good child's apparent lack of needs, and, often, on his overtly caretaking role. When the good child does finally express needs, his beleaguered parents become angered by what seems a betrayal. Uninfected men have become, in the haunted, beleaguered family of the gay and bisexual communities, something like the "needless" child.

During the first years of the epidemic, there was good sense in gay communities adopting such an arrangement with its needless children. Infected men suffered and died in ways that left one speechless. Resources were limited beyond reason, given the wealth of this and other nations. When and where demands on resources by the infected and the uninfected have overlapped, it has seemed unimaginable to direct them to the uninfected. This is all true, but it does not address the fact that we have not even acknowledged the problems of the uninfected, much less clarified them in useful ways. Furthermore, there are resources available to the uninfected that will not take away from the infected. As one example, few psychotherapists can work exclusively with HIV-positive men, both because the HIV-positive community seeking psychotherapy is too limited and because the work is too emotionally difficult. Therefore, therapists working with gay men in general have an opportunity to work with uninfected men, and this mandates some clear definition of their problems. But a report from the San Francisco AIDS Foundation makes public policy regarding survivors clear: "There appears to be no plan for assisting the gay community or city [of San Francisco] at large in coping with the resulting psychological consequences [of the AIDS epidemic].[5]

There is a second important reason that the distress of uninfected men has been denied. We now often hear about "survivor guilt," though much of what is meant by the term is unclear. It is, however, certainly one of the cornerstones of the psychological epidemic among uninfected men, and it has played a central role in the denial of psychological distress among negatives. If an individual feels ambivalence or guilt for having simply survived those dead from AIDS, imagine how impossible it will be to think and talk about the kinds of feelings now seen routinely in uninfected men: that they are depressed, anxious, and lonely in their "wellness"; they are having a hard time surviving, and for many survival is so difficult they sometimes wish they had not survived and sometimes hope they will not. Despite the contribution of survivor guilt to often disabling anxiety and depression—and, in complex ways, to unprotected sex—such feelings are difficult to think and talk about, and are virtually impossible to ask for help with in the middle of a disaster like the epidemic. Woody Castrodale, a San Franciscan who has thought deeply about HIV-negative issues, wrote me about an HIV-negative group he facilitated, and the difficulty the group had addressing its purposes. Clearly, feelings of survivor guilt are described here.

Thank you for sending me a copy of your paper, *The Impact of AIDS on Uninfected Gay and Bisexual Men* . . . all I had was the first four pages of an older version of the paper . . . which I am in the habit of reading to the group every four weeks or so, just to remind us all of our mandate, or "purpose" in meeting. . . . It serves to wake us up, once again, to the fact that we do have lives of our own to live.

It is so easy, and in some sense comfortable for us to slip into talking about friends who are sick, friends who are dying, or partners who are struggling with HIV. The drama of death and sickness attracts our attention. And I have to gently . . . remind them to talk about themselves, to address directly the issues of what it feels like to be living as an uninfected gay man. Reading the beginning of your paper together, as a group, helps [us] comprehend that our own lives are real, and that we need to talk about and express ideas which are "politically incorrect" in the outside world.

Many different issues continue to arise in the group. One which seems to always be there in the background is the issue of telling the truth about how we really feel, as opposed to how uninfected gay men are "supposed" to feel and act in the world. We have been startled at times to realize that how we actually feel, when we express it in words, comes out sounding not so nice, not so proper, and quite "incorrect."

But the expressing of our actual feelings has had some obvious effects, which almost everyone in the group has mentioned: most notably the reduction of anxiety and guilt feelings. . . . What I have noticed, myself, as facilitator, is that over a period of months certain men have "come to life" again, woken up, started to seem less confused, more alive, more actively engaged, and less depressed. And these things happen to me, also.[6]

It is not only the understandable draw of the AIDS epidemic itself, but survivor guilt—experienced as discomfort with a life that one values and wishes to improve, or with having a life *at all*—that motivates the "drift" Castrodale talks about. The group's difficulty with trying to remain on its own HIV-negative issues is apparent in the need for a monthly rereading of four pages that describes nothing more than what group members are *themselves* experiencing. Uninfected men routinely have difficulty recognizing, acknowledging, and addressing their own problems, even when those problems are obvious and close to destroying viable lives.

That complex and difficult but largely denied feelings exist commonly in gay HIV-negative communities should be apparent to any psychologically astute observer. Because so much denial has been exercised against the evidence, it is worth providing some data on the subject. Much literature—though most of it more concerned with issues of bereavement and grief than with HIV-negative issues per se—now exists to document a psychological epidemic among uninfected men.[7] James Dilley, director of the University of California at San Francisco's AIDS Health Project, summed up the situation in 1988:

> A critical concern is the impact of bereavement and anticipatory grief on a variety of populations: PWA's [persons with AIDS], PWARC's [persons with AIDS-related complex], seropositives *and those in their social networks* [emphasis added]. . . . Indications are that people undergoing stress of this magnitude show high levels of psychological distress, as well as physical illness. Among those harmful health outcomes are demoralization, a sense of helplessness, sleep disorders, irritability, increased use of tranquilizers and sleeping pills, and reliance on mental health and medical care.[8]

Other researchers describe anxiety-related symptoms, including panic attacks, obsessive-compulsive disorders, and hypochondriasis, sometimes of sufficient severity to impair social or occupational functioning.[9] Some men experience a "posttraumatic stress"-like syndrome, symptoms of demoralization, and sleep disturbance—all proportionate, in one study, to bereavement episodes.[10] In some men, recreational drug use and sedative use have been shown to increase proportionately to bereavement episodes, and men with one or more bereavements are four to five times more likely to seek mental health assistance in connection with concerns and anxiety about their own health than men who have suffered no bereavements.[11] In New York, a study attempting to recruit healthy gay men as control subjects found that one-third to one-half of this "healthy" group actually qualified for a psychiatric diagnosis of "Adjustment Disorder with Depressed or Anxious Features," a diagnosis describing reactions to stressful life events.[12]

Psychologist Rachel Schochet conducted a study of HIV-negative gay men living in San Francisco and found that *nearly half* those responding had sought counseling or psychotherapy within the prior year. Among all respondents there was a significant relationship between depression or anxiety in reaction to severe life trauma and the experiencing of multiple deaths. According to Schochet, multiple losses are significantly related to doubts that one is, himself, actually HIV-negative, and to engagement in unprotected sex. In total, more than half the respondents reported "possibly safe" or "clearly unsafe" sexual practices within the year prior to the study.[13]

My own clinical practice confirms all these observations. I have seen innumerable examples of psychological problems among gay men that seven years ago would have been unusual and noteworthy, but are now so common that they pass almost without comment. Men are completely isolated for the first time in their adult lives, afraid to become involved with anyone as friend or lover, for fear that he, too, will turn out to be positive or will die. Men with no psychiatric history now often appear profoundly depressed, anxious, uncertain about their futures, or sexually dysfunctional; some, despite their uninfected condition, engage repeatedly in unprotected sex; and some, despite their uninfected condition, live in nearly every detail like a dying man—disoriented, piecemeal, and with no assumption of a future. Such experiences are clear evidence of feelings not being talked about, feelings that are part of the current psychological epidemic in HIV-negative gay communities.

How widespread are such serious psychological difficulties among uninfected gay men? Does a false impression arise in the erroneous generalization from a self-selected "clinical" population (those who actually go for mental health assistance) to the population of uninfected gay men in general? Such questions are often raised legitimately, but are also often raised in the hope that such problems are not widespread, or in the unconscious hope that the problems of uninfected men—like so many feelings about the epidemic—can simply be denied. My impression of the psychological condition of gay communities today is certainly partially based on my clinical work with gay men. These men are in psychotherapy not only for serious problems arising from the epidemic, but also for developmental reasons—personal growth, relationship, and identity issues. Much of my impression also comes from personal, not clinical, experience with gay communities, and with nonclinical groups and organizations to whom I often speak. While many men seem to not now be experiencing serious psychological difficulty in response to the epidemic, *many are.* Among those who are, many are still not seeking or receiving mental health attention for all the traditional reasons that psychological help is shunned, because psychological distress has been normalized among gay men in the age of AIDS, and because gay communities have conspired within themselves to deny the impact of the epidemic, particularly for those who do not actually have HIV. We must explore the reasons why doubt might even be entertained about the potential psychological consequences of surviving a severe, sustained event that has destroyed thousands of men in their twenties, thirties, and forties, and threatens millions more lives in the United States alone. Many of the features of the psychological epidemic are unique to uninfected gay men. These include the "HIV-negative identity," both personal and social; feelings of disenfranchisement from the gay community; isolation from both HIV-positive men and the heterosexual mainstream; and certain aspects of survivor guilt. No other group shares these issues, on the whole, with uninfected gay men.

On the other hand, some of the experience of uninfected gay men is shared with many others living in and around the AIDS epidemic. Depression, anxiety, hypochondriasis, *some* aspects of survivor guilt, and loss and grief are experienced by many who are not uninfected gay men. Not the least among these are many HIV-positive gay men, who are frequently survivors over a considerable period of time, experience much loss, and must, at the same time, deal with the burden of HIV within their own bodies. There are others too: the lesbian communities, who have done so much for us in gay male communities; the bisexual communities that share much of our experience; and the health and mental health care providers of every sort, gay and straight, whose contributions defy any adequate expression of gratitude. All of these people are survivors too, and they share much of what I will be discussing in following chapters.

Woody Castrodale described to me his own and his group's efforts to navigate the shoals of personal experience as HIV-negatives living in the epidemic. It is a perceptive and apt narrative with which to introduce my discussion in chapter 2.

> We meet and talk and it's as if we're planting trees, but every once in a while we hit a gas main—we're digging around, and issues keep coming up which seem unresolvable. I imagine in my own mind that I should have figured it all out by now, but instead new issues keep coming up because we don't know how to respond or react in the modern world, as opposed to the world before AIDS. I often feel that we are just casting about in the dark, and a lot of the men in the group feel that, and while I know it does people a lot of good,

it is also very troubling—it raises so much anxiety, because we're digging around in material which has been so carefully repressed. There are so many things which keep sliding away on us. I try to sort them out in my mind—a taxonomy of issues—but I have only been moderately successful in sorting out what might be linked to what.[14]

Chapter 2
The Psychological Epidemic

The density of the
universe, if that
sort of thing interests you:
one atom of hydrogen to two and a half
gallons of nothing.
—Keith Waldrop, from
The Ruins of Providence [1]

In the winter of 1992, I was asked to speak to a group of San Francisco psychotherapists, all of whom worked with people with AIDS and their lovers and families. I began with a question: What did each count on, what assumptions did he hold, that allowed him to hope that any gay man in San Francisco—who did not die of AIDS itself—might have the resources or resilience to survive the epidemic in any relatively healthy or happy way? All sat silently. These men are bearing witness to an epidemic of psychological distress that, in its own way, often seems as hopeless as the AIDS epidemic itself.

Much of the distress of gay men living in the AIDS epidemic is like that of other individuals and groups—though rarely seen in such large numbers within discrete, isolated communities. Among these familiar elements are depression, anxiety, isolation, and sexual, social, and occupational "dysfunction." Such responses must be *expected* in reaction to an event like the AIDS epidemic, but our denial of both the predictability *and fact* of these responses is a measure of how little psychological resilience the epidemic has left us. To admit to any problems seems to threaten the opening of floodgates we will never be able to close.

The AIDS epidemic itself is an obvious source of psychological distress, and it is the foundation of the psychological epidemic, a grim decade of suffering and death that has not occurred as a discrete event on American soil in these proportions since the Civil War. But, as with every other aspect of the epidemic, the significance of simply living within the epidemic is so often denied by those within gay communities. Not only does the individual *not* have troubled feelings, he is not *supposed* to have them. This denial is colluded with by American society at large, which more or less ignores AIDS between sporadic public concern about celebrities who contract it. I am still struck by colleagues in psychology—particularly those relatively isolated from the gay and bisexual communities—who remain essentially ignorant of the major mental health crisis of twentieth-century America. This is a plague of historic proportions that will ultimately change the life experience of every human being on the planet. The human consequences of this catastrophe are movingly suggested by Barry, a 32-year-old psychotherapy patient:

> Driving to work the other morning, I watched people in a gas station pumping gas and putting air in their tires, and I thought, "It's amazing that people can still do things like that." It's like when I was a little kid, and my father would come home drunk and start yelling and throwing things around, and my mother would stand in the kitchen polishing the toaster. That's what it reminds me of— the world is crumbling around you and you don't even know if you can exist, and other people are putting gas in their car like nothing's happening. I think to myself, "How do we do this? How are we getting through this? Why do we keep going instead of just lying down and dying on the spot?"

If the AIDS epidemic itself, and the psychological issues of those with HIV, were not so necessarily overshadowing, it would surely be obvious that the psychological condition of uninfected men is a crisis that places in peril the health, mental health—and lives—of millions of men, and that threatens the future of gay communities as a whole.

Psychological Development

In psychological and social senses, human life changes throughout its course. These changes can be described as "stages" of development, and the work of psychologist Erik Erikson,[2] is one such description, a scheme of eight relatively progressive stages of development, each with a central "task." The stages proceed in sequence, and an adequate—though often incomplete—mastery of the task of one stage allows the individual to approach the task of the following stage. It should be said that Erikson was the first to warn that such schemes must not be taken too rigidly, for they lack, as one example, the predictability and precision of biological models of development.

While we generally progress psychologically and socially through developmental stages, human life does not proceed on tracks—or even a trajectory. We frequently return to earlier, incompletely mastered developmental tasks, and sometimes become fixed in one that we are not able to adequately master. Such common diversions in our development are referred to by psychologists as *regression* and *fixation*—meaning, respectively, a return to earlier developmental issues and getting stuck in an issue.

When we return to an earlier stage of development, this means that relatively satisfactory solutions to the tasks of that stage were accomplished when the stage was first transitted. Under stress, however the individual may "return" to that stage, meaning that he experiences the kinds of conflicts, and responds to them with the kinds of solutions that were available to him at that time. Such familiar, though largely outgrown, solutions to conflict provide one with a sense of safety, as they did at the time the developmental phase was first being transitted. We see this commonly, as one example, in the adult who sulks in response to conflict with a partner—perhaps not the most adult response, but one that is developmentally familiar and seems to offer safety from an otherwise unmanageable situation.

Getting "stuck" or fixated in a developmental task—as opposed to regressing to it—is usually a matter of degree. The adult who *typically* responds to relationship problems by sulking might be described as fixated in the developmental stage—around 18 to 36 months—when sulking is an expected and normal "solution" to conflict because the child does not have other resources. The adult is expected to have other resources, like the capacity to talk about and negotiate problems. If, as a small child, he substantially failed to develop these more mature solutions, he will have difficulty mustering them as an adult. When the failure is substantial in one developmental phase, subsequent development tasks may also be affected. The three-year-old who has not learned to discuss problems, rather than sulk, will be handicapped in solving other, later tasks that require discussion.

Fixation and regression are useful concepts for understanding the impact of the AIDS epidemic on all gay men, including uninfected men. In understanding psychological distress, it is helpful to have a sense of how it has originated, developmentally speaking. Is withdrawal in the face of loss, for example, purely a reaction to the epidemic in a man who rarely uses it in adult life? Has the man regressed to responding with withdrawal in the face of loss as he *sometimes* has with other significant loss? Or is this a man who characteristically uses withdrawal in the face of loss—or threatened loss—and always has, and for whom the epidemic is simply another reason to withdraw from others? The answer will depend on the individual. The epidemic certainly has the power to induce difficulty into the lives of men with no significant history of loss; and it has the power to exacerbate preexisting vulnerabilities or refocus serious lifelong problems. The idea that many men's psychological issues may have preexisted the epidemic is moot, but it is nevertheless often used to deny the importance of the event. Such individuals are all the more vulnerable to the epidemic. That the devastation of whole communities by AIDS has "merely" profoundly entrenched long-standing vulnerabilities is in no way reassuring.

The Psychological Problems Men Are Experiencing

Many are not really familiar with a clear description of common psychological problems, and denial, as well as the "normalization" of psychological distress among gay men in the age of AIDS, keeps many from noticing the most obvious features of their experience. Therefore I will briefly describe each of the psychological conditions most commonly experienced in the epidemic. Those familiar with these psychological concepts may wish to pass over this section.

DEPRESSION

Depression is commonplace in the lives of gay men. Before the epidemic, depression was often rooted in both ordinary sources, such as childhood loss, and in the often severe psychological and social pressures of growing up homosexual. These special developmental pressures often result in isolation and loneliness in adolescence that serve as a foundation for depression in later life. But depression may also grow out of the losses, isolation, and loneliness of adult life, and out of an adult sense of helplessness and hopelessness. The AIDS epidemic provides all of these adult experiences, and many gay men living in the epidemic have manifested developmentally unprecedented depression in response to the epidemic; have returned to familiar, developmentally rooted depression; or have refocused their lifelong depression on new loss and trauma. Much of the depression we see is a variable, synergistic, and destructive mix of old developmental problems and a reaction to current events.

In addition to loss, isolation, and hopelessness, there are other sources of depression for uninfected men living in the epidemic. Anger, rational and irrational, turned against itself, is one—anger about particular deaths, or how many deaths, and anger about a personal, social, and political revolution gone awry. There is also anger about the response of American society and the federal government to the epidemic, and anger about a myriad of other disappointments, abuses, and problems. A related source of depression is a sense of helplessness to do anything about the AIDS epidemic itself or about others in psychological distress. Linda Zaretsky, a colleague working with many gay men, described this to me early in the epidemic. "I find gay men experiencing an existential pessimism that is new: a feeling that the environment is not safe and the world is not as benign as they thought it was. The epidemic has brought a severe and sudden end to what was a new optimism about being gay and what kind of life that implied."[3]

Depression may be characterized by many different features. It may be *acute,* appearing suddenly and severely, or may be *chronic* and characteristic of the individual's longer-term experience. The specific signs and symptoms of depression include some or all of the following features, in both *acute* (shorter-term or reactive to events) and more *chronic* depression.[4]

1. A depressed or sad mood.
2. A diminished interest or loss of pleasure in daily activities.
3. Chronic anorexia or overeating or, in acute depression, a change in appetite or eating habits that results in significant weight change.
4. Difficulty sleeping, especially awakening early in the morning and being unable to go back to sleep; or oversleeping.
5. Either physical agitation (often experienced as anxiety) or physical slowing and inactivity.
6. A lack of energy or chronic fatigue.
7. Poor self-esteem, a sense of worthlessness, or inappropriate guilt.
8. Difficulty paying attention, concentrating, and remembering.

9. Recurrent thoughts about death, being dead, or suicide.
10. A chronic feeling of being out of control of one's life, or more acute feelings of helplessness and hopelessness.
11. An effort at "self-medication," either with alcohol or other depressants such as benzodiazepines (Valium, Xanax, Dalmane, Halcion, etc.), all of which usually exacerbate depression; or with stimulants such as cocaine or amphetamines (methamphetamine, Dexedrine, etc.), which provide a subjective, temporary relief from the depression but exacerbate it as their effects diminish ("rebound" depression). (Much of the substance abuse in gay communities rests on underlying mood disorders.)
12. A loss of interest in sex, or the inability to function sexually due to problems with arousal, erection, or attaining an orgasm.
13. Increased isolation due to reduced energy, loss of interest in social activities, a desire to conceal one's mood from others, or the avoidance of potentially sexual situations. Isolation exacerbates depression, which may in turn deepen the isolation.

Some features of depression, including a depressed or sad mood, are often so long-standing and familiar, that an individual may not even recognize the problem—precisely because it is chronic. When other expressions of depression—like anxiety or substance use—*are* perceived in themselves, they may not be understood as aspects of depression, and the possibility of a mood problem may be entirely overlooked.

MANIC RESPONSE

Manic responses, broadly speaking, span a range of intensity, but are all unconscious efforts to stimulate oneself out of depression with activity. They are thus a kind of psychological equivalent to stimulant drugs like cocaine and amphetamines, which are so often used to "self-medicate" depression. The specific features of full, clinical mania include some or all of the following features.[5] *Hypomania* (less intense than full mania) and *hyperactivity* (still less intense) will also include some of these features, though perhaps with less intensity.

1. Periods of elevated, expansive, or irritable mood.
2. Inflated self-esteem or grandiosity, often involving feelings that one is especially gifted or protected by some transcendent force.
3. In more acute cases, a decreased need for sleep.
4. Talkativeness, pressured speech, racing thoughts, and distractibility.

5. Physical agitation and an increased need for physical activity.
6. An increase in goal-directed activity, socially, occupationally, or sexually.
7. Exaggerated engagement in pleasurable activities with potential for pain, including buying sprees and sexual "indiscretions."
8. A general foreclosure on psychological experience, including a denial of feelings (especially painful ones), a loss of empathy for others, and an inability to engage intimately with others.

Manic responses, their personal significance for many gay men living in the epidemic, and their social implications for gay communities as a whole are important. The idea of mania provides some insight into a psychotherapy patient, Pat, who suffered multiple deaths at work, lost four friends in a single month, and yet continued to conduct a normal day's activities. The loss and loneliness Pat was experiencing were rarely the overt topic of conversation during therapy hours, and he only rarely subjectively experienced depression. Instead, we usually talked about the stresses involved in his twelve-hour workdays at a San Francisco AIDS services agency; his series of troubling and, for him, consistently unintelligible relationships; his inability to spend time alone or to sleep alone; his sudden, unaffordable shopping sprees; his sometimes twice daily aerobics classes; and, often, his inability to have any sense at all of what he was feeling about a person, event, or moment.

Periodically, however, Pat *would* collapse into an immobilizing depression, and would express puzzlement about its origins. During one session he described a sudden feeling of hopelessness and exhaustion the morning before.

> "Do you have any idea why this happened Tuesday morning?" I wondered.
> "None at all. I was feeling fine before that."
> "Could it have something to do with what happened on Monday or over the weekend?"
> "What happened on Monday?" Pat asked me.
> "I don't know. What happened on Monday? You are talking about your feelings Tuesday morning, as you often do, as if they came in with the weather—as if they had no *meaning*—and when we talk about these changes in your mood, we do usually find something. That's why I'm asking."
> "Well, I can tell you what happened on Monday, and whether it has to do with how I'm feeling . . . A lot happened on Monday. For

starters, Jim died." [Jim, a coworker of Pat's for several years, had died sitting at his desk in the office.]

"That seems like a very disturbing event to me. And, of course, one connected to a lot of others for you . . ."

"Oh yeah, it was—though I'd have to say I think the poor guy is better off. We weren't close, but, you know, I liked him. And he's number one hundred and twenty-seven or something."

"And do you think your feelings about Jim might have affected the way you felt Tuesday morning?"

"That night—after Jim died—Roger [whom Pat had been dating for a few months] and I went out. We broke up. It was hopeless, I mean, we just weren't connecting and it was too difficult to be with him. I was just irritated with him all the time. I wonder why we even waited so long to end it . . ."

"These seem like *two* big events for one day." I commented.

"Hmm—yeah."

"And what do you think of the idea that your feelings Tuesday morning had something to do with them? It seems to me that you are avoiding the connections here—and understandably—because it would likely produce a terrible sense of loss."

Pat sat quietly for a moment and then spoke cautiously.

"I don't know, I guess so. It's certainly possible. When I'm feeling this hopeless, these things are much harder to stand. Last week I could have dealt with it. Right now, I'm just thinking to myself, 'If one more person gets sick, it's going to push me right over the edge and I'll be a basket case.' They'll find *me* dead in the office."

"But you sound as if your feeling hopeless is something incidental that only makes the losses harder to bear. But this ignores the idea that you are feeling hopeless because you have to deal with such losses constantly . . ."

"If I felt this bad every time someone died, well, I would have no life left."

"You understandably don't *want* to feel this bad, but sometimes you do."

"Well, it's not something I'm going to dwell on when I don't have to."

As the preceding conversation suggests, manic responses rely heavily on denial, and Pat is partly working in the session to counter depression by denying the emotional meaning of the events of Monday. This denial also entails a fantasy of omnipotence, of being beyond the epidemic both physically and psychologically. While it is also true that denial is an aspect of normal psychological functioning, and is often a helpful adaptation to an overwhelming event, it is a psychological defense that entails great costs. Denial distorts both external and internal realities. With regard to external reality, there are facts that are problematic or dangerous to deny: Engaging in unprotected sex, substance abuse, and other self-destructive behaviors can be serious consequences of manic denial.

The distortions brought to internal realities by denial are more subtle, but also costly. Manic defenses work partly by helping one deny his internal life of reflection and feeling, including depression. While depression may be the "target" feeling, the denial of feelings is intrinsically indiscriminate. Sustained manic defenses against depression will broadly inhibit an individual's capacity to experience feelings in general. Ultimately, mania relies on a denial of one's whole internal life, including feelings of genuine happiness and of empathy for others. Unfortunately, such feelings serve as the basis for intimacy, and the denial that isolates the person from himself finally isolates him from others.

The developmental problems usually encountered by gay men often result in a tendency to deny feelings, to isolate, and to avoid intimacy. Most gay men have grown up with fantasies and feelings that include forbidden, homosexual ones. The internal conflict arising over such feelings is often resolved with isolation from others—or from anything that might evoke feelings of any kind. Manic defenses, marshalled against feelings arising out of the epidemic, unfortunately collude with such developmental predispositions.

Manic defenses and the isolation that result from them are a significant danger to gay communities. The few decades prior to the epidemic provided political and social freedoms that have allowed important psychological growth for gay men and women. The stresses of the AIDS epidemic may well reverse much of that. The important point about manic solutions is that many gay men are becoming isolated not only in the familiar and more recognizable form of depression, but in manic forms as well. Profound and ultimately painful isolation may lurk invisibly but destructively in the energetic man, busy in the world, and socially connected. In human terms, such a man may be disconnected from himself, from others, and from his capacity for intimacy.

ANXIETY

I have spoken about depression as an important response to the epidemic, but in men with certain kinds of problematic childhood development we often see a "depressive" response that is characterized more by anxiety, agitation, anger, or boredom than by a typically sad or depressed mood.[6] In such men, anxiety may be a kind of substitute for depression, or, in others, it may be the more usually expected direct response to anxiety-provoking features in life—which are abundant in the epidemic. Anxiety is usually more easily recognized than depression and is experienced as nervousness or fear, sometimes accompanied by obsessive (repetitive, senseless) thoughts, usually about all the things that might go wrong. Anxiety may be completely unfocused on specific things or events, or it may be narrower but still generalized, as in fear of leaving the house or being in crowds. It may also have a very specific focus, as in the fear of bridges or elevators. All forms of anxiety may be experienced in discrete, very severe episodes known as *panic attacks*. As elements of character—rather than as discrete problems—anxiety is familiar in the very compulsive person who habitually checks his door lock three or four times on returning home at night. Anxiety may include some or all of the following.[7]

1. An unrealistic or "excessive" subjective experience of agitation, anxiety, or worry.
2. Motor tension, which may include trembling, feeling shaky, muscle tension, restlessness, or easy fatigability.
3. Autonomic activity ("fight or flight" arousal), including shortness of breath, accelerated heart rate, sweating, dry mouth, dizziness or lightheadedness, nausea, diarrhea or other abdominal distress, frequent urination, or trouble swallowing (a "lump" in the throat).
4. Vigilance and scanning, including feeling on edge, an exaggerated startle response, and difficulty concentrating.
5. Difficulty falling asleep or staying asleep.
6. Irritability.
7. Panic attacks, which are discrete periods of intense fear or discomfort that include autonomic activity as described above and often a sense of depersonalization, a fear of dying, a fear of going crazy, or of being out of control in public.
8. Posttraumatic stress disorder, which includes anxiety symptoms connected with the reexperiencing of an extremely stressful event, or

the effort to avoid reexperiencing it. Additional features may include an estrangement from others, a restricted range of emotion, and the sense of a foreshortened future.

In her research with HIV-negative gay men in San Francisco, psychologist Rachel Schochet has found a high incidence of psychological distress that includes both severe episodes of anxiety and chronic depression. She feels it is consistent with the concept of *posttraumatic stress syndrome,* a diagnostic idea developed to describe the experience of returning Vietnam veterans, many of whom suffered such problems with an onset long after the traumatic event. Many other researchers also believe that anxiety disorders are the most common psychiatric complications among uninfected gay men.[8] During life in an epidemic, some anxiety is an expected and realistic response. But anxiety may become chronic and severe, and it can be a crippling source of reclusiveness and isolation, occupational dysfunction, and sexual dysfunction. Like depression, anxiety is both a cause of isolation and dysfunction and is in turn aggravated by them. Anxiety may keep us in the house, and the more we are isolated from social interaction, the more anxiety its anticipation evokes. How anxiety among gay men living in the epidemic should be interpreted is a difficult question. While anxiety experienced by uninfected men is, indeed, often appropriate and realistic under the circumstances, it is also often psychologically debilitating and, in any nonepidemic times would be the appropriate object of psychological attention. In clinical practice today, anxiety is considered problematic when it appears to be in excess of group norms, or when it is the basis of severe and "unusual" levels of dysfunction. Unfortunately, our standards have been radically altered by the epidemic.

HYPOCHONDRIASIS

Hypochondriasis is anxiety focused on the fear of serious disease. Such fear is supported by the interpretation of physical signs and symptoms, and the anxiety continues despite medical reassurance to the contrary. Like other forms of anxiety, it is often difficult to know in a particular instance whether the anxiety should be considered "problematic" or expected and appropriate among men who are living in an epidemic—and, no doubt, at real risk for disease. In the case of anxiety about HIV, we now often make the judgment by evaluating the individual's likelihood of actually having been at risk of infection. Regardless of what it is now called, what would have been perceived as true hypochondriasis before the AIDS epidemic is now commonly experienced by gay men. Greg, a 28-year-old psychotherapy patient, related his experience to me during a psychotherapy session:

> With all of my friends it started with the skin: there was always some little thing that didn't look like much, and then, *pow* you would find out they had AIDS. I mean, I don't even look at myself in the mirror any more, and I never look at my skin. I'm terrified that one day I'll find some little spot and the next thing you know, I'll be dead. I have just freaked out when I got a bruise or saw a birthmark I'd forgotten about, and I just don't look anymore. I used to look, and I'd run off to the doctor and it would be nothing. That was early on in the epidemic. And though I have the idea that these things don't bother me anymore, the truth is that I never look.

Similarly, another psychotherapy patient, John, in his early twenties, talks of his anxiety about AIDS and his insight into a hypochondriacal process. During this session he was recovering from a cold that had kept him in bed for a few days.

> "Lying in bed, I was just filled with these aches and pains, and I decided I had AIDS. I've asked all my friends and they say the same thing, that they get sick with anything and that's the first thing they think. I know I bitch a lot, but when I was lying there, I was really scared, and I was thinking, you know, I don't want to die, I don't want to die, I really don't."
>
> "And what do you think made you feel it was AIDS?" I asked.
>
> "I thought about that, because, you know, I've done so little, sex-wise, that you'd think I would be the last person to have AIDS. And I thought that it really had to do with my feelings about myself, about coming out, and that I thought I had AIDS because I was gay."
>
> "Because you were gay?"
>
> "Yes, because that's who gets AIDS, and if you're gay, that's what you get. But I think that it's about my fear of coming out, of being gay, and that fear somehow gets turned into fear of having AIDS. So instead of worrying about being gay, I worry about having AIDS."
>
> "And why would you experience the fear in that way, move it over to the issue of AIDS, so to speak?"

"Well, it's a lot simpler to think about AIDS than about being gay. And also, I know my mother would be very upset if I got AIDS, but I also think it would be easier for her to talk about [because she is a nurse], and you know, that it would be more acceptable to her. She is much weirder about sexual stuff."

Such hypochondriacal feelings have become a familiar, critical component of "AIDS anxiety," a phenomenon widely recognized—if often simplistically conceptualized—by mental health providers now working with gay men. The existence of unrealistic hypochondriacal anxiety is clearly seen in men who have tested HIV-negative but who so doubt the results that they test repeatedly to no rational purpose. Although medical personnel are beginning to discourage the practice, I have had psychotherapy patients test as many as six times in a year.

As I have already suggested, the traditional concept of hypochondriacal anxiety does not adequately describe the entire phenomenon we are now seeing. In the dialogue with John, we see the suggestion of a set of complications that are more subtle, unconscious, and pervasive than conventional hypochondriasis in itself. John's feelings are about more than fear of disease merely because there is a lot of it around or because a focus on physical problems provides some psychological benefit. Hypochondriacal anxiety among gay men today involves issues of personal and social identity, guilt, and a psychological response to a society that persists in destructively confusing homosexuality and AIDS and persecuting both. Such broad support for the gay man's "hypochondriasis" must be accounted for in our understandings.

Although convincing figures are unavailable because of anonymous testing and, in my impression, because of a decline in repeated testing, a large number of gay men in the U.S.—perhaps 40 percent—may still be untested or not recently tested for HIV antibodies and do not know their antibody status. We have "safer sex" guidelines, but they, as well as HIV antibody tests, provide only reassurance—not insurance and, often, not assurance—either emotionally or medically.[9] The epidemiology and biology of AIDS are immensely complex, and they are filled with contradictions, inconsistencies, and anomalies. Thus it is not only hypochondriacal anxiety, but a mix of irrational and rational ideas and feelings that contribute to many men's continuing doubt and anxiety about their health, whether the feelings are conscious or not. Hypochondriacal anxiety and reasonably founded doubt are now part of the experience of virtually all gay or bisexual men who have had sexual contact with other men in the last 15 or so years, who continue to have such contact, or who contemplate it, regardless of how "safely" the contact was or might be conducted.

The extent to which gay men have become involved in psychological distress about physical health and the complexity of that distress, is illustrated by an incident involving a psychotherapy patient, Bill. He was in a monogamous relationship and both men were uninfected.

> Bill developed randomly distributed itching of the skin, and the symptom became increasingly disturbing and severe. Much speculation was made about the cause, he made visits to his general practitioner and a dermatologist, and the medical consensus was that this was a case of dry skin. The diagnosis was called into question, however, when Bill's lover developed similar, though less severe, symptoms, and when Bill's condition continued to worsen despite the use of prescribed and unprescribed skin moisturizers. Finally, Bill was using sedatives several times a week to sleep, and was having to undress in the middle of the day to apply moisturizers to his entire body. He was preoccupied with the problem and spoke, not entirely seriously, but with genuine distress, of suicide.

> At this point, Bill's lover decided to go to *his* general practitioner, announcing the appointment to Bill with the joke, "Tomorrow I'm going to Doctor F. to see if we've got dry skin or we're really dying." This physician, a gay man with a large AIDS practice in San Francisco, was pleased to see a patient without HIV— although he expressed concern that the two apparently uninfected men were practicing unprotected sex. After a physical examination, he offered his diagnosis: The two had scabies, an infestation of the skin by a microscopic form of mite. Scabies had been relatively common in gay communities, especially during the sexually more active seventies. An antiparasitic lotion was prescribed for both men.

> Relieved at having a diagnosis and the prospect of cure, both used the conservative course of treatment, with initially good results. But four or five days after the second application, Bill's symptoms, though not his lover's, began to return. At this point, four months into his symptomatic condition, he was genuinely despairing. While he still had perspective on the inappropriateness of the idea, he was once again talking of suicide. Although he had experienced mild depression throughout his life, there was no question that the skin

problem was seriously exacerbating it. The itching was constant, it was disruptive of most activities, and it was creating a chronic sleep disturbance and chronic fatigue.

At this point, Bill was able to gain some insight into why these difficult but certainly not disabling or life-threatening symptoms were so profoundly disturbing. He connected the dermatologic problem to both his experience of life in the midst of San Francisco's plagued gay community and to feelings about a former lover ill with AIDS. He discovered that much of his distress arose from experiencing the skin problem as a metaphor for illness. His mostly unconscious terror of illness for himself, his former lover, and his current lover, as well as the appeal of illness because it connected him to those who were seriously ill, were all focused on the potent idea of an invisible organism, transmitted between two men by sexual contact, burrowing invisibly in the skin, hatching eggs, and creating undiagnosable symptoms.

Shortly after this insight, it occurred to Bill, still suffering from the itching, that a nonsteroidal anti-inflammatory drug he used regularly (and that is well known for allergic dermatologic complications) might have a role in the problem. He discontinued the drug, and within a few days the symptoms were entirely gone.

While the cause of Bill's skin problem is not certain, the possible role of the anti-inflammatory suggests that Bill's lover, as well as the lover's gay physician, might well have been participating in the metaphor of illness too. The physician, beleaguered by AIDS-related problems and concerned about the unprotected sex of the two men, seemed to have landed easily on the idea that his patient had been "infected" by another man. The scabies diagnosis seemed so obvious to him that he had conducted no microscopic examination of skin scrapings, a common procedure if there is doubt, which there was, because Bill did not have the expected scabies "tracks" on his hands.

As is almost always the case between gay lovers now, the two men both feared—partly unconsciously and partly not—being infected and infecting the other. They thus readily accepted the notion of mutual infection with scabies, for it was a diagnosis that expressed metaphorically important and preoccupying fears. That Bill's lover "contracted" the problem is an expression of his fears that he had been "infected," his identification with his lover, and his identification with the gay community and the important role that illness now plays in it.

SEXUAL DYSFUNCTIONS

I am using the term *sexual dysfunction* in its traditional sense. It encompasses a number of specific, familiar problems. These include a loss of interest in or aversion to sex, the inability to have an erection or to maintain one, and the inhibition or absence of orgasm. Gay men now commonly experience such problems, although they are rarely the reason for seeking psychotherapeutic attention in the age of AIDS. They are now too familiar to gay men and too well accepted to appear to warrant attention. Furthermore, it feels very difficult for any gay man to seek attention for *problematic* sex when others have contracted HIV or are dying from it.

Although the specific dysfunctions seen among gay men are similar to those seen with other men, there are some aspects of their expression today in gay communities that are unusual and especially concerning. Frequency is one important difference between gay and heterosexual men. The association of sexual dysfunction with anxiety, depression, and other feelings about the epidemic has made sexual dysfunction astonishingly common among gay men, both positive and negative. Most often, dysfunction occurs during sex with a partner, while masturbatory sex is normal. Physical contact between partners, *regardless of known antibody status,* elicits conscious and unconscious associations of sex and death that, in terms of known medical fact, run the gamut from realistic to ridiculous. Regardless, the association is immensely powerful, pervasive, and frightening both as medical fact and as metaphor. It looms hauntingly and destructively over—and between—the lives of virtually all gay men. Couples in "mixed antibody" relationships often have sexual problems because of fears, both rational and irrational, about HIV. But the specter of HIV is now so integral to the gay experience that it commonly haunts even the relationships of two monogamous, HIV-concordant men—two men who cannot possibly infect each other because neither has HIV or both *already* have it. It was precisely the largely unconscious association of sex and infecting, sex and being infected, and sex and illness, that provided the power of the scabies metaphor for Bill and his lover.

The pairing of sex and death in human life is a pairing of intimacy with betrayal, love with violence, and giving of oneself with the taking of life. It is a horribly destructive irony that a quirk of nature and timing has brought this epidemic to gay communities, which were beginning to clarify and correct a social legacy that for so many centuries brought despair to the lives of homosexual men. This prejudicial legacy paired homosexual intimacy and love with hurt, shame, and guilt. That the AIDS epidemic has appeared to make traditional social misrepresentations of homosexuality quite literally true threatens to reverse much or all of the psychological progress made by gay men over the last decades. "Noncontact sex," such as telephone sex and jack-off (group masturbation) clubs, are one outcome of AIDS. While they provide sex that is safe against the transmission of HIV, it is even more significant that they allow a gay man to have sex without having to touch another gay man. Homophobia is now widely experienced as anxiety about HIV; and, indeed, HIV provides a partially realistic basis for avoiding certain ways of expressing gay intimacy. As always, the realistic element confounds the clarification of psychological truth. Now hidden in the conscious and unconscious entanglements of AIDS and homosexuality lies an impoverishing confusion between avoiding HIV and avoiding being touched intimately by another homosexual man.

Chapter 3
Survivor Guilt and Related Family Matters

You read the obituaries and all these people who seemed like they just had so many gifts. . . . There are moments when I find myself thinking, "Oh, it should have taken me and not them. . . . Retrain me for another incarnation, and I'll be quite something."—Matt, a 34-year-old San Franciscan[1]

Although survivor guilt is intimately related to other psychological problems discussed in the previous chapter, I am giving it a chapter of its own because of its centrality to gay men living with the AIDS epidemic. In the second decade of the epidemic, one hears a lot about survivor guilt and gay men, but the term has remained too vaguely defined to be very useful to those experiencing it, and, indeed, to most mental health providers working with them. While the psychotherapist may recognize the existence of the phenomenon, if imprecisely, for the nonpsychotherapist the idea of survivor guilt is most often denied on the premise that it does not make sense: "What would I have to be guilty about?" is the common retort.

Steve, a gay man in his early forties, was referred to me after a hospitalization for depression and a suicide attempt. Over the previous five years he had lost most of his close friends to AIDS. The suicide attempt occurred a few days after Steve had been asked by his supervisor to write an employee, telling him that the employee's pay would have to be reduced because of poor attendance and performance. Ill with AIDS, the employee had been denying his disability, and had refused to discuss his problem with Steve or accept a change of position that might accommodate his disability.

"I was beside myself. The secretary gave me the letter to sign, and I looked at it, and I kept thinking, I can't do this, I can't. And suddenly I just started crying and screaming, really screaming, and everyone in the office was looking at me, and I ran out without telling my boss where I was going, and I went home and got in bed. I crawled under the covers head first, like a kid, and I thought, 'I'm not going to come out. I'm not going to come until this is all over.'"

"Can you tell me more what you were feeling at that moment, with the letter in front of you?" I asked.

"My last therapist told me that I have survivor guilt."

"What do you think of that idea?" I wondered.

"Well, I don't know. I shouldn't have guilt because Tom has AIDS and can't do his work. He couldn't do his work, he was too sick, and that's not my fault. It's that I couldn't hurt him when he was sick. He has AIDS. I'm fine, I have a zillion T-cells, and I already earn twice what he did. And then I'm supposed to take my money home, and pay my mortgage, and go into work and tell him that because he has AIDS, we can't pay him as much as he used to get, that we're going to cut his pay. It's impossible for me to do that. Is that survivor guilt? I think all the time, 'Why me?' but in reverse. 'Why not *me?*' That's what I say to myself all the time, 'Why not *me?*' Is that survivor guilt? It's not my fault that he's sick. I don't take responsibility for that."

Steve *is* experiencing survivor guilt, and despite the unclarity of the idea and the instinctive denials, it has become a critical component of the psychological epidemic that is engulfing seronegative gay male communities. Survivor guilt is a particularly destructive aspect of this psychological epidemic for many reasons, including the difficulty it creates for the survivor in recognizing and communicating his emotional distress.

Since the beginning of the epidemic, most agencies serving gay men have been tremendously resistant to addressing the needs—including psychological needs—of seronegative men. This has begun to change recently in San Francisco, but institutional resistance remains in most areas of the country with large gay populations. The reasons for this resistance are numerous. Earlier in the epidemic, money and resources were needed for HIV-positive men and those with AIDS, and these populations quite appropriately remained our priority. In those early years it also seemed possible that the epidemic would be medically limited, which would have limited the psychological damage to survivors— partly because it would have reduced the duration of the trauma and the number of dead, and partly because it would have allowed us to tend to the problems of survivors *after* the event was over. Things have not gone as planned. The epidemic is likely to continue for decades, and presumed survivors and nonsurvivors must coexist in their partly different realities. But potential survivors cannot live through decades of unaddressed emotional distress and then be successfully helped with psychological problems when the epidemic is over. Too much damage will have been done over too many years—and too many will not have survived because of the destructive consequences of psychological distress, including exposure to HIV.

The coexistence of possible survivors and presumed nonsurvivors creates significant psychological difficulty in itself. The lack of confidence that so many uninfected men feel about whether they really *can* survive is partly a consequence of living daily with those they believe are dying. Even for those who are convinced they will survive without HIV infection, the very nature of survivor guilt makes it difficult to acknowledge problems with survival in the presence of the nonsurvivor. Unlike those who lived through the Nazi Holocaust, the presumed survivors of the AIDS epidemic must examine their feelings and problems in the presence of those they presume will die. But if a man feels guilt or unworthiness for having had the good fortune to survive when another has not or will not, he will find it very difficult even to recognize his own distress and almost impossible to talk about it. In the early years of day-long workshops for HIV-negative men in San Francisco, those attending often said they lied to friends about where they were spending the day. "My friends, most of whom are positive, wouldn't understand, and I'd be embarrassed to tell them. I know what they'd say—'Going to discuss problems with your retirement investments?'"

Depression, anxiety, and social, occupational, or sexual dysfunctions are often a direct response to the experience of the epidemic. For example, men often experience depression in response to loss, anger, and feelings of helplessness arising from the epidemic; or anxiety may arise out of fear for one's own health and that of others. In other instances, however, survivor guilt may be a mediating element in the development of both depression and anxiety. For most, guilt itself is largely unconscious, is denied or rationalized, and is virtually never an explicit part of a person's reasons for seeking help in dealing with feelings about the epidemic. Psychotherapists unfamiliar with the concept of survivor guilt may overlook it in such patients. But ignorance of concepts is not the only reason psychotherapists overlook survivor guilt. They may be having similar feelings about the epidemic, and for developmental reasons psychotherapists as a group are probably particularly prone to experiencing survivor guilt. Regardless of how it comes about, the unwitting collusion of therapist with patient in ignoring issues of guilt is a common, and destructive, phenomenon in the epidemic.

Thus for the psychotherapist—and for the therapy patient himself—it is very important to distinguish between depression and anxiety that arise directly out of the experience of the epidemic and depression and anxiety that are "guilt-mediated." Among those men experiencing "direct" (non-guilt-mediated) depression, anxiety, and dysfunction, there are many who have already suffered such serious losses and other destructive events that no amount of clarification of the *meaning* of these feelings is likely to undo the damage. For these men, depression, anxiety, and dysfunction may become chronic and lifelong. Profound psychological transformations are common consequences of wars, plagues, and other huge and destructive social events, and the AIDS epidemic will not be an exception.

When shared by much of society, such events are given social reality and meaning, both of which, not unlike the ritual of the funeral, validate the individual's feelings and help him make at least some human sense of the tragedy. For the gay man in America, however, the AIDS epidemic has been a huge but relatively private hell, invisible to most of society, and kept invisible, for the most part, quite purposely. Invisibility specifically denies the validation of feelings, and both the enforced and inadvertent invisibility of the AIDS epidemic has badly exacerbated the personal costs for most gay men. While the meanings of the AIDS epidemic can be shared within gay communities—to the extent that sharing is not limited by denial—in relations with family and heterosexual friends, it can seem virtually a nonevent. Because the gay man's suffering is largely unrecognized and unsupported, it can feel wrong, unreal, and unwarranted. Bill, a psychotherapy patient in his late thirties, was close to his mother and had communicated and visited with her regularly throughout the years of the epidemic. In the summer of 1993, she telephoned to say hello.

"So she said the usual, you know, 'Hi, Bill, how are you doing?' and I said, 'OK.'" Bill hesitated here and was obviously quite upset.
"What is coming up?" I wondered.

"Then she said, 'Is there something wrong? Is there anything I can do to help?'" Bill began crying. "And I said to her, "Well, you know, Mom, all my friends are dead.'"

Depression and anxiety that are a direct response to the epidemic (uncomplicated by guilt) may or may not persist with psychological clarification, because they are often a realistic response to a real situation. The outcome will depend on the severity of the stress and the psychological resilience of the individual. In contrast, guilt-mediated feelings—which may be especially dangerous if unaddressed—are often responsive to psychological insight. Guilt and the depression, anxiety, and dysfunction that it can produce may be substantially reduced by insight because guilt is largely the product of unrealistic and unconscious interpretations of reality.

The following notes from a psychotherapy session with Allen illustrate the guilt-mediated problems an individual can experience in response to the epidemic. Allen was a long-term psychotherapy patient and a professional writer, and he speaks here about a visit with a former lover and close friend who had been diagnosed with AIDS a few months earlier. Allen, now dead of AIDS himself, thought himself uninfected at the time of this session. Perhaps his feelings led to his contracting HIV or perhaps he was already unknowingly infected. Regardless, knowing that he had HIV provided him a sense of relief from the conflict and loss he felt about John.

John was tired and was lying on the bed napping. I was watching him, from across the room, staring at him, and suddenly I imagined I could actually see the virus, like tiny dust particles, pumping through his veins and lodging in muscles and other parts of his body—contaminating him. I suddenly felt so completely repulsed, as if he had actually become physically repulsive—can you imagine, John, who was once so beautiful to me? I felt afraid to touch him because he was diseased, and I was afraid I would catch it just by touching his arm, or that he would wake up and want to touch me. He was still sleeping, but this panic just swept over me, and I felt, literally, like running out of his apartment. I started feeling so awful about these thoughts, of fearing him, of finding him repulsive, and of thinking about abandoning him while he was sick, that the idea came to me that I could be sick myself, or that I should be, that I could talk John into infecting me or do something else to get infected so that I would not have to feel torn between these feelings. I had the idea that if I lay down on the bed beside John, to take a nap with him, that would do it, and it seemed irresistible. I would just lie down and nap with him and not wake up.

There are many ways to interpret Allen's feelings. He is trying, in part, to ward off mourning John's (anticipated) death by "merging" with John, a kind of psychological "internalization" that would make the loss impossible. But guilt is another important unconscious feeling here—guilt not only about running out on John, but about not sharing his HIV and his fate. Merging with John would not only prevent his loss, but make Allen "like" John, allow Allen to share John's HIV and thus have nothing to be guilty about. It is characteristic of survivor guilt that, although Allen consciously experiences some guilt about running out on John, the more important guilt about not having John's HIV and dying with John is almost completely unconscious. It is this unconscious guilt that makes Allen feel like sharing John's illness and not being a survivor.

Survivor guilt like Allen's is experienced by many men, including those who are not in psychotherapy. A positive HIV-antibody test or AIDS diagnosis results in a *decrease* in anxiety for some men.[2] Conversely, at HIV test sites men often experience significant distress in response to negative blood test results. Scott Walton is the former executive director of both Wellness Networks, Michigan's largest AIDS service agency, and The Pacific Center for Human Growth, of Berkeley, California. Both provide counseling services for patients at HIV test sites. Walton cited four common, "paradoxical" responses to negative HIV tests, and estimated that together they comprise approximately one in twenty immediate responses.[3] He also felt that such responses rose significantly in the weeks following the test. These responses are: "My lover is positive, now what am I going to do?"; "If anyone deserved it, it is me"; "All my friends are positive—how can I relate to them?"; and "Now I'm going to have to deal with my life." According to Walton, "crisis" responses—those requiring intervention by a psychology supervisor—were generated by negative blood tests at about a three-to-one margin over positive tests.

Ralph, a 37-year-old psychotherapy patient discusses his first HIV-antibody test:

I had been a wreck for two weeks, but when I went in for the results, I knew I was positive, and I'd psyched myself up for it. I mean, I never thought about being negative, it hadn't even occurred to me. But when the nurse gave me the [negative] results,

I was really *shocked*. And for a minute I didn't react, and then the first thing I thought was, "Oh, my God, what am I going to tell all my positive friends?" And then all these things were rolling over in my head, like "Everyone's going to be very angry at me," and "They're right, I have no reason to be negative because I've done all the things they did." All of this was going through my mind like within one minute of the nurse telling me I was negative, and then suddenly I thought of Robert, and I just started crying, and I was thinking over and over, "Oh my God, Robert would never forgive me for this," and I just started sobbing right there. And the nurse, who was very confused, she just kept saying over and over, "I don't think you understand. *Negative* is *good, positive* is *bad*." And I just kept sobbing and thinking about Robert being dead and wanting to be with him, and she just kept repeating that. And I wanted to tell her about my feelings, but I couldn't think how to explain them.

Because of such confused feelings about negative test results, HIV status is often not revealed to friends. Another psychotherapy patient, Frank, describes such an event and the feelings behind it.

Kevin told me that a colleague of ours had just died, that it was sudden, and that he [Kevin] was positive too. I didn't tell him I was negative when he said this. I would have if he'd asked, but I didn't know what to say, and for me to have brought it up would have sounding like bragging—or so I felt at the time. After that I wondered what I would want to hear if I were positive, and I thought, "Well, if someone doesn't say anything when I tell them I'm positive, then they're negative. And that's OK with me, I wish them well, and I guess I also don't want to hear a lot about it." And that's why I keep my mouth shut about being negative.

Other evidence of survivor guilt in seronegative men is expressed in many seemingly irrational behaviors. A binge of unsafe sex, especially after the death of a friend, is something often described in psychotherapy. Such behavior is often motivated by guilt and the self-destructive impulses arising from it, as well as by the desire to internalize—and thus "prevent" the loss of—the dead friend. While a return to unprotected sex among many gay men after about 1987 is now widely recognized, the trend is still often treated as a problem of "complacency with the epidemic" or proof of a renewed need for traditional AIDS education. It is a much more complex issue than that. Tim, a 38-year-old

San Franciscan, told me about his first HIV test and his response to the negative results:

> The weekend after I got the first negative test, I went out and got completely shit-faced. I was still drinking then and using other stuff like cocaine, and I was *shit-faced*. I went out and picked up a guy, and I went home with him. And we fucked for hours—I mean we fucked without condoms both ways. I knew all about safe sex—I was in the [AIDS service] business. That had nothing to do with it. At the time I don't think it even occurred to me that this had anything to do with the negative test, but I see now that that's what it was all about. It's as if I was trying to go out and change the results. And I probably came pretty close to doing that, but I was lucky. Being negative was a great shock to me, and I didn't know how to understand it or what to do with it. It was a *big* shock.

Experiences like Tim's, which are common, do not occur *despite* the potential dangers of unprotected sex. For some—guilty, depressed, anxious, and living a life that often seems not worth living—the self-destructive aspects of unprotected sex are important incentives to practice it. This has nothing to do with complacency, nor will traditional AIDS education address it.

Guilt is a diverse and complex experience, and it is important to separate out and refine the idea of survivor guilt per se. The following description of survivors, by psychiatrist Michael Friedman, will be familiar to those living in the AIDS epidemic. The discussion is actually about survivors of the Nazi Holocaust. Friedman is discussing the work of another researcher, Niederland.

> Typically, after struggling to begin a new life and often succeeding, these people succumbed to a variety of symptoms like depression, anxiety, and psychosomatic conditions. . . . Niederland believed these symptoms to be identifications with loved ones who had not survived. His patients often appeared and felt as if they were living dead. Niederland believed that these identifications were motivated by guilt, which he called survivor guilt. The survivors experienced an "ever present feeling of guilt . . . for having survived the very calamity to which their loved ones succumbed."[4]

In an unpublished work,[5] San Francisco psychotherapist Tom Moon, provides a useful summary of the research into survivor guilt, including several studies that seem pertinent to the AIDS epidemic. They establish survivor guilt as a central issue for survivors of Hiroshima and as an important factor in suicidal behavior among Vietnam veterans, and physicians, medics, and nurses serving in Vietnam. Friedman, himself, expands the narrower conception of survivor guilt to include the idea that survivor guilt is not only guilt about having survived, but also feelings that one

> could have helped but failed. . . . It is a guilt of omission. It is the guilt of people who believe they have better lives than those of their parents or siblings. The greater the discrepancy between one's own fate and the fate of the loved person one failed to help, the greater the empathic distress and the more poignant one's guilt.[6]

Moon discusses this much broader conception of survivor guilt in a summary of the work of Arnold Modell and others.[7] Survivor guilt is not only a response to extraordinary events and disasters, but is also an ordinary and basic human conflict. It is expressed, for example, by those who sabotage their own adult relationships or occupational success in order to honor their feelings that they deserve no better a life than that of their parents. Guilt may be part of why low-income, first-generation college students have difficulty with academic achievement, for many of these students wonder why they should escape poverty if their families have failed to do so, and they exhibit typical signs of survivor guilt: depression, psychic numbing, and withdrawal. "If fate had dealt harshly with other members of the family, the survivor may experience guilt."[8] Modell expands his ideas further with the idea that survivor guilt includes conflict over whether one has a right to lead not only a successful life, but a separate and independent existence at all. The mere fact of separation from the family may be perceived as a deprivation of and injury to the family. Friedman further distinguishes such "separation guilt" from guilt based on the belief that taking is always at someone else's expense.[9]

Moon adds to the understanding of these theorists with a summary of Control-Mastery Theory (a contemporary psychotherapeutic approach) and its conceptualization of guilt. Here he quotes Friedman and, again, it is a clarification extremely pertinent to the AIDS epidemic:

> A child will compromise or even renounce his own developmental goals in order to maintain ties to his parents. Dysfunctional ties are maintained not because they are inherently gratifying, but rather

because letting go of them is believed to be harmful to [other family members]. . . . For Control-Mastery, it is a child's beliefs about his power to harm others which are crucial in the production of all forms of guilt, including survivor guilt.[10]

Survivor guilt reflects the social nature of human beings and it includes not only guilt about literal, physical survival, but guilt about separation from others, about being happier or more successful than others, and about failing to help others. These expanded understandings of survivor guilt help clarify the experience of many uninfected men living in the AIDS epidemic. Survivor guilt is often not simply about the public event, but is connected to developmentally earlier guilt about parents or siblings. One brings to the public event his personal history and development. Thus past and present, as well as internal and external realities, all engage each other powerfully. Particular difficulty with guilt in a man's history interacts synergistically with a public event like the AIDS epidemic, complicating and exacerbating the guilt experienced about the public event. It is only when the unconscious interaction of history and present life are clarified that the destructive grip of the current event may be reduced.

Allen, who spoke about visiting John in the earlier quotation, illustrates the interaction of an individual's psychological history with the epidemic. Allen grew up with a mother who had been mildly crippled by polio as a child and walked with a pronounced limp. His feelings about her were often discussed in therapy, and he quite consciously identified the similarity of certain feelings about John to many about his mother. The following is from a session about six months after his visit with John.

> "My mother called last night and I noticed this feeling that I often have with her—you know, I had friends over for dinner and we were having a good time, but when I heard it was her on the phone, I noticed that I toned down—as if I didn't want her to think I was having a good time."
>
> "Why would you do that?" I asked.
>
> "Well my guilt about her, which we've talked about a lot."
>
> "But how do you get from guilt to wanting to sound as if you're not having a good time?"
>
> Allen hesitated a moment. "Well, if she's not, then I shouldn't be, I guess. It would be like pushing it in her face, you know, 'You may

be depressed, but I'm out here in California having dinner with my boyfriend and having a ball.'"

"So you would be sort of showing her up by having a good time?"

"Yes, definitely," Allen said.

"And abandoning her to her bad times?" I wondered.

"Well, I have abandoned her . . . just by going to California, so far as she's concerned. I can tell you that she calls me up because she's depressed and she wants me, as you call it, to 'fix' her. This has been a lot of our relationship. My dad isn't going to do it. He's out bowling or yukking it up with his friends, anything to stay out of the house."

"And did you 'fix' her last night?"

"Well of course not . . ."

"And because you couldn't fix her, you thought it better to seem depressed yourself?"

"When you put it that way, it sounds ridiculous. But if I can't do anything about her depression, the next best thing seems like being depressed myself—to keep her company, I guess."

I reminded Allen of an earlier discussion we had had: "This is like your self-consciousness about running around in front of her or walking too fast when you were a child. We have speculated about your foot pain and limping [Allen often had foot and ankle pain as a child and this sometimes kept him from normal play activities—and at home, keeping his mother company].

"Yes—if she couldn't run, I did often feel that I shouldn't run in front of her. Showing her up again."

"And perhaps literally running away from her, leaving her behind?"

"Well, exactly, running away and leaving her behind, because that is what I often wanted to do. I often pretended I wasn't with her because of my embarrassment about her [being crippled] in front of other kids—I'm embarrassed by these feelings even now, as much as we've talked about them, it's disgusting really that I did this to her—but I would run ahead so people wouldn't think I was with her."

"You seem to feel a lot of remorse about this, that this was something you *did* to her. Almost as if your feelings of embarrassment caused the disability."

"It is only because I was a child that I can excuse myself."

"And it occurs to me that you still bring these feelings—I'm referring here to your disgust for yourself—to your relationship with John."

"I don't see that . . ."

"I'm thinking of the day you watched him sleep, of being disgusted by him, afraid of him, of wanting to run out on him, and how much that sounds like your feelings about your mother. It was as if the very fact of your being HIV-negative constituted your running out on him, and this made you so guilty about those feelings. And I'm thinking about your guilt about your relatively good health, and about coming up with the idea that you could have HIV too—that you could be crippled like your mother."

"Well, I'll take your word for it, but I don't really see this."

"I wonder if it isn't harder for you to look at your feelings about John than about your mother . . . that you are having difficulty with this because it's still hard for you to look at those feelings."

"Hmm."

It was only over the following months that this line of interpretation made sense to Allen, and that he began to see that some of the guilt he felt about his mother was now being experienced about John and his "disability." Allen's guilt about John and his disability was thus nominally connected to a specific developmental experience—a mother who was disabled in a literal sense. But for both Allen and his mother, the literal disability was a signifier for a more important emotional disability, his mother's depression and loneliness.

It is my impression that compared to the general population, gay men as a group suffer inordinate problems with guilt, beginning very early in life. Developmental descriptions of gay men and speculation about the psychological "causes" of homosexuality have become highly politicized among theorists of gay life, including psychologists. Developmental description is often shunned as a reductionistic effort with the explicit or covert aim of pathologizing homosexuality—and, indeed, this has often been the case. But such abuse does not explain why *any* developmental descriptions of homosexuality (as opposed to physiological causes) are treated as a political compromise and construed as implying that homosexuality is a "choice" of the gay person or "mistake" of the parents. Developmental description of heterosexual development is often useful, and comparable descriptions of homosexual development need not imply pathology, choice, or culpability—unless homosexuality really *is* an unacceptable form of life. We do not dismiss the role of choice or infer culpability if the outcome is desired. It is precisely the fear of unearthing pathology that has caused us to neglect full developmental descriptions of gay lives.

Exclusively genetic or in utero explanations of homosexuality have been consistently inadequate in themselves, and identical twin studies used to support genetic explanations of homosexuality are the clearest indictment of the idea that homosexuality is *exclusively* a genetic product. While concordance of sexuality is much higher in identical twins than fraternal twins, siblings, or adopted children, it is still only about 50 percent. This means there is a 50 percent chance that genetically *identical* individuals (with nearly identical in utero environments) may be sexually discordant. It is certain that early life experience accounts for this discordance, and that childhood plays a significant role in the development of homosexual people. An explanation that includes early human experience—perhaps the most influential occurring *before age five*—does not introduce the idea of choice in any ordinary sense of the word, but what *if* it did? Is homosexuality only humanly defensible if it is *not* a matter of choice? Is a homosexual life by choice less constitutionally defensible than that of a converted Jew? Although such assumptions seem to underlie the position of many in the vanguard of gay rights, they are profoundly homophobic. Why would it be unacceptable to be homosexual merely on a whim (the source, no doubt, of many fleeting, individually uncharacteristic homosexual acts)? Or, perhaps, because one is inclined by physiological factors and is influenced by life experience to honor the predisposition? Genetic and in utero consequences are something we *put up with* and merely validate after the fact—if at all— and we invoke their immutability to combat our own, often unconscious homophobia.

Among the developmental circumstances that make survivor guilt a significant issue in the lives of many gay men is being homosexual itself. Very often the simple fact of a homosexual son introduces survivor guilt into family relations. The son's homosexuality is experienced by the family as an abandonment, and by the son himself as the reason he must abandon others to survive as himself. *Psychologically* the abandonment is experienced because of emotional separation from the family necessitated by conflict—sometimes only anticipated conflict—over sexuality; and the abandonment is often made literal by the son's leaving home in order to live homosexually. Allen's mother's experience of his move to California reveals both the psychological and literal sources of her experience of abandonment.

Because abandonment of the family may be integral to being homosexual, survivor guilt may be too. Guilt arises from feelings that one has to take from the family in order to survive. The homosexual son is often felt to take from his parents the "normal" son they wanted and expected; and he may be experienced as taking their grandchildren and their respectability in their community as well. Thus, by implication, the son takes the family's sense of identity from it. Tim, a 38-year-old San Franciscan, illustrates a son's—and his parents'—feelings that his homosexuality is an abandonment of and injury to the family in many senses. After five years of a secret homosexual life—tortured by the need to reveal himself to his parents—Tim wrote them while in graduate school to tell them who he was.

> As soon as I'd written the letter I starting thinking about my mother and how she can't stand pain. And this letter was—no doubt *whatsoever*—going to be very painful for her. So I called her and told her it was on its way and not to read it. And she didn't. My father read it, but, of course, I heard nothing from him about it. Apparently over the following months my mother sensed that something was wrong with my father—and I guess that started when she saw him *burn* the letter—and she later told me that during this time he asked her whether she thought he had been a good father to "the boys." What she said to him, as I remember it, was, "Well, not really, because you were never around for them." Finally she asked him what was in the letter and when he told her, she wrote me on my grandmother's birthday—her mother's birthday— and she said, "This is grandma's birthday, and it is the blackest day of my life."
>
> Over the next year or so I tried to communicate with them, but it was impossible. Essentially my mother told me I was going to hell for this, and at one point I even asked her, "Aside from my going to hell, what do you have against my being gay?" But it was impossible to talk to them about it, and I finally gave up. They have actually never mentioned it again, and I even had the idea that they had completely forgotten about it. And years later when I was visiting them in Pennsylvania to celebrate their fortieth wedding anniver-

sary—in 1988—I was sitting on my mother's bed, talking to her. She suddenly pulled a dress on a hanger out of her closet and said, "What do you think of this dress?" It was very pretty, and I said that, and she said, "Well, I'm saving this for your wedding." Well my mouth just about fell on the floor, and I said the only thing I could thing of: "Well, I guess you're going to be waiting a very long time." [11]

It is clear that the family feels abandoned, betrayed, and injured by Tim's news that he is homosexual. But it is also evident that Tim feels he must take responsibility for his parent's feelings, particularly his mother's, and he feels it appropriate to warn her against experiencing pain at the potential cost of abandoning himself and his developmental needs. Coming out to others is part of a process of *internal* as well as interpersonal growth, and thus the inability to come out to others—particularly *important* others—may be a significant impediment to growth of all kinds. For Tim, as for most gay men, his very nature is an injury to his parents, and an abandonment of their needs and expectations.

One's homosexuality, itself, is not the only source of guilt for gay men. In my clinical experience, a particular family organization common among gay men frequently contributes to a gay man's feelings of survivor guilt in another way. The following vignette is an illustration of that family organization.

Greg was a psychotherapy patient in his early forties who had HIV but only mildly deteriorated health. He found himself chronically depressed and unable to enjoy any activities, and he came to see me because his physician felt that his fatigue and other physical limitations were not substantially medical problems. Greg talked a lot about his family. His parents, now in their seventies, were recently divorced after many years of separation, but as Greg described it to me, "They might as well have gotten divorced forty years ago. My father paid no attention to us— he had girlfriends on the side. To this day, I can hardly stand to have anything to do with him."

Growing up, Greg was the oldest of three siblings and was close to his mother. He and his mother shared a sense of abandonment by his father (like Tim's mother, for her suggestion that he was "never there" for his sons suggests that he was never there for her either). Greg empathized with his mother's loneliness and depression, was acutely sensitive as a child to her moods, and attempted in an emotional sense to serve as surrogate husband to her. He also helped care for his two younger siblings in an effort to unburden his mother, and he became "my family's psychologist," often mediating conflict between siblings, siblings and his father, and his mother and father.

His effort to mitigate his mother's loneliness and depression was, not unexpectedly, largely unsuccessful, and when he was nine, she was psychiatrically hospitalized for depression. During the three months of her hospitalization, Greg did all the housekeeping, caring for his siblings, grocery shopping, preparing meals for the family, and ironing the family's laundry. Thus the hospitalization gave Greg an opportunity not only to relieve his mother entirely of her family burdens, but to "become" her, an expression of their common experience and identity in the family.

In therapy it became clear that Greg experienced the hospitalization as a personal failure: This would not have happened to her had he been a better son. Furthermore, he felt he had also failed his father, for he unconsciously also understood his task to be caring for his mother so that his father, whom he idolized as a child but hardly knew, would not be burdened with her. Therapy further revealed that he unconsciously bore his father's guilt for being a failure as a husband. He thus felt he had failed both parents, not only in his conscious relationship with each of them, but in his unconscious role as surrogate spouse. As a result of this family experience, Greg had grown up with a profound sense of failure about relationships in general.

Greg's sexuality was the source of guilt too, for it seemed a further abandonment of both parents, particularly his mother, with whom his unconscious role as surrogate spouse included a "latent" and unconscious (heterosexual) relationship. In adult life, his guilt was exacerbated by any happiness that he experienced in homosexual relationships, for he only compounded his failure of his mother by being less depressed than she. Greg slowly became conscious of limiting himself in order not to have a better life than he felt his mother had, and his AIDS served admirably in this effort. He had never overtly discussed his sexuality with his parents, and at the time of the session quoted here, he had not yet told his mother of his two-year-old AIDS diagnosis for fear of hurting her.

"My mother's seventy-fifth birthday is coming up, and she's going to expect me to come East for it. Well, I can't go, because she'll see how I look [because of AIDS], and she'll know something is wrong. And of course, I'll have a lot of guilt about not going. You know I haven't lived with her for over fifteen years, and I still feel guilt about *that*."

At this point Greg became silent for several moments.

"What's going on?" I wondered.

"I'm thinking about when I left home. I was twenty-five, and I moved out here [to California]. It was to get away from her, from both of them, because it was the only way I could be gay. And the very first day I was here, my father called, and he said, "You know, Greg, you're breaking your mother's heart." And then two years later he left her too."

"And that is a burden that you continue to feel, I think."

"Oh, all I have to do is hear the phone ring and I assume it's her. She's depressed and she says she can't walk, but she doesn't walk because she doesn't want to. And I know that I use AIDS as an excuse not to do things—I sit in the house doing nothing, exactly like my mother."

"Yes, we've talked about how much you live like her."

"I've always felt that I was too much like her. But, you know, so long as I can't go out of the house, I also don't have to visit her."

"Just in the sense that it gives you an excuse?" I asked.

"No—in the sense that if I'm not doing any better than she is, I don't have to cave into my guilt and go back for her birthday. AIDS has kind of evened the score between us, and if neither one of is walking, so to speak, then I don't feel like I owe her anything."

Greg's guilt about his parents is largely an expression of survivor guilt. His illness with AIDS reduces his feelings of guilt because it "evens the score." He may have escaped his parents and their emotional difficulties, but he now has a different kind of limitation in his life, and, in his mind, it is comparable to his mother's limitation of loneliness and depression. In a family where suffering is a measure of the importance of one's life and of how much one deserves from others, Greg's life is made more important by having AIDS. His illness serves as penance too—for leaving home in pursuit of a happier life, for his father's leaving home two years later in pursuit of a happier life for himself, and for disappointing his parents by being gay. Unfortunately, Greg's longstanding, unresolved guilt seriously impaired his capacity to use his time enjoyably, if within his true physical limitations. An exaggeration of limitations was the only

way he knew to feel as unsuccessful as his mother, and to make amends
to everyone.

Many do not have the psychological "advantage" of Greg's guilt-
mediating impairment with HIV. For uninfected men the epidemic is
too often not mitigating of guilt, but exacerbating. Developmental guilt
may provide a predisposition that, in combination with AIDS-induced
survivor guilt, becomes a devastating, self-destructive—even fatal—experience. In addition to "surviving" parents, uninfected men must deal
with the possibility of literally surviving millions of other gay men over
the coming decades. Larry, an uninfected psychotherapy patient in an intense, difficult relationship with Mark, an HIV-positive man, illustrates
such an experience. Larry grew up with a chronically depressed father,
a mother whom he described as "cheerful but incredibly shallow," and
two younger sisters. From early childhood Larry had an acute sense of
his father's isolation and loneliness, and his anger and bitterness about
his failed career as an engineer. Early in his childhood, it had become
Larry's job to involve his sullen father in the dinner table conversation
each night. When Larry lapsed at his task, his father withdrew into a
sad, silent, sulking demeanor that Larry experienced as his own failure. He admired and idolized his father, but his father's sadness pained
him badly and felt like the product of Larry's failure in the relationship.
In twice-weekly therapy, Larry and I had talked often about his fear of
allowing himself to experience his feelings, which he said "Are mostly
just sadness, sadness, and sadness." We also speculated that his fear of
his feelings was partly fear of living in a permanent state of sadness like
his father.

> "Mark is coming home on Tuesday," Larry told me, "and I'm so
> glad, and yet when I thought about it over the weekend, I was just
> sad. All I felt was sadness."
>
> "Which was not what you thought you'd feel about his coming
> home?"
>
> "No, I wanted him home. I couldn't wait. And at the same time, I
> have this constant idea that it's just not going to work. I was think-
> ing about that, and it reminded me of when I was in college, before
> I came out. I would wander around campus at night, and I would
> walk by the rooms of guys I had crushes on—but you know it was
> hopeless, they were completely unobtainable. I felt the same sad-
> ness then, as if I had lost something that I had never even had.
> Sometimes it would be snowing, and it had that really silent, cush-

ioned quality it gets when it's snowing, and I would be looking into the rooms from outside . . ."

"This reminds me of your father at the dinner table," I said. "He sat there in his silence, outside. And this is what you're describing."

"Well, it really is a lot like that. I always felt outside like that. I feel outside, I still do, and, you know, I often have this feeling about men that I don't really know what they're up to, what the rules are, or how it all works, and that I'm outside and I have to sort of interpret what they're doing, and pretend that I understand it and sort of play along. And this gives me the same kind of loneliness and sadness."

I realized that Larry was also talking about feeling outside and isolated from me, but I decided for now to stay with the line we had been pursuing.

"This is like your father, self-absorbed and inattentive, trying to make sense out of what's going on at the dinner table. But is this true with Mark? Is it true that you are like your father with Mark, outside and trying to guess what's going on with him?"

"Well, in one sense, which is that he has HIV, and I can't really know what that's like. Recently when we were talking about my father, I realized that I kind of equate Mark's HIV with my father's depression, that they are alike in that way. They're outside, and I'm separated from them by their problems. And the sadness that Mark has had ever since he knew he had HIV is something I identify with, that connects us. And it's also what makes it OK for me to be connected to him, and to try and really make a relationship out of this."

"And how does the sadness make it OK?" I asked.

"Well, if I think about wandering around in the snow, and then going into a guy's room and making it with him, it's like just diving into what's going on at the dinner table, just getting into the conversation with everyone else. You know, I would leave my father behind when I did that—he would sit there and I knew he was getting depressed, that he wasn't part of what was going on."

"So getting into a relationship, and abandoning your sadness to the happiness you might have, feels like an abandonment of the sad parts of yourself?"

"Definitely. And of my father. And at the same time, I'd like to get rid of him. I don't want to think about him. All of that anger—he was always against the whole world—as if it were everyone else's fault his career was a failure. When Mark and I—when we first met and decided to have sex, and we talked about his being positive—my first reaction was, you know, I'm afraid of this, of getting HIV, or getting attached to someone who might die. I thought of just getting the hell out of there. And then I thought, 'No, I'll sleep with him one time.'"

"Why was that?"

"Well, I had to be sure that his being positive wasn't why I was ending it, I mean that I was not just afraid of his being positive. So I thought, 'Well, I'll sleep with him and then if I want to, I can end it.' This is just like taking care of my father because he's depressed. So I don't know if I want to leave because he's positive or I want to stay because he's positive. And my guilt is one of the things that makes me think I'm involved with Mark for the wrong reasons."

"But is it possible to respond with empathy to someone without guilt being part of the empathy?" I asked. "Or just to respond to Mark, HIV aside?"

"I imagine it is. But, as you say, these things are all tangled up together for me. When I think of Mark, and of leaving him, you know what my fantasy is? It's that he'll die next week, and if I stay it won't happen."

"Yes. For example, you might keep him alive by keeping him involved in the dinner conversation."

"If I'd been depressed too," Larry responded, "then he wouldn't have been alone. We would have just talked to each other, we would have had our own world together."

"And how does that relate to Mark?" I asked.

"It would be like my having HIV."

"And would that solve the conflict about whether to go or to stay?"

"Well, it would solve my guilt about him. I don't want to have AIDS, but it would mean a lot to us if I did."

In Larry's case the developmental guilt, like Allen's, is nominally focused on the specific limitation of a parent. But for Larry, the developmental guilt interacts powerfully with the guilt he feels in a relationship with a man who also has a limitation, HIV. Psychotherapeutic clarification can help reduce such interaction of historical conflict with life in the AIDS epidemic. Survivor guilt relies on entangled, unconscious, irrational feelings and beliefs—precisely those that psychotherapy can reveal, analyze, and clarify. As Larry felt less entangled in guilt, he described himself as feeling closer to Mark, and closer to the things that the two share emotionally—*including* a sense of sadness and irony about life.

Developmental conflicts that are *not* about guilt also interact with the psychological experience of seronegative men living in the epidemic. Histories of especially difficult conflict about homosexuality, serious depression, and long-standing personal isolation all interact destructively with the public event. The AIDS epidemic provides a versatile opportunity for playing out developmental problems of every kind. At the most difficult end of this interactive spectrum are men with extensive, serious conflict about their sexuality and consequent depression and isolation. Such men, living in the AIDS epidemic, find new reasons for remaining isolated, and perhaps sexually dysfunctional, and AIDS may be enlisted unconsciously to displace feelings from the private conflict about sexuality to the public matter of AIDS and the epidemic.

In the middle of the spectrum we see men with similar developmental problems that either are less severe or have been better worked through in adult life. For them, the AIDS epidemic may be a test of psychological "progress" or may entail some regression. Still other men, with more benign developmental problems, may find themselves with unprecedented depression, isolation, or sexual dysfunction—experiences, in this case, that are largely reactive to the epidemic. Finally, there are some men, possessing a fortuitous combination of a relatively benign history and sturdy psychological "constitution," who appear able to weather the AIDS epidemic with a minimum of serious problems.

Fortunately, survivor guilt is often responsive to psychotherapy.[12] Whether through individual psychotherapy, therapy or support groups, or prevention education, there are many reasons it is critical that we address survivor guilt in gay communities. Pragmatically, healthier survivors make better caretakers of those with AIDS, and this is now important work in gay communities. It is this idea that has allowed much of the initial attention to the distress of uninfected men, for it simultaneously acknowledges the needs of positive men, and thus reduces guilt. But there are also the independent issues of survivors themselves. Many will not survive for long because of self-destructive behaviors fueled by guilt, depression, and anxiety. For those who will survive, the epidemic has already wrought an immense amount of psychological damage through loss, and this damage is only compounded and exacerbated by guilt. The psychological futures of countless survivors, as well as the future of gay communities as a whole, depend partly on our ability to deal with these intense and complex psychological issues.

Ed Wolf, with whom I began facilitating workshops in 1990 for HIV-negative men at San Francisco's Shanti project, is a 42-year-old who has worked in AIDS services for nearly a decade at Shanti, Metropolitan Community Church, and The AIDS Health Project of the University of California at San Francisco. In discussing our upcoming first Shanti workshop, he told me of a visit he had made to Theresienstadt, a Nazi concentration camp in Czechoslovakia. Ed was clarifying for me his first understanding of the experience of being HIV-negative.

There was a very long road leading through acres and acres of cemeteries leading up to the camp. And finally going through the gate, you are suddenly standing in a courtyard where literally tens of thousands of people had been lined up in rows and shot. It was an incredible, very intense experience, and while I was standing there, and when I was walking through the rest of the camp, I could *feel* the really great suffering that had happened here. You could feel it in everything about the place. And amazingly, what I realized was that I felt comforted by it—because it validated for me all the suffering that has gone on in the epidemic. And I have never felt that kind of validation before for what we've been through. It was all there: people had suffered the way we are suffering, and just sharing that was very, very comforting for me. It was a feeling of being whole for the first time since the epidemic started, because it made sense of my suffering and I could let that be part of me.

After this whole tour through the camp, we started to walk toward the gate to leave, and I suddenly had this feeling of just overwhelming joy—it was joy about being able to leave and leave the suffering behind. And it occurred to me that this was something I had never felt in the epidemic. I had never felt that I could leave it behind the way I was able to leave behind the suffering that took place in Theresienstadt. And as I walked under the gate, I felt this incredible gratitude about being able to leave.

But then you are on the road again with all the tombstones. And that was it, that was the epidemic for me: this incredible—

profound—gratitude on the one hand, and miles and miles of tomb-stones on the other. And this was when I first had an idea of what the epidemic was doing to those of us who were [HIV] negative. That we were very, very grateful for being negative, but we were being left living with this incredible suffering. And there was abso-lutely no way to walk away from it. And I thought, my God, if this is ever over with, we are going to be left with these acres of tombstones. Tombstones and gratitude—this is my idea of being HIV-negative.[13]

Ed's powerful feelings about those murdered in the camp reveals human experience in transcendence of place and time—in this case, the complex and painful experience of witnessing the deaths of many but being a survivor. For Ed, these feelings had remained largely unrecog-nized and unvalidated in the AIDS epidemic. His gratitude at being able to walk out of the camp—to *not* perish there—is also something he was not able to experience as an uninfected man surviving the epidemic. That inability is partly due to guilt about HIV—the fate of fellow gay men—which he does not have about the Nazi holocaust and its victims.

Chapter 4
Life in the Shadow: Loss
and Mourning

He has been told that the number of stars in the sky, whatever it is, is just the right number.

Also, that before he goes away again, he should file a change of address. There is no bravery more stubborn than this: the dead lie where they fall.

But note, he does not tell us, or even himself, everything. And, besides, this world lasts only so long as it lacks balance—the veer preserves us.—Keith Waldrop, from Potential Random [1]

The first decade of the epidemic alone has made it certain that all gay men now live—or will live—with loss that is unimaginable to most Americans. The relentlessness of this loss raises doubt about what form of psychological and interpersonal life will be possible for those gay men who do not succumb to AIDS itself. For some, the losses of the epidemic will surely make even physical survival impossible.

Upon leaving a dinner party at the home of a heterosexual couple in San Francisco with a friend and sometimes lover, Tim, I commented to him that it became clear to me in the course of the evening that our hosts did not live in the epidemic.

"That's true," Tim acknowledged, "But they have many friends, like me, who do live in it, and they are very close to it."

"But they don't *live* in it," I said, "and you can feel that about them. It's evident in their speech, the way they sit in their chairs, in everything about them. They don't live in the shadow that we have lived in for so long—the shadow that you and I have loved each other in and that made our love so impossible. It's been so long now that I'm only conscious of this shadow when I see those who live free of it."

In discussing this perception, which Tim began to share, we agreed that there was a difference. Unconsciously we had come to live with a different set of expectations and assumptions about life, about what it means and what the possibilities are. We have a different sense of time, and of possible futures or the lack of them, and a different sense of what is important and what is not. We live with a habitual level of intensity that comes from existing daily with matters of life and death. *They* neither live with this intensity nor do they understand it—though I think they peripherally perceive it, and with some discomfort. It is as if we move through our troubled world walking in deep sand, while our hosts still walk on paved roads—perhaps not gold, but firm, relatively clean, and trustworthy nevertheless. What was so apparent in them during that dinner, was their ease, their easy sense of expectation and their trust that each step would follow the last, and that the road actually went somewhere. We have so little of that left. We move with so much more effort, and do it with so much doubt about its purpose. Too many men have already vanished, and too many more will surely follow. We live in a world of survivors—*we hope*—but also a world of ghosts, who, like invisible housemates, invade our solitude and complicate our lives. In our trek across the sand, we must negotiate paths between and around them, and between and around our feelings about them. This is the shadow that all gay men now live—and, if possible, love—in, whether they can acknowledge it or not, and it will remain a part of who we are for as long as we are each alive.

Jim, a San Franciscan working in AIDS services, describes a personal history with the epidemic beginning in the early years, and finally crossing over to life in the shadow.

"My three best friends from college—we were gay, but we didn't know it then—the three of them lived in Mill Valley [north of San Francisco] together, and Robbie and I were living in the city, and they had us over for Thanksgiving. This was the beginning for me— 1984, I guess—which was pretty early on in the epidemic for me. I remember that John wasn't feeling well that night, and before dinner was over, he went to lie down. I just thought he was tired. You know, I was working with AIDS people, and I just never thought about why he was tired. But two weeks later I had this message on my answering machine, and it was his lover, Bruce, and he said, 'John died last night. He got pneumonia. I thought I should tell you right away.' I was shocked, and mostly at the time, I just resented the way Bruce left that message on the machine.

"But in some way this didn't affect me that badly. John was the first one I knew, and I guess I just reacted to it like it was a fluke— you know, I was upset, but it wasn't that bad. But next year Bruce died, and then Mark, who was really my best friend of the three, and when this happened I realized that they were *all* dead—this whole group of my best friends was *completely* gone. And suddenly it just overwhelmed me, and I would picture their house empty or someone else living in it—I would wake up in the middle of the night and think about that—and this was the point that it really hit me: you know, we are all going to die, we are all going to be dead. And if I'm lucky, they won't leave me behind. How did we end up like this? But up to that point, the point when Mark died, I was just able to deny what was going on for me. It just didn't seem real until Mark died. But now it seems very, very real . . . and every day I must think about Mark and how much I miss him. It is something I think about every day one way or another. Their not being here is a part of my life in the way that they used to be part of my life. It's like *your hair*—one way or another you deal with it every day."

"But you and Robbie," I asserted, "You are both negative."

Yeah. But to me that seems like the *least* important thing about the epidemic. I guess if Robbie got sick, that would be the end for me. And at the same time I don't know how we've stayed together. It has been so hard because of the epidemic. We still love each other, I think, but it's become harder and harder. It's like the epidemic eats away at our relationship."

"Why do you think that is?" I asked.

"I don't know. In some ways AIDS has made us cling to each other—but that's not the same thing as love. I guess it's made it harder because you can see how easy it is to lose someone you love. Or how easy it is to let down someone you love."

"By dying?"

"By dying. Or by being afraid of dying, or being afraid of their dying. By not being able to stick it out with them. All of that. You're afraid to love someone or let them love you. Robbie and I—I guess I'd have to say that we're both much more afraid than we used to be. For myself, I'm also much less attached to life than I used to be, and that makes it hard to love too. It makes you feel like you can't keep your promises. You might be dead, or you might *want* to be dead. To love someone you have to be committed to being there for them, and you have to expect them to be there for you. And if you're not committed to life—I started to say, if you don't believe in life—then love finally becomes impossible. You just don't know if either of you can stay around for another week. It makes real love too scary."

Merely living and loving close to the AIDS epidemic does not place one in the shadow. Even someone as personally and professionally close to the epidemic as Jim was still able to fend off its personal meaning for a considerable period of time. It took the death of all three friends from college. On the other hand, for many men profoundly identified with their gay communities, the repeated losses of lovers and friends may finally make impersonal losses nearly as powerful as the personal ones. One begins to grieve the deaths of unknown men simply because they were gay and part of one's family, and even the man with no personal losses may finally be carried beyond life as a concerned observer to life in the shadow.

The Psychological Idea of Loss

. . . and then I put my finger into the hard, unflexible opening to search for what I knew wasn't there, just like what happened in Orlando, nothing's ever quite where you want it, a soul goes by and you haven't even taken a bite out of it—just like that, a thing can happen and dismiss itself and you're left with nothing. Rotten nothing. But you're not even back where you started from, you're back even further, back someplace no one's even gotten around to naming, never will, like an area in the throat even a physician can't stand to look at.—Ippy Gizzi, from Letters to Pauline [2]

The way the adult experiences loss, and his resilience against it, is partly a result of early life experience. Erik Erikson speaks eloquently about human psychological development and feelings of loss. The first year of life, he tells us, is concerned with the establishment of "basic trust," a foundation that provides the resilience to weather loss in later life. Such basic trust is established by a caretaking environment that is reasonably consistent and reasonably responsive to the infant's needs. This provides the child with a foundation that allows him to trust himself, others, and the world. [3]

At best, however, the first year of life also inevitably provides the first experiences of loss, and plants the seeds for difficulty with loss in adult life.

> Our clinical work indicates that this point in the individual's early
> history [the second six months of life] provides him with some
> sense of basic loss. . . . [This time] normally expresses itself in our
> dependencies and nostalgias, and in our all too hopeful and all too
> hopeless states.[4]

When the infant's environment during his first year is less than opti-
mal, for example, with a mother who cannot respond in a reasonably
reliable fashion to her infant's needs, the consequences can be serious
difficulties with loss in adult life.

> In adults the impairment of basic trust is expressed in a basic mis-
> trust. It characterizes individuals who withdraw into themselves in
> particular ways when at odds with themselves and with others. . . .
> A drastic loss of accustomed mother love without proper substitu-
> tion at this time can lead (under otherwise aggravating conditions)
> to acute infantile depression (Spitz, 1945) or to a mild but chronic
> state of mourning which may give a depressive undertone to the
> whole remainder of life. . . . It is against the combination of these
> impressions of having been deprived, of having been divided, and
> of having been abandoned, all of which leave a residue of basic
> mistrust, that basic trust must be established and maintained.[5]

Special Loss in the Development of Gay Men

Dear Mother
Do you think it is possible that life go on this way?—Ippy Gizzi, from Letters to Pauline[6]

In addition to universal, infantile sources of the adult experience of
loss and depression, there are others. Some stem from later childhood
development, and some from severe trauma in adulthood.[7] In my experience with adult gay men there is an unusual level and frequency of
sadness, nostalgia, and longing. Often this stems not only from infantile development, but from common developmental problems arising in
puberty and adolescence and, later, in the "coming-out" process. These
experiences contribute to many gay men finding loss especially difficult.
An illustration of adolescent sources of loss is described in the following session with Bill, a psychotherapy patient in his late twenties. This
session occurred several months after Bill came to therapy to work on
conflicts about his sexuality. We had talked for several sessions about

his lifelong, central masturbatory fantasy, which began in puberty and had continued to the present. The fantasy was about having sex with the same, idealized man who had come to represent all that Bill longed to be connected to emotionally and sexually—and all that was forbidden and impossible.

"It's been so much a part of my experience ever since I started masturbating that I've never noticed it before. But I just realized a few days ago that right after I have an orgasm, I feel terrible grief. I just never noticed it, but when I think back, that's always been the case."

"And this happens when you masturbate, but not when you have an orgasm with someone else?" I wondered.

"Not as much with someone else—sometimes. But masturbating, it's always true. I suddenly feel sad, and sometimes, if there is something bad going on in my life, I've started crying right after I come. It's just this intense sadness, really a feeling of loss, and I may attach it to something else going on, but I think it really comes from my sexual fantasy somehow."

"And do you have a sense of where this feeling of sadness or loss comes from? What it has to do with the fantasy?"

"It's that he disappears, I think."

"That your fantasy disappears?"

"Yes. And when I was a kid, it was only when I was masturbating that I could have him. I mean, I knew that I could never really have sex with a man, and I had this relationship with this beautiful man in my fantasy, which was the only one I could have, and when I came, he would be gone."

"You are obviously very moved right now," I interjected.

"Well, I'm feeling sad about this, I think I'm just feeling all the sadness of all the times this happened. It's as if every time I come, some part of me also dies, and I have died a thousand times by now. And I feel very angry about it—you know, about all this prohibition on gay sex, that it was something I could never really do, and all I would ever have was my fantasy. I had to hold onto that, because it was only in this fantasy that I could ever be who I really was."

"I'm wondering," I said, "if this sadness, and feeling of loss doesn't go beyond just what you experience in connection with orgasm during masturbation."

"Oh it does, and I've thought about that, because it really be-

comes my sense that if I ever get close to anyone—and that would
be a man, of course—well, it's not something I can have. So since
I've come out, and I really am having sex with men, then I just bring
this sadness along, because the sense is that this is still not something that you can really have, and that somehow you are going to
lose this just the way I'd lose the fantasy. It's very mixed up."

"Well you have a long-standing experience of feeling sadness and
loss in connection with homosexual intimacy," I tried to clarify.

"But now I don't have to lose the person—I mean there is a real
person, and I can have a relationship."

"But much of the capacity to have a relationship with a man is
something that you developed in your fantasy life, this is how we explore and develop our feelings and bring them to real life—through
fantasy. I think you are underestimating the power of the unconscious association that your fantasy life of many years established
between intimacy and loss."

Bill was silent for several moments. "It's very powerful, this entanglement, and I was thinking about your question about whether
I had this sadness when I was having sex with someone else."

"You said sometimes . . ."

"Yes, I do sometimes have that. I suppose it's the unconscious
connection you are talking about."

"But what about the times when you don't have it. The times you
come, and you're with someone. What is going on there? What are
the feelings then?"

"Those times—the times I feel OK afterwards—are when I really
stay connected to the person during sex."

"As opposed to what?" I asked.

"As opposed to being there having sex with someone else, but
really being in my fantasy. When I do that, well, then there is the
same feeling of loss afterwards, because I've really never connected.
You know, it can be like masturbating, I'm in my head, but there
happens to be someone else—I should say someone else's body—
there."

"And do you know what it is that allows you," I asked, "to 'stay
connected'? As opposed to staying in your fantasy even with someone else there?"

"I know exactly when it is—it's when I feel very close to someone . . ."

"You've left this observation hanging," I coaxed.

"I wanted to say—I started to say, that it is when I really trust someone. Because then I feel like I can expose my feelings to them, need them, be connected to them, really feel sexually stimulated because of who they are, and I'm not afraid of losing them. It is my trusting that they will not abandon me."

"And this must require your overcoming the expected feelings of sadness and loss that you anticipate after you come."

"I have said to myself sometimes, particularly with Dan, when we were together, 'This is someone I love very much, and your sadness is not about him, that is not what is going on here.' You know, 'This is Dan, and the sadness is about something else, something old.'"

"I had the idea when I asked you what allowed you to stay connected—you mentioned trust. But there was something else you started to say or were thinking about. Something drew your attention."

"Well, I started to say that I didn't feel the loss if I was connected to the person, and I realized that there was something else in there—that sometimes when I come, I think about AIDS, and about how it is spread, and when I come that's what I think of, and I feel very depressed about that. I thought of that once when Dan and I were having sex, and afterwards we were cleaning up, and he said, 'Let's wipe up this killer cum,' or something like that. And I got very angry, and I said, 'Why did you say that?' And he said, 'I was just making a joke, like killer kum, you know, K-U-M.' And I thought, 'Well here's a new reason to get depressed after sex.'"

"So that even if you are connected to a person you're making love with, AIDS, or the thought of HIV in the semen, can make you feel the sadness that you felt about your fantasy?"

"Yes."

I continued. "They are both about loss, aren't they?"

"Yes, they are both about losing the person that I love. And it's very hard to let yourself go when you are thinking about that."

In Bill's adolescent experience, in the interaction of feelings about AIDS with that adolescent experience, and perhaps in his earlier development, we see some sources of his difficulties with loss, trust, intimacy, and for his chronic depression.

Coming Out and the Experience of Loss

For many gay men, the second special developmental issue contributing to difficulties with loss is that of the *coming-out* process. Coming out is a complicated psychological and social process, but it is fair to say that it begins internally with the individual recognizing his erotic and emotional attachments. Briefly, the internal process proceeds from a first recognition of homosexual feelings—often very erratic or diffuse initially—to an assimilation of that recognition, a clarification of the meaning of the feelings, and a relative integration of the newly discovered feelings into other aspects of internal experience. This process is essentially what we mean when we say a man is "coming out to himself."

The man coming out to himself is also a person living in a social world. Others in his world reflect back their perceptions of him, responding to both his deliberate and unconscious representations of himself. This feedback from others is then incorporated into the internal process of recognition, assimilation, clarification, and integration. The actuality of this whole process, including both psychological and social elements, is that it flows in both directions simultaneously—not unlike a highly sensitive and refined feedback loop—and the two elements are much more integrated than either a psychological or sociological description might convey. We come to feel internally whole in being recognized by others as our real selves; and our feelings of internal wholeness allow us to relate to others "accurately" and honestly.

The objectives of coming out are much like those of any developmental process accomplished with reasonable success. One comes to feel relatively whole and relatively likeable within himself, and how one lives and relates to others reasonably reflects that internal experience of self. In this sense the coming-out process, when accomplished in adolescence, is much like the identity development of any teenager, with the important qualification that *who* he is, is completely unacceptable to many around him, both peer and adult. Thus the constant interaction of internal and social processes so important to successful development is almost always problematic—and is often traumatic—depending on the level of support the young man is able to garner from his particular environment. When the environment is indifferent or hostile to the emerging internal experience of homosexuality, there is a serious risk that the young man will find a partial solution in the isolation, encapsulation, or dissociation of the homosexual parts of his internal life from his emotional, intellectual, and social development as a whole. The consequence is a person whose feelings are unintegrated and divided, and whose internal and social lives do not accurately reflect or express each other. The result is *not* that two separate, but satisfactory, lives are led, but rather that the young man's internal and interpersonal lives are both impoverished by their lack of wholeness, and by their lack of integration with each other. He remains divided, inauthentic, and dissatisfied, both within himself and in the world.

There is an important relationship between the coming-out process and loss. Developmental theory can often seem to imply an idealized, linear, progressive process that misrepresents the reality. Human development—the growth and life of the psychosocial self—is immensely complex and subtle. The complexity is perhaps even more pronounced in homosexual development, for with some exceptions, there is an effort at one or many points in the individual's life to live heterosexually. This means many developmental false starts and elaborations and, often, the relatively complete development of a psychological and social "false self," which at some later point in life must often be abandoned.

Thus in the developmental process, loss is first experienced early in the homosexual child or adolescent as the *unattainability* of a real self, for this is a self connected to forbidden homosexual feelings. This "anticipatory" loss of an authentic and meaningful life leaves many gay men with a characteristic, lifelong experience of loss and nostalgia; an idealization of unattainable gay relationships; and more of a capacity to *long for* intimacy than the trust to really accomplish it. As the adolescent and postadolescent grows further into a false, heterosexual self, both within himself and in the world, the real self recedes further and further. Feelings about the loss of the real self continue, though often unconsciously, in an effort to minimize the pain of the loss and to deny its reasons. If the man does finally begin a coming-out process, it is invariably driven by a sense of loss about the real self, a loss that has finally become unbearable and unmanageable.

Once the coming-out process begins, new losses are encountered. These are losses of parts of the *false* self, and the older the man when coming out is initiated, the more false self there is to feel loss about. Loss is felt because within the "false" self are many feelings, experiences, identifications, and relationships that are authentic and important. Despite their authenticity and importance, psychological, social, and interpersonal pressures may require their abandonment. For example, a married, homosexual man coming out in later life may deeply love his wife and may even have significant, though secondary, sexual feelings for her. He will also have a form of life built around his marriage, including close friends, and perhaps children and a home. But his wife's feelings about his sexuality and those of friends—as well as the homosexual man's projections of his own feelings onto others—may isolate him from those who are important to him, and thus from parts of himself that were authentic in those relationships. The shedding of even a largely "false" self—one with very little authenticity—may create a serious experience of loss. For many men, coming out entails the loss of an entire form of life, and this may lay shaky foundations for the experience of loss in the epidemic.

Life in the Epidemic: Feelings about Loss and Death

If this city, and this
city alone (*it is such a small thing to ask—surely*
to Universal Cause-and-Effect an
infraction beneath notice) if only
this single city might
escape . . .

No:
there shall not be left here one
board nailed to another.
—Keith Waldrop, *from* The Ruins of Providence [8]

The failure to acquire an adequate foundation of basic trust in infancy, specific childhood problems with separation and loss (such as parental divorce or death), the developmental problems discussed in chapters 2 and 3, and the special experiences with loss of most gay men, all contribute to the predisposition of the gay man trying to survive the epidemic. Loss, above all the other consequences of the epidemic, may reverse even a relatively sound psychological predisposition. The epidemic has created a profoundly untrustworthy world that requires a substantial reservoir of trust to offset it. The consequences for those who have failed to develop basic trust, or who have lost it because of later trauma, will be isolation, depression or mania, and compulsions, addiction, or substance abuse. All these suggest a person who has lost—or failed to develop—a capacity to trust his own feelings, to rely on others, to be emotionally vulnerable, and to be intimate.

The extent to which many gay men have acclimated themselves to death is a measure of how much loss has occurred in the epidemic. Many gay men have lost a half-dozen, a dozen, or even two dozen friends, and the familiarity of such stories can make them seem routine and unremarkable—even to the survivor himself. Intimacy with loss and death is an important part of life in the shadow. For the larger society, still gripped by an aversive and avoidant relationship to death, still grieving the deaths of 80-year-olds, and still viscerally ignorant of the AIDS epidemic, the life of the gay man has no reality and makes no sense. Gay men have experienced an unprecedented decade of death among young peers that has transformed their assumptions and feelings about life and death and that has further isolated them from mainstream society. If gay men were at one time isolated and alone because of their sexuality, they now have profound, new reasons to feel a loss of connection to mainstream ideas of meaningful life. But how could gay men's assumptions, feelings, and values not be changed by this experience? Gay community organizer Ben Schatz, described to me a personal vision of the epidemic:

> I sometimes feel like gay men are dangling by their fingers from the edges of a roof, and every minute or so you can look over at the man next to you just in time to see him let go and drop. But up on top of the roof, the rest of the country is having a cocktail party— and except for those people who are walking around stepping on our fingers, they're not even aware we're hanging there. Yet man after man lets go and falls, and you're dangling there and thinking, "Can I really hang on? How long can I hang on? This seems impossible." And man after man loses his grip and falls to his death, and up above you hear ice tinkling in the glasses, but the pile of bodies down below is just getting higher and higher.

The Denial of Loss and Grief

I must take the liberty which adjoins itself to your own fluent body to tell you now about a small seed of depression in my head. I often cannot distinguish between lassitude, lack of thyroid and absence of my contact lenses, etc. A dimness which I am familiar as a relative with is liable to thicken inside me even before I have the opportunity to rise from bed, installing its limpness in the very delicate and impressionable areas behind my

*corneas. I hate that dimness, and thank God on occasion something sweet and audible
like your letter arrives.—Ippy Gizzi, from* Letters to Pauline[9]

Despite widespread recognition of the *fact* of loss and death in the epidemic, feelings about the facts are often denied, even by those living in the middle of the disaster. Some of the denial is psychologically naive and primitive, as expressed in the 1991 statement of a gay man living in San Francisco:

> The possibilities are limitless. See, I am not willing to give the disease power. And just take dis-ease, going to Louise Hay: "Dis-ease, the condition of being uneasy," and the whole scenario behind that. Her experience, what I've gotten through her is, AIDS is just another opportunity, it's another thing that we've created on this planet at this time to learn from.[10]

Psychotherapy patients, whose authentic feelings are generally more accessible than those of this man, often report multiple losses. They also often acknowledge that they do not know how they are affected by them. One psychotherapy patient, Carl, was in his early forties, and had lived in San Francisco since the beginning of the epidemic. He told me that he was lonely but would no longer try to make gay friends. I wondered why.

> "Because they turn out to be positive and then they die, and I don't want to do that anymore," he told me. "Most of my friends are dead, except Bill, or they are positive and there are too many things I can't talk to them about."
>
> "I'm wondering why it's been so hard for you to talk about this here," I asked.
>
> "I don't know. Larry and Bob [the patient's two ex-lovers] are both positive. I must have had fifty people die," Carl answered, now beginning to cry.
>
> "You are obviously very upset by this," I commented.
>
> "But what's *the point* of getting upset about this? It won't help anything—I can only say . . ."
>
> "What did you start to say?"
>
> "I started to say something that I don't believe, which is that they all got what they deserved. And sometimes I'd like to believe that, so that I don't have to miss them so much. But I know that's not the reason. My friends and I just talk about the details: 'Oh, did you

hear that so-and-so died,' or something like that. But we never talk about how we feel about it, or about the big effect, the accumulation of it all. I think I just have to keep to myself at this point."

There are many who expect not to be affected by the losses of the epidemic and who feel they are not. Such assertions, at best, express the desire not to be affected, and, at worst, a loss of the capacity for any feelings because life in the epidemic has become overwhelming. Denial receives some profound, if often covert, social support. If homophobia denies the existence of a relationship between two men—or simply its importance—it also denies the importance of the loss when a partner dies. Psychotherapy patients who have lost partners to AIDS speak often of their family's surprise at the depth of their grief. The family wishes to deny the grief, for to recognize it would be to acknowledge the relationship for what it was—an acknowledgment often refused for the duration of the relationship. Men experiencing profound grief thus often remain socially isolated and unsupported in the most rudimentary ways. Gary, a 38-year-old psychotherapy patient, described a weekend at the family cabin with his parents, sisters, and several nieces and nephews. The weekend occurred about six weeks after his lover of four years, Robin, died suddenly at home after two years of illness.

"I suppose it was ridiculous of me to go, but I've been in the house alone since Robin died, and I wanted to get out, and I especially wanted to see Claire [Gary's twin sister, with whom he was close]. We'd talked on the phone a couple of times about Robin, but there was so much else I wanted to tell her. But what happened was that all weekend everyone was running around the cabin cooking or cleaning or playing cards, and I just sat at the table crying. And half the time they'd pretend they didn't notice, and then someone, Claire usually, would come over to me and say, "Gary, are you *sure* you're all right?" and I'd say "No, I'm not all right. I feel terrible," and she would walk away because she didn't know what to say. My mother did not say one thing about Robin all weekend, and it was clear that she just wanted the whole thing to go away. This was the loneliest time I can remember. I wish I'd just stayed home by myself."

"How were you feeling about Claire and the others while this was going on?" I asked.

"Well, I felt foolish sitting there crying. And sometimes I would just feel furious at them, because they made it very clear that they didn't know how I was feeling and they didn't want to. When Claire's husband had an operation—I mean, it was about *nothing*—my mother was all over her with sympathy. But Claire is straight, and I'm a queer, and my mother knows that, but she's never been able to talk about it. So I guess there's no surprise that she can't talk about Robin. But I feel a lot of anger about that, a lot of resentment, and our relationship will never be the same after this. All of them, even Claire, just haven't been able to give me anything over this, and I don't see how I could forgive them for it. They have really given me nothing."

Many men, unable to experience feelings through their own overload, denial, or lack of social support, are nevertheless aware of the problem. Steve, a 36-year-old psychotherapy patient, discussed his reasons for going to Washington, D.C., in 1992 to see the Names Project quilt:

"I have often thought that living in the epidemic is like living on your MasterCard: you can go on your merry way, but eventually the bill arrives. And I know I haven't been paying my bills as I go along, because I have lost so many friends and acquaintances, and most of the time I just haven't had feelings about it. Going to Washington was my way of trying to catch up, to pay my bill—and it worked in spades. I mean it was horrible and it was wonderful at the same time, because I walked around and saw maybe a half dozen people I'd known [represented in quilt panels] and I was just overwhelmed. And as horrible as it was, it was a big relief . . ."

"How was it a relief?" I asked.

"It was a relief because I got it out. I cried for the last eight years, and not only about people I knew. I mean, I cried when I saw quilts of people I'd never known —something would set me off. I was crying for everyone, for the whole thing, the whole epidemic. And it was a great relief to find out that I had feelings about it, that I could have them. And I guess to find out I could survive them, which so far I think I have."

The costs of broadly repressing and denying feelings are incurred in the narrower repression and denial of feelings about loss. One necessarily loses a capacity for all feeling, including happy feelings, and feelings that allow intimacy. In the case of feelings about loss, repression creates specific additional problems because the "grieving process" is inhibited or prevented entirely if feelings cannot be allowed. Some men seem to know intuitively that feelings of loss and grief will inhibit the grieving process. Tom, a 35-year-old psychotherapy patient, speaking of his dead lover Sean, is an example of someone who worked deliberately to keep feelings available so that he could assimilate the death.

> After Sean died, I felt dead—I mean, I had no feelings at all about his being dead. Except that in the middle of the night I would wake up and suddenly I would panic: you know, "Oh my God, Sean is *dead!*" It would be a realization of that fact, but it would also be this sense that I *had* to do something about it. At first I thought this was about wanting to make him alive again, but I began to think, "What I have to do about this is *think* about it—I've got to get it into my head that Sean's dead," because the truth of it was that I wasn't accepting that at all. I accepted the facts of it, but none of the feelings about it. So I would go around in the daytime, and I'd repeat it to myself, "Sean is dead. This is true. Sean is dead." And I would start to cry. I would look at his things and this would make me cry, and I'd replay the tape of his voice on our answering machine, which I'd saved. All of this has helped me a lot. But sometimes I still feel as if he's not dead. I see something, and I think, "Oh, I should buy that for Sean. He'd really like it. It's just the kind of thing he likes." And now sometimes I just have the idea that I can't buy it for him because he's dead, but sometimes I cry or feel sad. I've really had to work on this to get at the feelings.

Tom's deliberateness reveals that he has had difficulty experiencing feelings, and that he is concerned this will inhibit his mourning of Sean's death. Those with historical difficulty allowing feelings in general, and those with significant historical losses, including losses in the epidemic, are likely to experience their pain and grief as especially unbearable and forbidding. For many of these men, loss and grief are experienced profoundly, but unconsciously, and the conscious feelings are denied for fear that they will be overwhelming or irreparably damaging. One must respect an individual's sense of his capacity to experience painful feelings. People come to a recognition of their feelings about loss in different ways and on different time schedules.

A 28-year-old psychotherapy patient, Steve, illustrates how profoundly the loss of the epidemic can effect an individual, and how necessary denial may be. Steve also experienced the inhibition of grieving that may result from such denial and repression. Steve's lover had died about eighteen months before this therapy session. For the intervening year and a half, Steve had been struggling with his feelings, mostly trying to contain and deny them. As therapy continued and his losses to the epidemic increased—another three close friends had died in the eighteen months following his lover's death—these efforts became more and more futile. Having been very hyperactive for over a year, Steve had become more and more depressed over the few months prior to this session.

"I had an awful night last night—I don't know if I slept four hours all put together. I couldn't stop thinking about Robert—the last year he was alive. He was twenty-eight that year."

"What is it you were trying to get rid of?" I asked.

"Well, I was thinking of him sitting at the table with his plate in front of him, with his hands in his lap, just sitting there staring at the plate. Every now and then he would take a single bite and put his hands back in his lap and sit there. For a moment he would look peaceful, and then I would think, I wonder if he is peaceful or if this is just how he looks when he's dying. When I thought of that, he looked empty or like he was methodically emptying himself of life, slowly—like his hair falling out hair by hair. I would think, he is taking in a little bit of food, but it is going out much faster than he's taking it in. He got thinner and thinner just sitting staring at his plate, and he was nauseated and vomiting all the time, and he had diarrhea for over a year. All these painful little bites would just end up in the toilet again and he would be so disappointed in himself. He would be contrite, like a child who was being yelled at for not finishing his peas."

"This is such a painful image," I interjected. Steve, very absorbed in his distress, ignored me.

"I didn't know if I was dreaming this, or I was half-awake or what. But sometimes I would suddenly look at him differently during that year, I would think he was peaceful again, that the thinness of his chin and neck looked very beautiful, that his eyes looked transparent rather than vacant or frightened . . ."

"You certainly felt that he was beautiful," I said. "But were you also trying not to see him as he really was?"

"When I would be alone with friends who had seen him, they would say, 'Poor Robert, he looks terrible,' and then I would realize that I had only wanted him to look beautiful and peaceful. It would then suddenly come back to me that at the table I had noticed how terrible his hair looked—dry, very thin, and a different color altogether than it used to be."

"It would have been very painful for you to see Robert the way he looked to others."

"Very painful. He sat in front of his plate for most of the last year—he was always trying to *eat, eat, eat.* I wish we had spent less time talking about eating, and talked more about our lives or other things that seem so much more important now that he's dead. I miss him so much, and I have only really started to feel it, but I sometimes feel like I'm going to explode with—I don't know with what . . ."

"Perhaps with grief?"

"But Robert died a year and a half ago, two years ago—no, a year and a half," Steve protested. "I don't see why I should be feeling like this now. Should it take this long? Does everyone take this long to get over this?"

"I think your question is an expression of not *wanting* to feel the way you actually do feel, which I can understand."

"Last night, imagining him sitting in front of his plate with his hands in his lap, staring at the food, and then at me, and taking another bite. Just over and over, this same scene . . ."

"You know, I have the idea that Robert's eating was what you thought would keep him alive," I commented. "That if he could only eat enough, you *both* believed that he wouldn't die." Steve started crying.

"And he did anyway. It is unbearable to me that he is dead—*I* feel unbearable, and it just gets worse and worse instead of better. I feel like this is *impossible,* that I can't go on feeling like this. I don't *want* to feel like this. But I also can't give up my feelings about him. I would be denying them now, and in some way I'd just be denying my whole life—*everything.* I don't know if I would be anyone if I didn't have the feelings about him, if there would be anything left over. His being dead is *me* now, and I will always live with that. I just hope it doesn't stay so unbearable—*it can't.* When I'm feeling this bad, my life is impossible."

"It has been very hard for you to acknowledge these feelings. You have understandably needed to avoid the pain."

"Joni Mitchell has a song, 'I wish I had a river I could skate away on,' and I've been listening to it all the time, and that's exactly how I feel. It's making me think of a Jack London story I read when I was a kid—a guy with his dogsled freezes to death and it was very warm and peaceful, and I guess that's what I'm thinking of when I hear the song—skating off down a frozen river and lying down on the ice. I could never say this before, I never told you this. But the morning I found Robert dead, lying in our bed—it's very hard for me to say."

Steve sat silently for several minutes looking frightened and despairing, and suddenly he started to speak again. "I kept saying, 'How can he be so *cold*, how can he be so *cold?*' just over and over. I was kneeling on the floor touching him all over and thinking, how can he be so cold?"

We sat silently for several minutes, and I finally spoke. "This is a very, very sad memory. Why would you doubt that it would all so profoundly affect you?"

"It's what you've said—that I don't want it to, and I never got it until just now. It's just that I didn't want it to. But it really came in through my fingers when I touched him that morning. Touching him is when it became completely real, and I've just been denying it ever since. Because then, I remember thinking, 'You will never forget this, there is no way you will ever forget this. He is completely cold, he is so cold, and there is nothing you will ever do in your life that will get you over this.'"

It was over the next few months that Steve began to allow himself to really experience for the first time his feelings about Robert, and to begin a process of grieving Robert's death and the deaths of others who had died before and since.

The Process of Grief

It is
possible to look, neither at surfaces nor beneath them,
but geometrically, squinting slightly to accommodate
things to our net of vision, robbing raw objects

of their atrocity. The only danger being that
the whole world may convert and you be left
with nothing but the music of, say,
(if you're lucky) Mozart or (if you aren't) Liszt.
A formidable danger. Still,
beauty is nothing to sneeze at.
—Keith Waldrop, *from* A Windmill Near Calvary [11]

Because the loss of loved ones is such a universal human experience, psychology has devoted much attention over the last century to the subject of grieving. Freud's "Mourning and Melancholia," written in 1917,[12] is an effort to distinguish "normal" grief from *melancholic* reactions to loss, and it is, arguably, as fine a piece as has ever been written on the subject.

A relationship with a partner involves both an actual experience of him in the world and an internal experience of him, including one's perceptions, feelings, and thoughts "about" him. Who one *is,* and what the world *is,* grows partly from one's relationships. When a partner dies, a man must become someone new, and must understand the world, which is now a different set of facts, in new ways. Thus grieving is partly the process of recreating the meaning of one's life in ways that account for the loss. The outcome is—more or less—a "resolution" of that loss. This process can also be understood as an effort to make an entirely internal relationship out of one that previously existed both in the world and in the survivor's internal life. In grieving, the survivor becomes someone new, living in a new world. He thus transforms a self and world experienced as damaged into a self and world experienced as relatively whole again. In response to a skin laceration, we do not "repair" old skin, we grow *new* skin, and thus our body is constantly regenerating itself in meaningful, but slightly different forms. When the reparative process of grieving is seriously inhibited or arrested, there are lasting, destructive psychological consequences.

Immediately after a death, the survivor generally enters an acute state of powerful and overwhelming feelings, often characterized by a combination of violent grief and denial of the loss—or numbness—which is a protection from such feelings. These normal initial reactions are not part of the grieving process per se, but rather a necessary inhibition of the grieving process to follow. Like shock after a severe physical trauma, these initial reactions are a way of protecting the individual from unmanageable psychic pain, but they are without any explicit reparative purpose. Such reactions are the psychological equivalent of emergency medical treatment, as opposed to the complex, long-term reconstructive surgery that may follow after the patient is stabilized and no longer in danger of death from acute injury. While this acute initial reaction may include explicit grief, it often does not, and this is what we observe when we say that a survivor is "in denial," or that "it hasn't hit him yet."

In addition to numb denial, the shock of a loss is sometimes contained with manic feelings, often expressed in the energetic management of the business of death, such as funeral and estate matters. A week after the death of his lover of seventeen years, a psychotherapy patient, Michael, said to me:

> I know that you're going to be expecting me to feel grief, but I have no time for that—I'm too busy taking care of things, and that's how Jack would have wanted it. He always relied on me to handle the business matters in our relationship.

Following the acute period after a loss,[13] the grieving process per se begins. It is initiated with a fuller acknowledgment of the loss, and is the point at which we observe that "It's finally hit him." About eight weeks after Jack's death, Michael said to me:

> Now that things have calmed down, I have these evenings when I'm home alone, and it's the first time that I've realized that Jack is gone, that he's actually not *here*. And I suddenly start to cry, because I think, my God, he's actually not here and I'm completely alone. I'm actually going to have to exist by myself, and I don't think I can do that.

Initiated by a recognition of the new facts of the world, this first phase of grieving may last a considerable time. The survivor may experience powerful feelings that are characterized by typical signs and symptoms of depression: sad or melancholic mood, a loss of interest in normally pleasurable activities, isolation, difficulty with sleep, bouts of anxiety, and changes in appetite and body weight.[14]

In instances of relatively "normal" grieving, reparative processes are very slowly introduced into this depressive state. These processes begin changes in the individual and in his world that account for the new reality. This complex, subtle, and extended process is partly a "disconnecting" from the lost person. This disconnecting entails giving the lost person up, and thus entails the repeated psychological reexperiencing of the loss. This is one reason grieving is so painful and so often avoided. The disconnecting, however, helps establish the death as a fact—internally—and helps to understand it, give it meaning, and slowly repair the emotional lacerations—the sense of no longer being whole in oneself—that it has created.

Disconnection is itself a complicated process. Ironically, it is partly accomplished by making the lost person part of oneself. This is done by *internalizing* aspects of the lost person, and by *identifying* with him. Both serve to make parts of the relationship that previously existed in the world aspects of the survivor himself. Concurrent with internalization and identification, the survivor slowly begins to make new connections with people and things in the world that, in some senses, replace the lost person. All of these processes are illustrated in the following condensation of several psychotherapy sessions with Michael about fourteen months after his lover Jack's death. I identify in brackets the processes described above.

"I have finally managed to sell Jack's Saab. You know, I never liked it, but after he died, I couldn't sell it—it just seemed like it would be getting rid of him by doing that [*there is some denial of Jack's death in this*]. I just had to keep it, and I actually found myself driving it a lot [*an internalization of Jack*], even though I couldn't stand the shifting business. That was something Jack loved, he loved cars and loved to drive and to shift the thing, and I never really did. So I sold it [*a disconnection*]."

I asked Michael what feelings selling the car might have brought up.

"Well, I was relieved in some ways, it unburdened me, as if I were finally making some sense out of this whole thing [*the reparative effects of disconnection*]. But you know, when I see Jack's side of the garage and the Saab isn't there, it's as if he's died all over again, and I can feel the most awful grief, which you know I've been feeling less and less [*the feelings of loss produced by disconnecting*]. It just seemed that it was time, and that I had to do it [Michael's *sense of the reparative nature of disconnection*]."

"Selling Jack's car," I commented, "is a part of separating from him, and I would think that would be painful."

"Well, driving that crazy car was a way I kept Jack in my life [*the internalization*]. But do you know you have to put it in reverse before you can pull out the ignition key? I mean, I never knew why Jack always left his car in reverse. The car is very complicated and eccentric—I mean it can be a very hard car to get along with—kind of like Jack, and some of these were things I could have done without in Jack. But in a car, you know, it's too much. My Honda is much more straightforward, and you don't have to get along with it. You don't have to have a relationship to it at all, and that's much more my idea of a car [*an inability to identify with Jack in this regard*].

"So there's some relief in not having the car, too," I commented. "Even though it means giving up part of Jack."

"Oh, definitely. I have plenty of Jack's things, things that I like [*that represent aspects of Jack that Michael could identify with*]. On Saturday afternoon after the guy drove the Saab away, I stood in the driveway for quite a while, just feeling sad about the whole thing, watching him back down the driveway, and knowing that I would never see it again. It made me realize that I will never see Jack again. But I went in the house and started working on his recipe file—you know, he would make things up and write them on 3 × 5 cards, and he kept them in a little wooden file box in the kitchen. And I've been reorganizing them, and I've used quite a few of the recipes lately [*an internalization and identification*].

"So you're not still eating in restaurants every night?" I asked.

"No. Actually I decided a few months ago that now that I'm alone, I'm going to have to learn to cook, and I find that I actually enjoy it. When Jack was around, I wouldn't boil eggs. But I am actually starting to like cooking now, and I've even been thinking about taking some classes in Italian cooking, which is what Jack really liked [*an identification with Jack and a concrete internalization of him by eating his food*]."

"So this is a way of keeping him in your life in a very positive way."

"Yes, and, you know, when I cook something from his file, it's a little like having dinner with him, I mean that I feel I am able to share something with him that was important to him [*identification*]. And I'm just getting to the point where I can really connect with our friends again [*a reconnection allowed by the internalization and identification with Jack*], and a few times I've invited people over and had a small dinner party, and they—you know, they recognize

Jack's cooking—and we've talked about it, that it's like having dinner with Jack in a way, that he's still a part of our lives. And we all feel very good about that, that Jack has meant so much to us as a group, and that he still does. He is definitely going to always be a part of our lives, of who we are [*a reorganization of self and the world that makes sense of Jack's death*].

Michael was silent for several moments, and I finally said, "You're describing a way of making sense of his death, and of having a life that acknowledges it—but also includes Jack in a way."

"Yes, I suppose so. At first, I thought his death meant that I was going to have to be completely without him. And in some little ways I can see that's not necessarily true."

Michael, who had entered therapy about six months before Jack's death to work on his feelings about the impending loss, finished his work to our mutual satisfaction within a few months of these sessions. By this time, he only rarely suffered significant depression, and was able to do some casual dating. We agreed that we would stop therapy, with the possibility of his returning if he felt a need (which he did not do).

Anticipatory Grief

Nothing, nothing will I
surrender. There is little enough as it is.
—Keith Waldrop, *from* A Windmill Near Calvary[15]

Anticipatory grief is a term like survivor guilt—it is often mentioned, but its meanings are not completely clear. It is unquestionably real, it is common, and it is particularly destructive both for the dying and the surviving.

In its simplest meaning, the idea of anticipatory grief refers to the experience of grief, sadness, depression, or loss in anticipation of another's death. Often, however, it is an experience that would be more correctly described as anticipatory *grieving*. The importance of this distinction is that in the latter case, it is not merely anticipatory feelings of grief or sadness that the dying and the survivor-to-be must manage, it is the "premature" initiation of an entire grieving process. Premature grieving entails disconnection between the dying and the survivor, and the possible reconnection of the survivor to someone else.

Anticipatory grieving occurs for many reasons. The survivor may feel inadequate in caretaking the dying man—indeed, for not saving his life—and thus withdraws from a task that makes him feel a failure. The survivor may feel the need to repair the psychic damage he anticipates as a result of the death before the death actually occurs. This is especially common among men who have survived many deaths or anticipate many more. Or the survivor may feel anger about what is experienced as abandonment, and withdraw both in punitive retaliation and in an effort to protect the dying man from his anger. Because of these largely unconscious processes, and numerous others, internalization and identification may be largely absent from anticipatory grieving. Unfortunately, these are precisely the processes in "normal" grieving that might bring the dying man and the "premature survivor" closer together. Instead, both are left largely with experiences of abandonment and abandoning.

The consequences of premature grieving are experienced routinely in the AIDS epidemic. Familiarity with death and loss does not make the process easier, but more difficult, and the withdrawal implicit in premature grieving is used by many men to protect themselves from events they know all too well. In the face of familiar and repeated death, intimate relationships become distant, perfunctory, asexual, hostile, or fall apart; and friendships evaporate. The ill person may be abandoned precisely when he most needs intimacy and support, and the survivor may be left with troubling guilt about his premature withdrawal after the death actually occurs. Such guilt is often a component of survivor guilt and, like survivor guilt, is often obstructive to any grieving process that might otherwise be possible.

There are two psychological insights that often help mitigate the destructiveness of anticipatory grieving for both the one who is ill and the premature survivor. For the purposes of this discussion, I will assume a couple in an intimate relationship, but the concepts are equally appropriate to the many other kinds of relationships that are now troubled by the effects of anticipatory grieving. The first insight involves clarification and discussion of the feelings of the survivor-to-be. These feelings— largely unconscious—may include his fear of loss, his anger at feeling abandoned, his desire to self-protectively withdraw from the relationship, and his sense of failure. The more clarity the ill person can have about these feelings of his partner—although he will have fear and anger of his own that may inhibit the process—the less likely he will be to experience his partner's withdrawal as an abandonment and an injury to his self-esteem. For the survivor, this clarification may help reveal continuing love for his partner that fear and anger are causing him, unconsciously, to deny. As a result, he may be able to tolerate more intimacy, and remain more a partner. If that is possible, his post-death guilt will be lessened. Implicit in the clarification of such unconscious feelings, is a recognition by both parties that the process is a normal one.

The second insight concerns anticipatory grieving on the part of the ill partner. He may feel hurt and angry and withdraw, and some of this may be reactive to his partner's withdrawal. The injury to self-esteem that motivates these feelings, however, is caused not only by the partner's withdrawal, but by AIDS itself and its destruction of the body, which is a tremendous blow to the self-esteem of most men. In addition to these interactive and reactive feelings, it should be clarified that the idea of anticipatory grieving—as a *premature* process—has no meaning for the ill and dying man. The process of dying, when it is not obstructed by denial, inevitably involves anticipatory grief, as well as grief about what has already been lost, often including physical and mental competence. What has not been lost prior to death will be lost at death, and the dying man *realistically* anticipates this final and complete loss of whatever remains of his life. Detachment from a partner who will survive is thus part of a normal process of resolution for many dying men, and it must be supported. It may, however, be experienced as an abandonment by the survivor, which may in turn intensify *his* abandonment of the dying partner. The important point is that the dying partner is often, understandably, an important source of waning intimacy in the relationship. The surviving partner's guilt is thus not always a realistic response to what has occurred, and he must understand that detachment is one way men arrive at resolution about their own deaths.

Michael, feeling distanced from Jack in the last months of Jack's life, and anticipating the imminent, complete loss of Jack, decided to buy a dog. Jack objected to this, and Michael talked about that in a psychotherapy session.

"When I first brought this idea up to Jack, he was very angry, and he put it as a question of his not getting enough from me as it was—and his not needing any 'competition' in the house. But he was feeling other things, and one night when he was very depressed he told me." Michael became silent at this point, and, waiting several moments, I finally asked him what was happening. He began crying at this point.

It's just painful for me to think about it. Jack said to me, "I know that it's important to you to get a dog, but I don't think I can stand it. I will probably get very attached to him too"—Jack always loved dogs, and he had wanted one for all the years we were too busy to raise it. So I said, "Well, why not get one then, because this will be something for you too." And he said to me, "No I can't stand it, because it will only be something else that I know I'm going to lose. And I just don't want something else that is important to me when I know I'm just going to lose it.'"

Michael and Jack were is a process of withdrawing from each other. Jack's withdrawal, however, involved a withdrawal from everything in his life that might increase his grief about his own anticipated death.

Multiple Loss as an Impediment to Grieving

The world is a weary place. Even short trips annoy me.
—Keith Waldrop, from The Quest for Mount Misery [16]

Denial and repression inhibit the grieving process because they deny that there are feelings about the loss that must be worked through. In addition to these general inhibitions to the grieving process, there are two additional, important experiences particular to the AIDS epidemic that interfere with grieving. These are multiple losses and survivor guilt. Unlike Michael, for whom Jack was the only significant loss in the epidemic, another psychotherapy patient in his early forties, Wally, had experienced multiple losses spanning several years. Very much in the mainstream of the gay community and its devastated condition, Wally had worked in AIDS services for many years. Prior to the death of his lover, Robert, he had suffered the loss of six very close friends. As a result, Wally's grieving was much more complex than Michael's, and the outcome considerably less resolved.

"I remember that in the couple of months after Robert died I had hardly any feelings about it. People would call up and say to me, 'How are you *feeling?*' and I would just say, 'I don't know. I'm eating dinner.' And I would also think to myself, 'Well, you've already done a lot of grieving over the years he was sick, and so you've gotten a lot of it out of your system.' Whatever that means. And I know that my feelings about Robert's death were mixed up with a lot of other things too—all the other people who have died and who I know are going to die. The whole thing was a mess, tangled up on itself—it was like gridlock for me, and I always had this feeling, despite the rationalizations I could come up with, that I just couldn't get untangled and have my feelings about it.

"I started dating again about two years after Robert died, but the effect it had was that I would discover this incredible love for Robert that I never knew I had. And I felt incredible *guilt* too, because I would think, 'What would Robert think of me dating this person?' and I often had the idea that Robert would find him unworthy and resent him. If someone spent the night with me, I would be relieved one minute to have someone to hold on to—someone who was *alive*—and the next minute I'd be angry because he was lying on Robert's side of the bed. He didn't belong there. And sometimes I would think, 'Well he's just another one who's going to end up dead anyway. Why get involved with him?' But I was never sure if this was just an excuse, and I would think, 'Wally, you've got to start letting go of Robert,' because I had this feeling that holding on to him was a way of not going on with my life. But in the next minute I'd think, 'You haven't cried enough for Robert yet, you haven't even really accepted that he's dead.' And how do you go on with the next piece of work in life if you haven't really done that one? I've been very stuck about this. I still am."

Wally's statement describes a grieving process that is complicated, inhibited, or arrested by both multiple losses and survivor guilt. Wally's difficulty in allowing himself to grieve Robert, and his hope that he will not have to go through it, express a denial of the effects of loss that is characteristic of those experiencing multiple losses. Multiple losses are more likely to be denied than single losses because they arouse fear that the allowance of *any* grief will overwhelm the survivor; and they do not receive the social recognition that single losses do. "How many times a year can you call up a friend and say, 'Oh, I'm so *sorry* to hear that so-and-so died'?" a psychotherapy patient once asked. Wally's discovery of his profound love for Robert, years after his death, suggests that there was some inability to allow his feelings for Robert while he was alive, and some disconnection from him prior to his death. Wally's guilt is expressed in his feelings about someone being "on Robert's side of the bed" and his anticipation of Robert's disapproval. This guilt is probably partly the result of Wally's feeling that he failed Robert by prematurely grieving his death while he was still alive. The guilt inhibited Wally's capacity to grieve, for it added to the painful issues that had to be dealt with; and it inhibited Wally's ability to make new attachments, because Robert remained a part of any new relationship. In fact, Wally made amends to Robert by keeping Robert a part of new relationships. In continuing therapy, it became clear that Wally's concern that anyone new would "end up dead anyway" both expressed that fear and expressed anger at anyone trying to replace Robert. Wally's life had become one limited by his unresolved feelings about Robert. This is characteristic of a grieving process complicated and inhibited by multiple losses and guilt.

A "standard" model of grieving—like that described earlier for Michael after Jack's death—does not fully describe the experience of men who have lived through multiple losses and can only anticipate more in the future. The standard model describes a process of assimilating single losses, and does not address the question of how much repeated loss a man can bear and still process the experience in a psychologically meaningful way. Terry, a 27-year-old psychotherapy patient, discusses multiple losses and his fears about the impact they may have on him.

> People talk about getting hit by the epidemic, but I can tell you that in my case it really snuck up on me. In 1987 I didn't know a single person—or I didn't think I did—who was even positive. But late in that year Charles got PCP [pneumocystis pneumonia] and he was dead in a couple of weeks. It was a big shock, but that was only the start, because from then on people I knew started dying like flies. In the last four years it has been one after another, and it's happened too fast for me even to get a picture of it. I don't even try to count it. It's like someone who keeps shooting at you—you, know you're too busy getting ready to dodge the next one to think about the one that just hit you. But what I think about is, when this is over, I'm going to *have* to think about it. And it just seems like too much, it will be too much to deal with. And in that sense, I'd have to say that I'm not looking forward to the epidemic being over with, because I don't think I'll know what to do about it—about the whole goddamned thing. I just don't know what to make of it.

Losses of this magnitude can present immense, sometimes insurmountable, difficulties for the survivor.[17] The exact psychological consequences for men subjected to repeated loss are difficult to predict. The accumulation of numerous personal losses, and the constant exposure to community losses—which, through identification and the displacement of feelings, are often experienced nearly as deeply as personal ones— combine to create an immensely complex process that is not entirely within the historical purview of psychological thought. What is apparent, however, is that many men living in the epidemic are accumulating loss that is substantially unameliorated by the reparative process of grieving. The inability to grieve spans a range from inhibition to foreclosure, and I would expect to see the consequences of repeated, ungrieved losses span a similar range of psychological injury from destructive to irreparable.

In some sense—though the physical metaphor is inadequate—ungrieved loss must be contained or encapsulated within an individual if it is not to interfere too destructively in daily life. When *some* reparative grieving has been possible because of developmental strengths or fortunate circumstances, the feelings arising from ungrieved loss will remain partially unconscious and isolated from other experience of the individual. Such isolated feelings may be opened up and grieved at a later time, or they may become part of a permanent discontinuity in emotional and interpersonal experience. In the latter case, the discontinuity will probably reduce the capacity for a sense of wholeness in oneself and for intimacy with others.

For individuals who have had to foreclose on virtually all grieving because of developmental weaknesses or especially numerous and difficult losses, the consequences may be much more serious. For such people the feelings of loss and grief must be radically dissociated from experience as a whole. The psychological "crypts" that contain these large, important realms of emotional life become aspects of permanent changes in character. Bodies delivered to the morgue go unacknowledged and unprepared for burial. Though themselves largely unconscious, such encrypted "corpses" of experience make themselves known in a range of symptomatology, including depression, anxiety, a lack of vitality, an incapacity for intimacy, or manic rallies launched against mounting feelings of depression, numbness, deadness, and isolation.[18]

Finally, there is a third broad possibility in response to repeated loss. This is an attempt at the reparative process of grieving, without the capacities to follow through to reasonably successful resolution. In psychological terms, the loss is acknowledged, and an attempt at disconnection from the deceased is made, but internalization, identification, reconnection, and reintegration of self are not adequately achieved. Ted, a 39-year-old San Franciscan, talks about the possible range of emotional responses to loss:

> "I wonder what the world will be like for me and other gay men around my age who are seronegative. In other words, people who have been around since the epidemic's been around. What are we going to be like? Are we going to be like the survivors of the camps? Are we going to be like the survivors of the ghetto in Warsaw? What will our relationships be like? The fear is, what don't I know about? —what is this doing to me that's going to show up years later? I could be having this huge thing sitting there and I'm not even aware of it because I'm still in the middle of it. Oh, I look at the *B.A.R.* [San Francisco gay paper]. The reason I pick up the *B.A.R.* every single week is to see who died. "Oh, I don't know anybody. Okay, *next.*" Or I see somebody walking down the hall [at work] or see somebody on the street whom I know is sick, and I say, 'Well, he doesn't have long.'
>
> "I am covering up a lot of pain about all this. I can't function in this world and continue to move my own life forward and be caught in grief about the impact of this epidemic all the time. Because I know people who are. And guess what? Their lives don't work.
>
> "There's one woman who used to work at Shanti [a San Francisco AIDS service provider], and she has made grief a specialty for herself, and it's clear to me that she doesn't have any interest in letting go of grief. She wants to be there because it fuels her. . . . But I'll tell you what: It's really draining to be in her presence. What are the rules here? Should I be more compassionate where this is concerned? Should I be more in my feelings about this? Should I move out of San Francisco?"[19]

Survivor Guilt as an Impediment to Grieving

My arms around you—to give you some idea of what time it was—the hour struck me as already past.—Keith Waldrop, from The Quest for Mount Misery[20]

Grieving of loss is especially complicated by the concurrent experience of survivor guilt. Although different in many ways, both grieving and survivor guilt involve an attachment to and ambivalence about separating from those who are dead; and the two often become destructively entangled in the survivor's experience. Depression and anxiety are a natural response to important loss and thus part of a "normal" grieving process. But depression and anxiety may also be an expression of guilt, including survivor guilt. Normal grieving does not, by definition, include survivor guilt, although survivor guilt always includes an element of grieving. Survivor guilt is most usefully understood as an adjunctive complication of a normal grieving process.

Although both normal grieving and guilt-complicated grieving may be expressed in depression, anxiety, and remorse, there are some clear differences between the two. In normal grieving the feelings are largely about the loss, while in grief complicated by survivor guilt, clarification will reveal additional features that are not usually part of normal grief alone. These may include especially powerful internalizations of and identifications with the dead person (or dead people in general) that lead to a number of special experiences. Among them are feelings that one would like to take the dead person's place, bewilderment at having survived the deceased, irrational feelings or ideas that one may die or is responsible for the death of the deceased, or feelings that one is not worthy of survival.

Because of such complications introduced by guilt, there is often an inordinate extension of the grieving process. The mourner feels persistently unsuccessful in attempts to begin separation from the dead person, or he cannot even think about making attempts to separate. But the impediment to grieving does not lie merely in the inability to separate. In a guilt-complicated grieving process, some of the remorse is not about the loss of the dead person, but about *the survivor's survival*. This is an ongoing event—the survivor's life—and cannot be grieved, because it is not over. It is the survivor's life that is partly the object of grief, a life grieved because it is a life in survival of someone else. Grief about the loss of the deceased may also be obscured by grief about survival, and in this sense, the grieving of survival may become a defense against feelings about the loss. This complication, too, is an impediment to grieving, for it represents a basic denial of the loss.

Anger may also be useful in making the distinction between more ordinary grief and grief complicated by survivor guilt. Anger, including anger at the deceased for leaving the survivor behind, is a common experience in normal grieving. It is rarely among the feelings of the person experiencing survivor guilt. Rather, there is remorse and sadness about being left behind, and often the feeling that it is one's own fault, rather than the deceased's, that this has happened. While those experiencing ordinary grief usually wish the deceased back in life, those feeling survivor guilt often wish to repair the situation by joining the dead.

The introduction of survivor guilt into grieving is not only complicating, but potentially very destructive. The inability to grieve a loss sustains depression and isolation that would otherwise eventually be resolved, and these experiences combine with the self-destructive feelings—regret about one's own survival—that are intrinsic to survivor guilt. When combined with survivor guilt, it is often difficult to know whether grief is about the loss of the deceased or the survivor's survival, and this confusion extends and entrenches the grief.

Fortunately, psychological clarifications are often useful when a man is ensnared in such feelings. Because we all begin life as infants entirely dependent upon the care of an apparently omnipotent and (hopefully) benevolent adult, and because such infantile relationships must change and ultimately be lost, there is no serious psychotherapy that does not finally—and perhaps immediately—deal with feelings of loss and grief. The issue often comes up early in the therapy in the form of anticipated loss of the therapist when the therapy is completed, and it will always be an issue at the actual end of therapy. The epidemic has added immensely to developmentally derived feelings about loss, and this real-world adult experience of loss must be acknowledged and respected by any psychotherapist working with gay men today. Not doing so expresses disrespect for the psychotherapy patient, and it colludes with his own possible denial about the AIDS epidemic and the feelings of loss it has created.

This comment is not intended to discourage the interpretation of any adult experience in the light of developmental experience. Adult life is always given meaning by its connections to childhood experience. Interpretations of meaning in therapy must account for the reality of the psychotherapy patient's current life experience, without diluting or dissipating the meaning of either developmental experience or current experience—or their interaction. *Meaning* is always the issue, and fact always remains merely a standard against which meaning is interpreted. How childhood and adult experiences of loss may become entangled in the life of a gay man are illustrated by Jerry, a 29-year-old in long-term psychotherapy. In the year and a half prior to this session we had talked many times about the significant unreliabilities of Jerry's parents throughout his childhood, and the anxiety, depression, and grief the experience had created for him. We had also spoken of his development of competence and independence as a way of dealing with those feelings.

Jerry started one session by saying, "I have been thinking about what we talked about last time—about my feeling like I need you, and not wanting to. It's true. I can't accept that."

"Can't accept what?"

"I can accept some of it, and then some seems too dangerous. All the things we've talked about—I just get pain when I rely on other people, and I can't accept doing that with you."

"How will you get pain with me?"

"The therapy will end. I stop coming here, and that will be that."

"And?"

"And that will be too painful," Jerry responded.

"I'm thinking of your dream of about a year ago that I closed my practice and moved to Africa to live in a hut. At that time you had the idea that I might have AIDS. Do you think about that anymore?"

"No."

"Why not?" I challenged him.

"Because you told me then that you weren't sick."

"And in a year you've never thought about it again?"

"Well, I was sitting in the waiting room today, and I just started thinking, 'I wonder if he was in the hospital . . . ' "

"He?"

"You. I meant you—that if you were in the hospital. Could I come and say goodbye and thank you. And I thought, 'No, that's ridiculous.' "

"What's ridiculous?"

"Well, my first thought was, 'No, you can't do that because that would be taking the relationship out of here.' Then I thought, 'Well, what the hell, he's dying and it would be important for me to do, and what difference would it make?' I would want to thank you, because I think you know how I've changed since I've been seeing you."

"So you are thinking about our relationship, and how it might be dangerous. And also about how AIDS might make it dangerous?"

Jerry hesitated a moment. "I'm very resistant to thinking about it. I was sitting out there, and I was thinking, 'I don't want to think about it, and you can't make me.' It's too painful."

"But you *were* thinking about it—about your feelings of gratitude to me, and your fear that I would get sick. What's too painful?" I asked. "Our relationship, losing it, my having AIDS?"

"All of it. I've had all this pain whenever I relied on people. Everyone has an excuse. My mother had to go away. She had to die. My father had to go away to work. I think of your having AIDS as an excuse. I have all these feelings and AIDS is just an add-on. It's another excuse everyone can have. Are you sick?"

"I'll answer your question, because I know it's important, and you ask it because you care about me and our relationship. But first, let's understand it. I'm thinking particularly about your difficulty in recognizing that you think about me."

"I don't."

"But you were sitting in the waiting room wondering if you could visit me in the hospital to say goodbye."

"Well I think about it as little as possible," Jerry retorted.

"It's always been very hard for you to think that we have a relationship at all. Do you think about AIDS when you meet someone, and are thinking about a possible relationship?"

"No."

"I'm thinking about all of your volunteer work with AIDS patients. You are certainly not naive about AIDS . . ."

"I don't think about it. It's too painful to think about it and I don't."

I continued: "But I wonder if your not thinking about it really changes how you feel. I know that you know the statistics here in the Bay Area. There's about a fifty-fifty chance I have HIV, or that someone you meet might have it. This makes me feel that you must have unconscious concerns about this that you are not allowing yourself to think about."

"This is too difficult for me to think about," Jerry insisted again.

At this point we were near the end of the hour, and I said, "We are going to have to stop in a few minutes, but I want to answer your original question. I believe I'm HIV-negative."

"I'm glad to hear that," Jerry responded.[21]

Ron Henderson, a longtime worker in San Francisco AIDS services, expressed himself in a diary entry on the subject of multiple loss:

January 11, 1990: Several Xmas cards came back with "NO FORWARDING ADDRESS" . . . Gay friends who have just dropped out? Or old buddies who have died of AIDS without my even knowing it this last year? Another crazy sign of the times: My lover's former lover died on the second floor of Ralph K. Davies [Medical Center]. George's ex-lover died there, now George is there. So much death in the 80's and many "endings" on the same floor of one building. It's haunting and hurting. The feeling of being in a death march . . .

Repeated loss—Louie, Doug, Mike, Don, Val, Joe, Tommy, Mark, Tom, Sean, Hugh, Sheppard, Don, Bill, Gary, Phil, Joey, Dick, Mark, Jimmy, Steve, Steve, Bruce, Ray, William, Joe, Rick, Ron, Lenny, Jim, Dan, John, Michael, Richard, Wayne, Paul, Ricardo, Ben, John, Scott, Karl, Ken, Mike, Dale, Noel, Bobby, Joe, Michael, Dale, Ron, German, Todd, Dennis, David, Rick, Tul, Rudy, Rusty, Demetrius, Steve, Tim, David, Carver, Starr, David, Doug, John, Michael, Walter, Ronnie, Tracey, Sheldon, Joe, Roger, Robert, Len, Ron, Nick, Chris, Ben, Cliff, David, David, Steve, Steve, Richard, Jeff, Jud, Paulo, Keith, Bill, Andrew, Chris, Sylvester, Bob, Al, Andy, Jason, Michael, Nick, Roy, Gilbert, Brad, Bill, Skip, Gordon, Joe, John, Gordon, Ed, Jim, Jack, Rob, Zyrus, Bob, Mark, Dave, Marc, Joe, Bill, Reinhart, Dennis, Andrew, George. Repeated loss.[22]

Chapter 5
Being Outsiders: The
"HIV-Negative" Identity

As if at a distance—he
lives, not in
life, but across from it.

And it comes to pass.

And he tries to distinguish
life and its contents.

And they wheel around him, the cars, as
if he were standing still.
—Keith Waldrop,
from Potential Random[1]

Being gay and uninfected in America today is an identity, not the absence of one, and it is often a profoundly troubled identity. The extended social impact of the epidemic within gay communities, the number of losses endured by uninfected survivors, difficult prospects for the future, and the divisions and conflicts between positive and negative men conspire to make being HIV-negative a complex identity and form of life. Within the gay community in San Francisco, a minority in itself, being uninfected is probably also a minority condition. The San Francisco Department of Health has consistently reported over the past eight or ten years that among gay-identified men in the city, about 50 percent are HIV-positive. Similar figures are likely in the gay communities of New York and Los Angeles. The prevalence of HIV-positive men in these communities not only makes it altogether difficult to define an HIV-negative identity, it makes it particularly difficult to define one that is independent of the issue of HIV: Witness the fact that we now describe *ordinary* (uninfected) gay men in terms of HIV, by labeling them "HIV-negative."[2]

There are many issues shared by uninfected and HIV-positive men, just as there are many shared by all survivors, whether inside or outside gay communities. But there is a form of life unique to uninfected gay men, most of whom are still at significant risk for contracting HIV. This chapter is for and about them. In its simplest form, "being HIV-negative" is the lack of a medical condition, a fact that could only be experienced with thankfulness—rationally speaking. Being uninfected, however, also entails special problems of personal and social identity and, often, a feeling of disenfranchisement from the minority community that has provided the uninfected gay man with acceptance and a sense of who he is and where he belongs. For these reasons, being uninfected is often fraught with conflict and ambivalence. Woody Castrodale eloquently expresses the irony and pain of this situation:

> I ran into a very old friend, Jerry, on Castro street. He [sero] converted—oh, I don't even know anymore—within the last year, and we started to talk and he seemed like a child to me. We just didn't connect at all, I couldn't really get through to him. When I left, it was as if I'd been drugged—I felt flat and empty, and I could barely move my legs to walk up the street. On the way home, thinking about my feelings, I suddenly had the insight, "Well, you're angry," and the minute I said that, I could suddenly feel rage. It was rage because Jerry had abandoned me, and every word of our conversation confirmed that. This rage was a feeling in my whole body, and the minute I felt that rage, I didn't feel drugged anymore. It was as if I could talk and move around and sing, and I wasn't under this terrible weight.
>
> I was thinking about how *gross* feelings are, how indiscriminate, how big, and about how everything gets buried under them. In our HIV-negative group, there is this very subtle thing: People keep saying, "I thought this would go away, I thought it would stop, that at some point I would have paid my dues. Is five years enough? Is seven?" One guy said, "I thought at some point I wouldn't have any more friends who were positive or dying, and my life would be *free* again." It's the idea that if we "suffer" enough—I can't say exactly what I mean by that word—but, if we go through enough of this stuff, eventually there won't be anyone left to be confused about, and our lives will be free again. Of course, then there will be this

terrible anger that we've lost all our friends. But gradually it's become obvious that it isn't happening that way. I have more friends who are positive now than I did five years ago, and when I wake up in the morning and remember that, I think, "Well the whole culture's in a state of denial. Years ago there were headlines in the [San Francisco] *Examiner* about how many people were being infected each month, and it was a shocking thing. But I know now that the numbers are much larger, *grossly* larger, and now you never read anything about it.

All of this makes it difficult for me to make any sense of my life—I don't know what the reality of my life is, and sometimes I just think, "Well Woody, you're delusional." It's very, very confusing. Isn't it natural that Jerry, knowing that he's going to get sick and die, would live in a strange mode? Or, perhaps I should say, one that's just strange *to me*. He wants to do all the things he can do, right now, while he's healthy, and this gives him the affect of a young high school kid, though he's in his late thirties. I can't help but agree with him. But this raving discontinuity between my own life and feelings about myself, when cast in the light of the lives of the people who are dying, it is all too strange. There is a split happening in my mind, and the split just gets worse and worse. It is a split between having my own feelings and then sort of denying them, and going back and forth, back and forth, into the world of these people who are sick, and then back into my own life, where I am trying to be "normal," whatever that means. Sometimes I can do that, and sometimes I feel like I'm straddling a chasm that has become impossibly wide and deep.[3]

The Homosexualization of AIDS

To understand the impact of the AIDS epidemic on gay communities, we must look at the psychological and social significance of an epidemic hitting these particular communities, and at the way this epidemic manifests itself in those who are infected. The disproportionate concentration of AIDS in minority communities is, in itself, of significance. Gay and bisexual men have borne, to date, the brunt of the infection in the United States. The heterosexual majority of the country has experienced some anxiety and concern, has had its infections and deaths, and has responded helpfully, if unevenly, to the plight of gay men. Nevertheless, few heterosexuals even marginally perceive life in the shadow of AIDS and the loss and grief it has produced. Nor have many heterosexuals suffered the personal concern about infection that virtually all gay men now experience routinely. AIDS is a habitual way of life for gay men, and, in this regard, these relatively small communities are still alone.

Gay men have always been separated from mainstream society and alone in much of their experience. Historically this has had nothing to do with AIDS, but with being homosexual and the form of life that often entailed. That gay men are now isolated for new reasons, and that the isolation is associated with a substantially new form of life, suggests that the AIDS epidemic has widely engaged the special psychological and social histories of gay men. This engagement is evidenced in the fact that AIDS was so easily *homosexualized* by the larger society, and that gay men have so easily identified with AIDS. Society's assignment of AIDS to gay men is intelligible—it is another example of the projection of self-hatred and fear onto others. Through socialization and other learning, gay men have always internalized such projections, and in internalizing society's homosexualization of the epidemic, gay men have thoroughly "AIDSified" homosexuality. An identification with AIDS and with the HIV-positive community is often—perhaps almost invariably—experienced by uninfected gay men. A gay, HIV-negative friend summed up such feelings succinctly in telling me, "People with HIV, that is where my heart is. I feel like I'm being left out of the great event of our time."

In this social and psychological climate, we are now also seeing younger gay men who are often unable to make any distinction at all between being gay and being at risk for, or actually contracting HIV. For younger men, AIDS has been a reality of their entire adult lives, and the identification with AIDS is natural and seamless. AIDS has developed, from the beginning, as an integral component of the gay identity of most young men. Ken, a 28-year-old psychotherapy patient who had self-identified as gay at age 26, spent two years exploring his sense of gay identity and community by volunteering at San Francisco's Shanti Project, an agency providing services for those with HIV. In deciding to leave Shanti, he said,

> All my gay relationships have been with people who have AIDS, who I knew had AIDS, and there you know what's going on, and what the relationship is about. It's very defined and it's simpler. But when I start thinking about just going out and dating, things

are just all over the place, and I don't know where to start. You
know, I've never thought about having a relationship for more than
a couple of years, because I've never dated anyone who was going
to live longer than that.

AIDS first emerged in the United States in gay communities, and it can
be transmitted sexually, including homosexually. But this does not adequately explain how AIDS has come to so completely characterize what
it now means to be gay, or how being gay—psychologically, socially, and
often occupationally—has seemingly come to be so completely about
AIDS. In discussing the homosexualization of AIDS and AIDSification
of homosexuality, it is the psychological and social meanings of AIDS
that are of concern. This is a matter entirely aside from the medical
phenomenon of AIDS and the undeniable reality of so many gay men
being infected with HIV and dying of AIDS. Psychologist Linda Zaretsky has spoken to me about the widely experienced stigma attached to
any chronic illness.[4] Susan Sontag has talked about some of the general metaphors for which AIDS has served.[5] In an article in *The Nation*,
Darrell Yates Rist has discussed some aspects of the meanings of AIDS
with more focus on gay communities and has pondered gay communities having so uncompromisingly embraced AIDS.[6] While much of his
article suggests an effort to deny the huge emotional impact of the AIDS
epidemic—including, perhaps, his own experience of loss and grief—he
nevertheless makes the important point that AIDS and homosexuality
are not at all the same issue, socially or politically.

What Rist does not discuss is that AIDS and homosexuality are also
not the same issue psychologically. Some of the psychological confusion
between AIDS and homosexuality that is within the psyche of most gay
men is a result of society's projections. Having projected this horrific disease onto a reviled minority—in order for it to be *other*—society is most
likely to acknowledge its relationship to AIDS when infection strikes
celebrities. Media stories about Kimberly Bergalis, Magic Johnson, and
even Ryan White have been an affront to gay communities. They provide constant reminders that the public can respond compassionately to
those with AIDS, but generally does not, because it is a "gay problem."

Many gay communities have colluded with such prejudice by internalizing the homosexualization of AIDS. This is subtly expressed in taking
on AIDS issues as if they were specifically gay issues, rather than human
issues—albeit human issues that also happen to be overwhelming gay

communities. This has happened partly out of human and political necessity, because if gay communities had not taken on the needs of those with AIDS, it is clear that it would not have been done. But it is members of gay communities who often fight for "AIDS rights" as if they were synonymous with gay rights, citing an AIDS-related, anti-housing-discrimination victory as if it were a triumph for gay communities. Why should we, within gay communities, accept the mainstream description of this victory as a "gay rights" victory? It is a victory *against* homophobia to be sure, but the most profound homophobia lies in putting gay people in charge of defending against AIDS discrimination. As long as we continue to accept this task without protest, we collude with homophobia while fighting it in other incarnations on other fronts. In this light such a victory is a victory *for* human rights and a victory won by gay communities on behalf of all human beings, because the burden has been thrown in its lap. It is this kind of entanglement of concerns, interests, purposes, and particularly *identities* that expresses the homosexualization of AIDS and gay communities' corresponding AIDSification of homosexuality.

Although substantial individual and social changes were accomplished by gay communities in the decades prior to the epidemic, homophobia within the hearts of gay men themselves remains a significant problem. We can see more clearly what AIDS and homosexuality can feel like they have in common—and how the two might become confused in the social and psychological identity of gay men—if we focus on this "internalized" homophobia and its application to AIDS. Homosexuals have been considered "sick," have homophobically considered themselves sick, and are now sick with AIDS. Homosexuals have often been threatened with, and expected punishment for, their sexuality, and they now often feel, consciously or unconsciously, punished with HIV or AIDS. Getting AIDS may be experienced as a form of redemption, a way of paying dues for one's transgressions. Gays have been shunned by mainstream society, and, in homophobic identification, have often shunned other homosexuals. Gay men now often shun each other because some carry HIV, or are ill, or because some do not carry HIV. Finally, AIDS has given many gay men the opportunity to shift familiar and traditional guilt about thinking, feeling, or living homosexually, to guilt about having HIV, not having HIV, or not doing enough to help others survive. In *Second Son*, Robert Ferro's last novel (1988) before his death of AIDS, the protagonist tells his family he has AIDS: "Nothing, I see, has much changed: it is still a question of coming out of the closet with something vile about yourself".[7]

   Through such dovetailing with the familiar psychosocial histories of gay men, AIDS has allowed a subtle reassignment of familiar, powerful, psychological conflicts to a new issue. Though subtle and unconscious, this is a process with important consequences. "Being gay" comes to mean not only being homosexual, but being infected with HIV or being fatally ill. Furthermore, HIV and AIDS may come not only to be *part* of the gay identity, but to supplant traditional parts of the identity. When this happens, illness substitutes for sexuality. To come out today, a gay man in heterosexual company need merely reveal an interest in the topic of AIDS. Yet, coming out as a person interested in AIDS—or, for that matter, *having* AIDS—has nothing, in itself, to do with coming out as gay in any meaningful psychological, interpersonal, social, or political sense. One merely implies his homosexuality by having AIDS, and implies that AIDS *tells the whole story.* Coming-out in this way is often taken to imply additionally that one is a contrite, reformed, and responsible homosexual, no longer engaging in the sexual practices that spread HIV. Because much of society, including the Pope, is now willing to accept people as "gay" if they do not express it sexually, the internalized homophobia of gay men collaborates comfortably in these implications. Many gay men now seem willing to allow or support the public impression that gays, after all, subscribe to asexuality as a personal and social virtue. The epidemic has proved an ideal event for the nurturing of homophobia—external and internal.

The AIDSification of Homosexuality

There is no doubt that gay communities talk about HIV because they must, and that is not, in itself, an expression of homophobia. It would be difficult to overestimate the realistic personal, social, and political demands of the epidemic or the grief that the epidemic has brought to so many gay men. These are things that must be talked about. But when AIDS *substitutes* for homosexuality in conversation or in personal and social identity, the confusion must be clarified. Elizabeth Taylor, through her support of AmFAR (the American Foundation for AIDS Research), has been immensely helpful to those with HIV and AIDS. But it is also significant that she became a friend, and said so on television, only after gay men came out with AIDS. This is something she could never have done when men suffered merely because of persecuted, secret homosexual lives. While coming out with AIDS is, as Ferro says, certainly difficult and "vile," that is because AIDS is associated with homosexuality, intravenous drug use, and social disenfranchisement—the perfect embodiment of the "ravages of sin." But in the minds of most, AIDS, *in and of itself,* would be no more vile than some of the more horrific degenerative diseases that have not become as narrowly attached to social prejudice. AIDS in itself is not nearly so vile as the homosexuality—and particularly the receptive anal sex—with which it has become associated.

AIDS, as compared to homosexuality, benefits from being part of the amoral and respectable worlds of science and medicine. Having any disease, AIDS included, is much more respectable than being homosexual; and many who do not "condone" homosexuality but are not profoundly homophobic have been able to separate AIDS from homosexuality and treat it as simply disease. We in gay communities have easily used these perceptions. Having AIDS can be treated as a matter of medical science. Being gay, even with the current effort to "legitimize" homosexuality with genetic and in utero etiologic explanations, inevitably requires acknowledgment of the much more difficult and frightening matters of feelings, intimate relationships, and sexuality. Disease allows one to *have* something rather than *be* it, and one can have AIDS—if only collectively in the cases of the uninfected—rather than be gay. Having AIDS, individually and collectively, is something many of us are finding frighteningly easy to do.

For gay men, accustomed to life on the fringes of a rejecting heterosexual society, the acceptance gained by having AIDS—genuine or begrudging—can feel irresistible. Apparently, many gay men are finding it is easier to be threatened by AIDS, to die of it, or to be guilty for not dying of it, than they have ever found being gay. This is at the heart of the homosexualization-AIDSification of the epidemic: AIDS has given many gay men a disease that, in all its horror, can provide an easier identity than being homosexual. Having AIDS provides many men a life as medical patient that is more accepted and supported—both by larger society and by gay communities—than was ever the case when they were merely physically healthy homosexuals.

The confused identification with AIDS rather than with being gay has made too many men too attached—in irrational, unconscious ways—to the meanings of AIDS, or too guilty about not being attached enough. It is an aspect of survivor guilt that one feels so profoundly identified with the dying that surviving is betraying. This identification with AIDS is part of what a 23-year-old gay man, contemplating his relationship to the gay community, was experiencing when he said to me, "I feel as if I won't really have come-out until I'm HIV-positive. That's when you know you've really thrown your hat into the ring and stood up as gay." This is the notion that being gay means having AIDS, or, at the very least, that one's life be defined by the epidemic. It is an expression of the feeling, often unconscious, that one is straying from his true identity, and thus betraying himself and his community, by not having a life made intolerable—or simply ended—by AIDS.

A day after receiving negative results from a much postponed, much debated HIV test, a 39-year-old psychotherapy patient, Tim, discussed his complex feelings.

> I got my HIV test back, and it was negative. I'm pleased of course, but I'm also very sad. I'm actually quite confused and don't know what I feel. When I got the results I felt like crying, though I can't say why, and I didn't do it. It wasn't just relief. I called Mike with the news and he wanted to go out and celebrate, and I thought, "Well how can you celebrate this?" I couldn't imagine. There are too many positive people, and I can't imagine talking about being negative. It's not the kind of thing you could go around and say, "You know, I'm negative." I've expected for so long, at least four or five years, to be positive—I'm talking about *allegiance,* I guess. I realize that I have to rethink what the gay community is. I don't know anymore what it is because HIV has changed it all, and I have no idea where I fit anymore.

In the week following the blood test, Tim found he was fearful of being alone, and he had several acute anxiety episodes (panic attacks), the first in his car the evening after his blood test results. He had just had dinner with a positive friend and his AIDS-symptomatic roommate. These were relatively new friends, and since his own test—which he had pointedly not mentioned to his dinner companions—Tim suddenly found himself afraid to make new friends "to replace those who have died" for fear that the new friends would turn out to be positive, and he would lose them too. "When I was positive—I mean, when I thought I was positive— this never worried me," he said. In our sessions, he realized that he was not only afraid of losing friends to illness and death. He felt that he had already "lost" his positive friends by being uninfected.

> "I'm no longer sharing, or thinking I'm sharing with them the most important thing in our lives. Now it's just the most important part of *their* lives. I'd like to escape from that now, or sometimes I'd

like to. I can suddenly see, just for a minute, that I could actually have a normal life, instead of a life with death everywhere. Part of me really wants a life like that."

Tim lapsed into several minutes of silence, and finally I asked him, "Why is it hard for you to imagine that—to imagine that you could have a 'normal' life?" Again he was silent for several minutes.

"You know, I'm trying to think about your question, and I just get so far with it, and run into confusion. It's like I can't even re-member what you asked me. I know there are feelings here that I don't want to have. It's the confusion, and I know that when I have this kind of confusion, it's because there's something I don't want to know about."

"I think some of the feelings," I commented, "are about your am-bivalence about being negative, and about being separated from your positive friends by that."

"I wonder all the time about how I ended up negative. I've never counted, but I'll bet I've been fucked by 20 guys whose pictures I've seen in the *B.A.R.* [obituaries of a San Francisco gay paper]. And I've wondered again and again, how it is I could be negative. I haven't done anything to *deserve* being negative."

"I'm wondering about the idea that being negative is something you feel you have to *deserve*—rather than *expect,* for example. It's also my impression that you went to protected sex very early on in the epidemic," I said. "You seem to discount that as a possible explanation for your being negative."

"Maybe I do. Maybe I should give myself more credit for that. You know, that was my reaction to the epidemic—I just pulled *way* back. But I know a lot of guys who just got more and more flagrant with sex as the epidemic went on. It was their way of dealing with their feelings, and I know a lot of these people are dead now. But I couldn't do that, I was too afraid of the whole thing."

"So that is a difference between you and many of the people who are dead."

"But I don't want there to be a difference. I want to be with my friends, to be part of their lives, and I guess I sometimes think that means being sick. In that way—I have to say that I don't feel coura-geous about this, I don't always think that what I did was the best thing. It was living in fear, and it's easy now to say, 'Oh, that was very smart of me,' but it wasn't smart when it happened, it was just *fear*. And a lot of my friends who are dead just refused to live in that fear. And I've got to say about them . . ."

After several moments of silence I prompted him. "Say what about them?"

"I *don't* know."

"You say that with anger."

"I feel angry. I feel very angry."

"Do you know why?"

"No."

"You said a while ago that sometimes you "wanted a life like that."

"I don't remember that."

"Well it's something else connected to very strong feelings," I responded. "But you were talking about having a 'normal' life or a life filled with death. And you said something like, 'I sometimes want a life like that.'"

"I don't know what I meant. I meant, I guess, a life with death and without death. I meant both. I'm very confused about my feelings about this. Obviously it doesn't make any sense to want to live with all this death if you don't have to. And it doesn't make any sense to want to be positive."

"Whether it makes sense or not, your feelings about whether you want to be negative or positive seem very complicated. And I have the feeling that some of your anger right now is about that."

"Part of it is that I just feel like it's very risky to hope I could be free of AIDS and this whole life it's made for all of us."

Tim again lapsed into several minutes of silence, and I finally asked if he could say why that seemed risky.

"I guess because it doesn't seem possible. I still feel, if I'm really honest with myself, as if I've got HIV, and to hope that I don't—to really *live* as if I don't—will be pushing my luck. The minute I feel reasonably O.K., that I'm safe, it will get me."

I commented: "But Tim, isn't there some confusion here between half wanting HIV, and feeling that you're going to get it *anyway*— as if your ambivalence about not having it might bring it about. And this idea makes me wonder if part of your anxiety isn't that you might expose yourself—that it is your ambivalence that poses the danger. You seem to feel a lot of motivation to have HIV, and I'm wondering why you *wouldn't* try to contract it."

Tim responded almost immediately: "The part that I haven't said,

is that I also have the feeling—and I *know* this isn't true, I think—
that I wonder if it would be O.K. with my friends who are positive,
or who are sick. I wonder if it would *really* be O.K. with them if
I were negative. I'm thinking of Rob, and I wonder if he will ever
forgive me for being negative."

"Why would he have to forgive you?" I asked.

"I don't know. Because I have abandoned him?" Tim asked.

"You are asking me."

"Because I don't know."

"You sound as if you feel you have."

"Oh, I know I feel I have—but I haven't."

"If you had," I asked, "What would that mean? How would you
make that up to Rob?"

"There is no way. But if I were sick I wouldn't have to—there'd
be nothing to make up, and believe it or not I *have* often thought
I would rather be sick. I hate to say it, because I know so many
people who would give anything not to be sick. I would never tell
them this either. I would never tell them I'm negative, and I would
never tell them that I wanted to be positive. There is no way I can
see to make this up to anybody."

What came up most often in the days following the HIV test were Tim's
feelings of loneliness and disorientation. The negative results meant that
he was not who he had thought he was and did not belong among those
he had thought he belonged among. He also now felt that, in all probability, he had to deal with the demands and complexity of a normal life
span, which was something he had not been counting on. This was a
burden that most of his friends, dealing with the prospect of worsening
illness and death, did not have.

Tim closed one session during this posttest period by announcing
that he was thinking of moving to Seattle, a subject he had never even
mentioned before.

"Why now?" I asked.

"I don't know. I never thought of it when I thought I was positive, but I have the idea there will be a gay community there that I
can be part of. Almost everyone here has died or moved away."

We were able to clarify that Tim's desire to move to Seattle lay in the
hopeful fantasy that gay people in Seattle would be free of HIV. There,

with his negative condition, Tim could belong, and would no longer feel the ambivalence he felt about being uninfected. Most importantly, Tim discovered that in his fantasy he would not be able to put himself at risk for contracting HIV.

Tim's fear of contracting HIV because of his own ambivalence about not having it, is expressed by another psychotherapy patient in his late twenties, Don. Don also expresses common feelings among uninfected men about the implied meanings of being HIV-negative. Don had received a similarly unexpected negative HIV test, and told me a few weeks later.

"I haven't told anyone about my test, because I'm not really certain about it. I just feel like there's too much weird stuff going on with HIV, and if I'm really positive, I don't want to go around telling people I'm negative."

"And if you really are negative?" I wondered.

"I wouldn't tell anyone anyway."

"Why not?"

"I just don't want to be different," he responded. "And I'm not going to push it in anyone's face. I guess I'm ashamed of it. It would be like saying, 'You know I've got something you want.' "

"Who wants what?"

"Being HIV-negative. *Being HIV-negative.* It would be like saying that I had an advantage, and I'm not going to push that in other people's faces—guys who are positive."

"Is it an advantage?" I wondered.

"Not really."

"Not really?"

"What do you mean?"

"I'm wondering if you feel there is an advantage in being HIV-negative."

"If you mean is there a privilege in it, the answer is no."

"I think you've introduced a new idea. I was asking about *advantage,* which would be something for yourself. When you bring up *privilege,* then I think of you in relation to others—others who are less fortunate."

"I don't think it's any of those things."

"Is the possibility of avoiding AIDS—even with all the other unhappy possibilities in life—not an advantage?" Don did not answer and was silent for several minutes. "Is it difficult for you to think about this?"

"I feel like you're trying to make me say something I don't want to say . . . I'm not going to say to Howard [Don's closest HIV-positive friend] that I don't want to be like him. *That* is what you're trying to get me to say—that I don't want to be like Howard, that I never want to see him again, that I never want to touch him again, that I never want to think about AIDS again—that I just want to get the fuck out of here and never think about any of this again."

Don began to cry and we sat for several minutes without speaking.

"Those sound like things *you're* feeling."

"Well if I'm supposed to be so overjoyed about being negative . . . what *does* it say about Howard's life. It says it's down the tubes. I feel *too guilty* to think that."

"That if it's important to you to be negative, it invalidates Howard in some way?"

"Yeah. Because Howard thinks he's going to survive, and sometimes what I feel like saying to him is, 'You know, Howard, you're going to die like all the others—*and I don't want to be like you.*' That is what I feel like saying. Howard *eats seaweed.* He eats seaweed and zinc because he thinks it's going to save his life. And every time I see him do that, I feel *guilty.* And if I'm HIV-negative, I feel like it's going to make him feel like all of that is hopeless and that I should support his hope."

"Your being HIV-negative, in itself, will make him feel hopeless?"

"It will if it's *important* to me to be negative. I mean, otherwise, I'd just get HIV and eat seaweed and zinc. Like Howard."

With great difficulty and pain, Don was able to clarify some of these feelings over the next few sessions. He felt very strongly that wanting to be HIV-negative, feeling that it was an advantage, or asserting explicitly that he did not want HIV injured and abandoned Howard and other positive men.

A few months later, Don "admitted" to me with great difficulty that he had been having unprotected sex with Richard, his boyfriend of several months. Their dating had started shortly after the HIV test. Although we had discussed Richard often, this was the first mention of unprotected sex. Don "assumed," he said, that he would not infect Richard because of his negative test; and he assumed Richard was uninfected "because of his [social and sexual] history." But as he discussed this with me, he doubted the reliability of the assumption, and wondered how he had made this judgment. They had never explicitly discussed their antibody statuses.

I said that we had spent much time discussing why Don had assumed he was positive before the antibody test, why he sometimes still thought he was positive despite the test, but that we had not yet completely clarified why he *wanted* to be positive. Don was surprised at the idea.

> "Why would I want to be positive?"
>
> "Since your HIV test, you've talked mostly about feeling shame and disenfranchisement; and if you can't feel any advantage in being HIV-negative, it seems to me that you will have little incentive to stay that way. And, I should add, if you get HIV, maybe you and Howard can eat seaweed *together.* That would mean a lot to both of you."
>
> Don responded immediately: "Yesterday I went to A Different Light [San Francisco's largest gay and lesbian bookstore], and I looked over an entire wall of books on AIDS. But there was nothing about being HIV-negative. It's like we don't exist, I mean there wasn't even a *chapter* in a book about negative men. And the message I get from that is that it isn't important to be negative. And I definitely get the message that I shouldn't be talking about being negative. When I told Mark [an HIV-negative friend] about this, he just told me I was confused. And I could see that *he* was confused, that he didn't want to talk about it, that it made him uncomfortable just like it makes me uncomfortable. And do you know what he said? He said, 'Don, you sound as if you want some *privilege* for being HIV-negative.'"

The subject of AIDS and disenfranchisement is poignantly addressed in an Albert Innaurato short story "Solidarity." The protagonist *has no information about his HIV status,* but, like Don and his friend Mark, he assumes an association and identity with HIV-positive people which subsumes his possible identity as one who does not have HIV:

> Though I don't know how much longer I'll survive, I have some survivor guilt. . . . Could I have been a better friend to [those already dead] knowing I'd live a little longer? And would that have made a difference to them, given they were to die? But after all, I tell my-

self, people die, consciousness ceases, and that's it. . . . Somehow I
don't want to accept that our only solidarity is with death.[8]

The identifications of Tim and Don with HIV-positive men are partly a
result of unconscious, *individual* psychological issues. They are also identifications that arise within the social context of being gay. For many gay
men, an identification with HIV is a natural consequence of membership
in the "gay community," a marginalized *set* of communities that encourage support of what are often felt to be their own marginalized members.
In many small gay communities, HIV-positive men are severely marginalized in social fact—ignored or actively shunned by other gay men,
unrecognized by the larger society, and provided few services and little
attention by either. In San Francisco, New York, and Los Angeles, which
have a near *majority* of gay men HIV-infected or with AIDS, there is
a natural identification by most members of the gay communities with
the infected, ill, and dying, and with their needs and values. Within
these communities, *uninfected* men have, in social fact, become marginalized and relatively ignored—like the family's good child. Gay Pride
parades are dominated by AIDS service contingents, and "community
awareness" is now more about the epidemic than anything else. That
there is much—I believe, self-evident—advantage to being uninfected
does not mean that uninfected men actually experience themselves as
advantaged—any more than positive men experience themselves as advantaged because services and community awareness are focused on
them. *Both* groups feel disadvantaged and marginalized, and the universally acknowledged horror and psychological complexity of actually
having HIV within one's body allows only positive men to say that.
Uninfected men thus find themselves unable to talk about important
feelings. Regardless of the comparability or noncomparability of the two
experiences, uninfected men are in many very important ways marginalized by both gay communities and larger society because they live in the
epidemic, if not actually with HIV. This is partly the source of Woody
Castrodale's conflict, quoted at the beginning of this chapter, in speaking
about "a split between having my own feelings and then sort of denying
them, and going back and forth, back and forth, into the world of these
people who are sick, and then back into my own life, where I am trying
to be 'normal,' whatever that means."

Shifting Identities and Values

The inability to acknowledge one's own identity—or the loss of it because of personal and social identifications—often results in a corresponding shift in personal values. This shift is described in the following
session with Paul, a 34-year-old, HIV-negative psychotherapy patient.
Paul had had a lover, Robert, diagnosed with AIDS several years before:

"I went to Roxanne's today [Paul's physician], because, as you
know, I've been having trouble breathing. It's really gotten so that I
walk across the room to get my socks and I'm panting. And as I was
sitting on the table with her stethoscope on my back, breathing in
and out for her, I suddenly felt so angry and sad about all the people
who have died of PCP [pneumocystis pneumonia] and KS [Kaposi's
sarcoma] in their lungs that I felt like crying. Well, she thought I
was concerned about these things for myself, that I thought I might
have PCP or KS . . .

"What had you said to her?" I asked.

"I said something like, 'I'm sitting here and I suddenly feel overwhelmed thinking about all the people with PCP and KS who can't
breathe.' And she said, 'Well you're not likely to have those problems if you're HIV-negative—and, by the way, I see here that it's
been well over a year since you've had an HIV test. Don't you think
it's time to get another one?' I said no, I wasn't interested, and
she was very surprised and asked why. I said, 'I'm not interested
because there isn't much I'd be interested in doing with that information,' and she said, 'Oh, you're wrong. You can live a lot longer
asymptomatically with AZT and the other antivirals.' I asked her
how much longer and she said she didn't know.

"While this is going on, I'm breathing in and out, and she definitely hears the wheezing, and I was thinking of the Jimmy Somer-
ville song, 'you know, 'I never thought I'd be sitting here watching
you, lying on the sheets, *drowning*.' And I had such intense feelings
about this song while I was sitting there *being sick* . . ."

Paul trailed off into several moments of silence at this point.
Finally, I said, "This reminds me of your sitting up all night with
Robert in the hospital—watching him breathe into the oxygen
mask—when he first had PCP." Paul didn't respond, but started up
a few minutes later, as if he hadn't heard me.

"So then she said—she was going through my chart at this

point—'We really should talk again about your cholesterol levels.'
I said, 'What about them?' and she said, 'Well these are among the
highest levels I've seen in my entire medical practice,' and she was
asking about my diet, and so on, and finally I said, 'You know, I
don't care what my cholesterol is, and if I think about having a
heart attack in 10 or 20 years, it just doesn't mean anything in the
context of HIV.' To me this was like living in a war, and she's saying
to me, 'You know you should really think about getting a nose job.' "

"What would you have liked her to say?" I wondered.

"Oh she was doing the right thing. But she's got her program,
and I've got mine." Paul started to laugh at this point.

"I told her that. But the whole thing made me incredibly angry,
at just the whole situation, and my thinking, 'God, maybe I should
take her advice,' and then thinking, 'Shit, cheese is practically the
only thing I do for fun anymore, and here we are in the middle of
a plague, and practically everyone I know is dying of AIDS.' But I
would just flop back and forth, and finally, I said to her, 'Just look
at the walls in this room. Do you ever think about what's gone on
in here over the last ten years? The amount of suffering that's gone
on in here?' Which of course she didn't answer.

"I was very agitated for the rest of the day, and I called Tim and
told him this story and how little sense I had been able to make of
my feelings, and he said, 'Well, God, you don't want to keel over
dead of a heart attack, and what does this have to do with the epidemic anyway? Don't you think you're a little confused?' I said,
'Well I know it doesn't have anything to do with the epidemic, but
it's also true that I'm not going to say to Robert, "Oh, by the way,
I'm reducing the cholesterol in my diet so I don't have a heart attack in 2020, twenty-five years after HIV has wasted you away into
a little pile of sores and vomit." ' Tim was very alarmed by this, by
my extremeness, and I said to him, 'You know, I don't mind saying
that I have been *affected* by life in this epidemic, and if there's *one
thing* I've learned, it's don't give up your cheese—or anything else
you care about.' "

"What do you make of Tim's concern for your health?" I wondered.

"I make of it that he cares about me, but also—just like myself
half the time—he's living in a lot of denial about what's going on
and how he's affected by it. I mean, the idea that people are drop-

ping dead right and left, and my problem is cheese. Are we going to try to survive this epidemic by denying our feelings and sitting around talking about cholesterol? We'll be zombies by the time this thing is over, if we do that—truly the walking dead. I'd rather be among the *real* dead than end up like that. Cholesterol and insurance. The other thing is insurance—we should take out more insurance while we're at it. We can all live to be eighty-five, and we can move in with my Aunt Florence in Leisure World. She's more afraid of animal fat than I ever have been of AIDS, and I wouldn't trade you one piece of cheese for her *whole* life.

"So how do you reconcile these differences in values?" I wondered. Paul suddenly became quite serious.

"It occurs to me that normal life, or perhaps normal *American* life like the kind we see on TV—life outside of the plague—lets us grow into a lot of deadness. I don't know if we come to take life for granted, or if normal life just supports more denial, but I feel lucky to have learned this, and I'm going to live it. I don't want a *normal* life anymore, and I'm not going to have one. To have a normal life now just means denying everyone's suffering—*everyone's.*

At this point Paul stopped, and I waited a few moments before commenting: "I respect the insight you have about this, Paul, and your conviction about it. But I'm also wondering about the conflict that this brings up—not only between you and Roxanne and Tim, but within yourself. You talk about going back and forth on this, even within yourself, and I see that you have a lot of anger at those who are trying to lead "normal" lives. And—I must point this out—Robert is actually dying right now, and you're not. And I'm wondering about that difference and how you account for that."

Paul was obviously feeling intensely at this moment and he sat silently for several moments again.

"I felt completely alone after talking to Tim. I don't belong in a normal world—I *can't* and I won't live there—and I know that I'm not in Robert's either. I'm *not* dying, and he won't allow me to share a certain part of his life that has to do with that. He has HIV and I don't, and that is a lot of my anger . . .

"*What* is a lot of your anger?" I asked him.

"I don't know exactly what I mean. Part of me doesn't think it's OK to take care of myself—in the normal sense—when Robert is dying. This is the guilt, I know. But part of me doesn't want to, and

I also know part of that is just feeling angry about the epidemic. But part of me doesn't want to because I can see through it—God, when I think about what empty lives people are willing to put up with, how little people will settle for, how much we value safety. It *disgusts* me. I'm left with a jumble of these feelings, but they have one thing in common, and that is that only half of me is in the normal world. What I really wanted to say to Roxanne was 'You know, I don't want to live that long—I've had *enough*. We're living in a war, and I'm at risk, everyone is at risk, so leave me alone.' Sometimes I feel that I suffer as much about Robert's HIV as he does. And I won't even have the relief of finally dying from it."

We sat for several moments after this, and I finally commented before the end of the hour: "Your identification with Robert and with others who have HIV seems quite natural to me. I accept that at face value, I find it valid, and I accept your right to live a life that makes sense and has meaning for you. I only think we have to clarify the other elements—your anger, and your guilt, because we haven't gotten to the bottom of that one either. They are entangled in there with the 'valid' feelings; and they can be destructive."

Coming Out as HIV-Negative

To this point in my discussion of the HIV-negative experience, I have emphasized the forces within the gay communities and internal sources of conflict that underlie common experiences of being HIV-negative: marginalized members of marginalized communities experiencing internalized homophobia, the transfer of psychological conflict from homosexuality to AIDS, identifications, disenfranchisement, guilt, and the seeking of acceptance by others. Such forces within gay communities and "internal" psychological phenomena also have their external roots and connections. For example, homophobia is "internalized" from others within the larger society, and psychological conflict exists in a matrix of internalized social values, ideas, and feelings. The larger social context of the uninfected gay man makes important contributions to the internal condition of being HIV-negative.

Although there are large disenfranchised elements of American society that suffer continuous economic, social, and psychological trauma, the AIDS epidemic is unparalleled in the experience of most Americans alive today. We cannot continue to entertain the idea that survivors—in all senses of the idea—might *not* find their lives profoundly affected and conflicted. As a psychologist, I feel much more concern about those who are without the emotional capacity to be affected, or those who are so profoundly affected that they can respond only with denial. For the HIV-negative man, denial of the very existence of his condition arises out of attitudes from society at large, which has refused to recognize the plight of *positive* men; from many positive men; and from other uninfected men who would deny their own pain. Except that being HIV-negative is much more precarious than being gay, the struggle to make sense of an HIV-negative life has many parallels to the struggle of the adolescent who is trying to be homosexual. Both are struggles with a difficult, diffuse, and conflicting internal experience that require societal recognition to be successfully consolidated as an identity. Both being uninfected and being homosexual require a coming-out process that is the more or less coordinated consolidation of internal experience and societal acknowledgment of who one is and how one feels. That being uninfected is a socially unsupported—usually unrecognized—condition is evident in the conflict of Richard, a 32-year-old psychotherapy patient:

> When I found out that I was negative—well, this is something I definitely keep to myself. The chances are anyone you'd admit that to is positive. And that's completely inappropriate. To me it would be like running down the hallway at [San Francisco] General yelling, "I'm healthy, I'm healthy!" You just wouldn't do that. You'd say, "Well that guy is a real *creep*."

The difficulty in coming out as uninfected is also immensely complicated by the common feeling that HIV status may be a relatively ephemeral condition. Many men doubt the permanence—and often reality—of their HIV status. The coming-out process, whether it be about sexuality or HIV status, is difficult and conflicted because it usually involves a fundamental realignment of one's self experience, internal identifications, and social affiliations. To feel that one might do all this work only to find that he really belongs among HIV-positives, is a frightening possibility. "Being HIV-negative is not a permanent state," Woody Castrodale, HIV peer-group leader, reminded me. "At any moment we could lose it, and it's scary to hang an identity on that."

"Do you mean that if the epidemic ended, there would no longer be positives and negatives?" I asked Woody.

> Oh no, I never even thought of that. I just meant that being HIV-negative isn't permanent, like being gay, or straight, or black. We

all—all gay men who are negative—realize in our unconscious that
being negative is a precarious state. We could lose it, and it makes
for a feeling of uncertainty. We could be on the other side of the
fence, and it's pretty frightening.[9]

Such doubt about HIV status seriously inhibits the coming-out process of many uninfected men, and thus compromises their commitment
to that identity—and thus to their actual physical condition. Just as
a positive man's life is changed by his knowledge of serostatus and
anticipation of illness, many uninfected men appear to lead lives that
express their anticipation that they will—somehow—become infected
in the future. Feelings of possibly or inevitably becoming infected arise
out of a mix of irrational and perfectly rational ideas. In addition to
the psychological complexities surrounding HIV, many biological and
medical uncertainties foreclose on complete rational confidence in the
impossibility of future infection. Both the feelings and the ideas are compelling, and they keep many men from hanging their hats on pegs that
so often seem illusory or tenuous.

The idea that being HIV-negative required a coming out was first put
to me so succinctly by Ed Wolf, with whom I facilitated San Francisco
Shanti Project's first workshops for HIV-negative men. For many of these
men, the experience of the workshops was like the experience of a gay
man's first visit to a gay venue. They were astonished, validated, grati-
fied, and bedazzled by the company of so many others like themselves.
They were profoundly relieved to find that they were not alone, and that
their futures might hold more than isolation and loneliness. Living in
an epidemic that will span decades, all inside and outside the gay communities must acknowledge *being uninfected* as both a condition in life
and a social identity. As with being gay, uninfected men require societal
recognition for their condition and feelings, and need social structures
within gay communities that support them.

The homosexualization of AIDS is an external phenomenon with internal correlates. The larger society has homosexualized AIDS to project
its fear about disease and its self-loathing about sexuality onto a traditionally persecuted minority group that has born the initial brunt
of a viral infection. When this homosexualization of AIDS is internalized by gay men—both positives and negatives—as the AIDSification
of homosexuality, it reveals, like internalized homophobia itself, a vein
of self-hatred. This self-hatred is demonstrated most clearly not by the

appropriate efforts of the gay communities to fight both AIDS and homophobic hatred, but in the irrational, unconscious, and destructive confusions that entangle feelings about being gay with feelings about having
HIV.

If uninfected gay men cannot clarify these confusions, cannot re-
establish individual and social identities that are not dominated by this
extreme unconscious and irrational entanglement with AIDS, it will
cost gay communities decades of psychological, social, and political
growth—as well as an even larger medical catastrophe. Because of the
social and psychological gains made by the gay liberation movement in
the 1970s, it is easy to overlook the depression, anxiety, isolation, and
loneliness that were experienced routinely by a majority of homosexual
men twenty-five years ago. The AIDS epidemic, with its ill, its dead, and
its potential survivors, has already returned depression, anxiety, isolation, and loneliness to the lives of too many. Historically these problems
have had to do with the difficulties of being homosexual in a disap-
proving society. None of these old problems have disappeared; but now
gay men must struggle with them in the context of life in an epidemic.
Some men have never been able to find peace with their sexuality, and
those refractory problems will become buried in the new problems of
the epidemic.

Many others, especially in the last two decades, who have been able
to accomplish relatively whole identities that include their real sexuality, are being badly damaged by the psychological toll of the AIDS
epidemic. Although we will always have the powerful legacies of many
lost to AIDS, it is those who are HIV-uninfected and can stay that way
who will be the gay citizens of the future. This group requires a community—and AIDS education—that can acknowledge advantages in being
uninfected and can offer incentives to stay that way; and this group requires acknowledgment of its effort to survive, not only medically, but
humanly. But *surviving humanly* means that we must find ways not only
to sustain survival, but to maintain or restore our capacity to *enjoy* that
survival—to live with the human capacity to create reasonably fulfilled
and satisfying lives. Ben Schatz, San Francisco attorney and gay rights
activist, conveyed this concern when he said to me,

> I'm pretty sure within myself that it's OK to be HIV-negative and
> to stay that way. But where I run into trouble is in enjoying being
> alive, and I include in that being sexual. Then I often feel that it's

not OK, that with so many people suffering and dead, I shouldn't be happy, I shouldn't enjoy sex. This is the point where my survivor guilt really clicks in, and it sometimes makes it very hard for me to enjoy the life I'm lucky enough to have.[10]

Gay men now often express such feelings. They reflect a profound division within many of us about whether or not it is acceptable to really *live* rather than merely be alive. Rick, an uninfected psychotherapy patient in his mid-thirties, and his lover Tom, also uninfected, had lost most of their friends to AIDS, and felt increasingly isolated. Rick told me about returning home the night before our session to their flat in the Castro:

Tom and I went to dinner last night in the Haight [Ashbury district of San Francisco], and on the way home, when we came to the crest of the hill—where you can see down into the Castro, and the street climbs up the other side into Noe [Valley]—I said to Tom, "You know, we're really just visitors here now." Tom said, "What do you mean?" And I said, "We're just visitors, we're interlopers— because we don't have HIV." And he said, "Oh, that's true. I think our fantasies about moving are really about where we could go and feel like we were part of things again." And I started thinking to myself how often we've talked about whether we should move— back to New York, to New Mexico, to Seattle. And the question we're really asking ourselves is whether we should leave now, when almost all our friends are dead, or wait until *everyone* is dead. But do you know what I said to him? It just came out of my mouth, and I said, "There's nowhere we can move, because we're not visitors in San Francisco. We're visitors in our hearts."

Chapter 6
Being Alone

Doctor, if you tell me that you have HIV, I will stay with you until you tell me that it's time, that you are too sick and I have to find a new therapist. But in the meantime, I will have to put the shell back around my heart.—A psychotherapy patient to the author

In the earlier years of the epidemic, I often thought our greatest danger would be that many gay men might perish under the unbearable weight of loss, grief, and depression. People die of sadness too, even in the age of HIV. But this was a fear, it now seems, that underestimated both the duration of the epidemic and the power of the psychological defenses that would be brought to bear on the experience. I now understand that our central problem is not depression, but the profound and destructive effects of denial and repression that we are erecting against fear, grief, and depression. These defenses are leaving too many of us in isolation from our own internal lives and feelings, in isolation from one another, and without the capacity for emotional or physical intimacy. What could a man mean, as so many now often say, that he is "getting used to the deaths?" I will try to describe some of the psychological processes underlying this feeling, and the costs—most importantly, isolation—that such processes will exact from us as individuals and as communities. All of the psychological and social problems I have discussed—depression, anxiety, social and occupational dysfunction, hyperactivity, hypochondriasis, sexual dysfunction, feelings of disenfranchisement, and identity confusions—have one important result in common. They all ultimately conspire to isolate the individual from his feelings—which is to say, from himself—and thus from the possibility of intimate connections to others.

The terms are largely metaphorical and the meanings imprecise, but we deal with forbidden or painful feelings by *suppressing* them, *encapsulating* them, *containing* them, *denying* them, *splitting* them off, or *repressing* them. These are ways of trying "not to have" feelings, which is to say, not experiencing them consciously. We are thus not aware of them, or if we are, feel less affected by them. We often notice them almost as if they belonged to someone else, but do not live them. Such psychological processes have immense value in normal life, for they allow us to get through the day, to function competently, and to not be overwhelmed by feelings when it would seem to be undesirable or dangerous.

All these ways of not having feelings, however, share two serious consequences. The first is that they are intrinsically nonselective. A person experiencing significant stress or conflict about a particular situation, cannot contain only feelings related to that situation. Essentially, he must contain, dissociate, or repress feelings *in general*. When feelings are a response to a huge, enduring event like the AIDS epidemic, these intrinsically indiscriminate and global defenses thus impoverish the entire emotional life of the individual by limiting his capacity for all feelings. This impoverishment includes loss of the capacity to know oneself, to have empathetic friendships and intimate relationships, and to take pleasure in life.

Consequences of defensive operations are exacted not only by our losing a capacity to experience our own feelings, but by the necessity of protecting ourselves from *others'* feelings as well. Every gay man is familiar with the homophobe who, unable to deal with his own homosexual feelings, cannot tolerate them in others. The homophobe must deny or reject *our* homosexual feelings in order to maintain control over his own. When trying to contain one's own feelings, others' feelings are stimulating, inciting, and dangerous. Thus if we attempt to protect ourselves from the emotional impact of the epidemic, we must separate ourselves from others, both negative and positive, who are having feelings about this event that we cannot allow ourselves. This is a further source of social and psychological isolation.

The AIDS epidemic is an event that holds the potential to easily produce painful and overwhelming feelings for many. Thus we must look at those who are apparently not being overwhelmed and ask what costs they are paying for their nominal peace. Unfortunately, we often will find that these costs include their very capacities to be connected to themselves and thus to others. It is to be expected that people protecting themselves with the containment of feelings are not only unaware of the contained feelings, but also often deny the costs of containment. To acknowledge the costs would be to acknowledge that there was a problem, and tantamount to acknowledging the nature of the problem itself. Sometimes the costs are so huge that they cannot be denied, and they may then force themselves into consciousness. If the costs are recognized consciously—in the experience of loneliness, for example—they are dissociated from both the process of containment and the feelings being contained, and are attributed to something else. The lonely man living in the epidemic might attribute his loneliness to the lack of social opportunities, a fear of contracting HIV, or the unreliable nature of gay men, as examples, and this rationale will help keep from him the painful truth that he is no longer present within himself, and thus no longer there for connections to others. Gay men commonly experience the emotional costs of the epidemic as unconnected to the epidemic.

The individual is often assisted in his containment of feelings about the epidemic, and in his denial of the costs of the containment, by social institutions. One result is that the isolation of gay men living in the epidemic has become widely institutionalized, with the creation of specific social forms that assist the isolated man in tolerating his life. Because containment of our own feelings relies on not being exposed to others' feelings, it is important that we associate with others involved in similar psychological operations. Social organizations may be useful for the sharing and reinforcement of various ways of containing feelings. It is such an organization's purpose to support the containment of forbidden feelings, by mutually assisting members in excluding their own feelings from subjective experience. Organizationally approved and shared feelings are substituted for genuine ones. These organizational substitutes serve to help conceal the individual's experience of emotional impoverishment, and provide him with a stand-in for an authentic internal life. What is not permitted is the individual's access to his own feelings, for group purpose and cohesion relies precisely on the individual not having that capacity. A religious group, as one example, may derive part of its cohesion from the denial of individual feelings about the possible non-existence of God, or about unspoken—often completely unconscious—desires to behave in forbidden ways. Political groups may help suppress ambivalence by demanding loyalty that requires denying the potentially useful ideas of anyone who is a political threat.

In addition to the contributions of social institutions—a subject I will pursue shortly in more detail—there are important developmental sources of many gay men's difficulties allowing feelings. Gay men, as a group, grow up with three problematic developmental focuses pertinent to the capacity for intimacy and connection to others. These are difficulty experiencing feelings in general, deficits of self-esteem, and anxiety. The results of these developmental difficulties, when severe or protracted, are often seen in adult character as what psychological nomenclature labels *schizoid, narcissistic,* and *obsessive-compulsive* "personality disorders."[1] Here I will discuss only the first of the three, the difficulty with feelings in general, and its expression in character style. Problems with self-esteem and anxiety, and their expressions in the lives of gay men, are discussed in chapter 7 because they bear directly on the relations between positive and negative men.

The term *schizoid* derives from *schism,* and the schism implied is between a person and his internal life of feelings and emotion. For a young man growing up homosexual, many feelings are homosexual feelings. These are forbidden and profoundly conflicted, become the source of much internal pain, and threaten abandonment by others if discovered. Because of this very central emotional conflict, the young man feels danger in allowing any feelings, and often substitutes other feelings in the effort to contain and conceal the homosexual ones. If the child, adolescent, or young adult attempts to focally contain or repress only the conflicted homosexual feelings, the results will nevertheless be substantially global because of the nature of psychological operations.

In addition to these specific conflicts within the homosexual individual, there are broadly sanctioned cultural forces that influence psychological development as well. Men, homosexual or not, are acculturated to neither experience nor express feelings; and if it is a parent's perception that a son is deficient in masculine characteristics or skills, the parent's efforts to acculturate the child to traditional gender models may be even more forceful. Alternatives to experiencing and expressing feelings are learned early in childhood. A boy learns to physically or verbally "act out," often hyperactively or aggressively, instead of focusing inwardly and living in his feelings. Sometimes he may be allowed to become depressed rather than aggressive, but usually with an internal experience of emptiness, agitation, anger, or boredom, rather than with the experience of sadness, empathy, or tenderness more often allowed girls and women.[2]

If an isolation from feelings is common in gay men because of developmental pressures, the painful feelings arising out of the epidemic tend to entrench residual developmental problems in many and force their reemergence in others. This synergistic coincidence of troubled psychological development and the psychological impact of the epidemic is now an extremely serious threat for gay communities. The usual developmental problems of the gay man and the shallow American conceptualization of the male have both been exacerbated by the AIDS epidemic—ironically an epidemic perceived as a consequence of men sexually expressing internal lives in ways that only women are supposed to. As the father of a psychotherapy patient said to his newly "out" son, "If you want to call yourself gay, I can live with that. But, I warn you, no son of mine is going to take it up the ass."

"And what did you say?" I wondered.

"I said that I had already 'taken it up the ass,' as he called it, and that it was *wonderful*."

An expression of the synergy between an individual's earlier development and life in the epidemic is expressed by San Franciscan Ed Wolf. He had a long-standing sense of isolation from the mainstream of the gay community and in 1983, feeling that the epidemic had worsened his isolation, he decided to volunteer as a Shanti emotional support volunteer for people with AIDS. In the opening session of the training, the facilitator asked each of the seventy people present to say why he or she wanted to serve as an emotional support volunteer and what he or she expected to get from the training.

> To that time, I had never been in a group of gay people as large as this, and . . . I suddenly realized when I was sitting there, that I was going to have to *show up*. And I mean this for myself, within myself, and also myself as part of the gay community. We did a check in, and because I was sitting next to the facilitator, I was going to be the last to speak. As they went around the room people talked about these very big things: you know, it was that they wanted to be part of the response to AIDS or that they wanted to make an important contribution to the gay community. Things like that. I didn't doubt that this was genuine, but I was thinking all this while what I was going to say, and I couldn't think what it was going to be except that I realized that I was there for myself. When it finally came to me to speak, I just opened my mouth and it came out: "I'm sitting here and I feel like—I feel that I have ice on my heart. And I hope it melts, but I'm afraid it won't." I have no idea where that came

from, and I was as surprised as everyone else. But this realization is something that I have never forgotten. I had been very alone with being gay, and I needed a community, and I saw that this was going to be it.[3]

Ed's lifelong sense of isolation from his own feelings and from others —ice on his heart—reached a critical level in the early years of the epidemic. His hope that he could overcome his isolation, and his fear that he could not, are something shared by many gay men.

Institutionalized Isolation

When blood rides us like a destroyer,
then what we want's not just an erection
but the ensuing dereliction. Still,
it makes some difference how the clay is turned. Not just
any hole is worth poking around in. There
was a Werewolf, in days gone,
refused to put his trousers on
while anyone was watching, so embarrassing
it is to lay aside the beast and be man again.
—Keith Waldrop, *from* To Define Oblivion [4]

Because only about 10 percent of the population is gay, the gay communities have always needed special social institutions for meeting and congregating safely. In part for similar reasons, the gay communities have also had special institutions, such as bathhouses, for sexual interaction. These venues for sexual interaction have served some distinct psychological purposes as well. One has been to provide men who are coming out, or coming out sexually, an opportunity for the exploration of their sexuality; and another has been to allow gay men to openly have fun together. Importantly, they are also venues—if usually disappointing and sometimes brutalizing—for men seeking real intimacy who, because of developmental deficits, do not know how else to go about it. In the new sexual freedom of the seventies and early eighties, these were important, if not always fruitful, opportunities for many.

Bathhouses, however, have also provided a venue, without peer, for the needs of men whose sexuality is relatively unintegrated into feelings or relationships. The bathhouse environment allows purely sexual interactions disconnected from more whole human interactions, an idea taken to literal expression in the "glory hole," through which you can insert your penis into an adjoining room and have it sucked by you-never-had-to-know-who. This is sex with a mouth—or, for the receptive partner, a penis—rather than with a person. Needless to say, such sex is free of the complexities, problems, and anxiety provoked by feelings, which become an inescapable part of more complex human interactions. It is also sex readily available for the sexually compulsive, because it involves no time wasted on "courtship" whatsoever. A psychotherapy patient, very active in the bathhouse scene of the seventies, said that it was his standard practice on entering a bathhouse "to get an erection immediately, so that I didn't spend too much time talking and risk getting intimate with anyone."

Today we again have such social institutions, though they are now usually not bathhouses, but sex clubs, jack-off clubs, or telephone sex lines. All allow for the same kind of emotion-free sex—or sex with highly ritualized and limited emotions. But with many of these new institutions, there are some new twists and restrictions. While bathhouses permitted any kind of physical contact, many of the newer sexual venues prescribe restrictions in behavior. The most liberal prohibit—though not always diligently—only unprotected anal sex. At the other end of the spectrum, some jack-off clubs prohibit any contact between patrons, other than visual. Telephone sex obviously involves no physical contact, and it offers the often brutal possibility of simply hanging up—or "switching lines" by pressing a phone button—to get rid of another man if he seems not to be meeting one's sexual needs. In San Francisco, the public policy rationale for permitting, if not always overtly supporting, such institutions is that they allow men to be sexual without danger of HIV transmission.

Allowing people to remain sexual, helping them to become sexual, or to become sexual again, must be central to our psychological efforts on behalf of gay men. Such institutionalized, feeling-free forms of sex are perfectly legitimate and have a place in the sexuality of many gay men. These forms of sexuality are troubling, however, when they become a man's *exclusive* form of sexual activity, and limit or replace entirely richer, more intimate interpersonal forms of sexual expression. We must also acknowledge that our new sexual institutions, like the old ones, may cater to those with long-standing—as well as epidemic-induced—psychological issues that prevent the integration of sexuality into feelings and relationships. Some men with conflict about intimacy are thankful for the new restrictions. Michael, a 36-year-old psycho-therapy patient, told me:

> "When I first came out [in 1978] there was this tremendous pres-sure [in the gay community] to have sex—I mean, you name it, but especially anal sex, which is something that I've never been into. And if you weren't into it, well then, your growth was stunted or something like that, and people would tell you to get into a group to work it out. There was this idea that you just hadn't gotten over your own homophobia if you weren't into a lot of sex, and especially anal sex. But with AIDS—well, the epidemic has gotten people into the kind of sex that I always wanted and couldn't have.
>
> "And can you talk about what that is?" I asked.
>
> "It's mostly masturbation. That's what I always liked, and that's what everybody does now. And if people want to touch each other during sex, that's OK with me, but mostly I'm into masturbation, which people accept now. I can't come if someone else is mastur-bating me anyway, and that's OK with people now—lots of people don't like to get your cum on their hands now anyway, because, you know, you might be positive. In this way AIDS has been a big benefit for me, because I don't have this pressure all the time to have sex with other people where there is a lot of contact. I mean, it's better not to touch people anyway because of AIDS."

The sexual preferences of Michael are certainly to be respected, and are harmless in themselves. But Michael began therapy to "work on my isolation," and much of our discussion revealed that Michael suffered long-standing conflict about his homosexuality, as well as a lifelong dis-trust of intimacy. Although Michael did not initially see any connection, his preference for sex "with others" in which there is a minimum of physical contact and he stimulates himself to orgasm expressed these long-standing problems—and exacerbated them. Such a psychological background is often revealed by men with a preference for essentially solitary sex; and typical of such men, Michael often expressed pain-ful feelings of isolation and loneliness that motivated sexual contact but were worsened, rather than relieved, by the sexual experience. The psychological clarification of Michael's feelings of isolation and loneli-ness partly involved clarifying the relationship between those painful feelings and his sexual preferences. This was a connection Michael ini-tially denied because his distance from others—supported by his sexual practices—protected him from what he anticipated as the even more painful experience of intimacy. As is often the case, it was only when his isolation became more painful than the anticipated pain of intimacy that Michael was able to begin to change.

Sexuality like Michael's, as an exclusive expression of sexuality, is of concern, because it is so often connected to painful feelings and a lonely and unhappy form of life. The epidemic, with its fear and anxiety, its sensible requirements for protected sex, and its new sexual institutions, conspires to maintain and strengthen limitations like Michael's by providing them with plausibility. This plausibility too easily disguises underlying psychological conflict and pain and too easily provides a pretext for not trying to address lives that could change.

A similar entanglement of preexisting problems of isolation with the reality of the epidemic is expressed in the following letter to the editors of *Out/Look* magazine. The letter's author writes in response to an article of mine[5] about the psychological distress of many gay survivors of the AIDS epidemic:

> Odets knows better than I whether there is a death-wish among [San Francisco's young gay population]. I would like to comment, in a constructive spirit, on only one of his statements: that safe-sex information has reached these men.
>
> It is true, or very likely, that they have all been exposed to some type of safe-sex guidelines. However, the safe-sex situation is confusing even to doctors. Some cases of HIV transmission remain unexplained. . . . Besides the strictly medical questions, there is anything but a full consensus about what degree of risk is tolerable, and how risky behavior must be before we deem it unsafe, and those who indulge in it neurotic.
>
> To my knowledge, partnered and group masturbation is 100% safe, and it's the only partnered sexual activity that is 100% safe. Those who indulge in it tend to speak rapturously about it. . . . It would seem to me the solution for these young men who want to have sex and also to belong. Yet outside the largest cities organized group masturbation is unavailable, and it's not very available even there. Wouldn't it . . . give frustrated men a place to go and be safely sexual? What is there to lose by trying it?[6]

The letter's author is responding to real concerns about the transmission of HIV. But his proposed solutions are disturbing in two important ways. When he speaks of *the* solution for young men, he fails to acknowledge that sex may be connected to feelings and relationships, and that different sexual interactions have different meanings for given individuals. Mutual masturbation as an exclusive form of sexuality may not allow expression of what needs to be expressed by many people, and the focus on "100% safety" provides a plausibility that obscures this. Beyond that limitation, the letter's author ignores all the other pertinent psychological issues—other than anxiety about HIV transmission—in responding to an article that is about loss, depression, guilt, and grief. These feelings will hardly be addressed by 100 percent safe sex, by masturbation, or through the absolute control of our anxiety about HIV transmission. Unfortunately, much of our AIDS education has supported the vision expressed in this letter, including its misconception of gay sex. Education too often supports the idea that gay sex is without human meaning, by portraying men who appear to be having casual or anonymous sex, and it almost invariably proposes ridiculously simple solutions—"a condom every time"—for complex psychological and interpersonal issues as expressed in sexuality. If we were to believe much of our AIDS education, the gay man who simply "plays it safe" can carry on with a "normal" life in the epidemic without a care in the world.

Surely the image of men in institutionalized masturbation circles is not an adequate vision of the future of the gay communities. Telephone sex allows men to have sex "together," without even the inconvenience— or "danger," in many senses of the idea—of being together. That such sexual expressions are medically safe provides no assurance about the total future health of gay communities, and there are much more intimate, relatively safe alternatives that might contribute to, rather than hinder, psychological growth. While masturbation and telephone sex have their useful and enjoyable places in the sexual lives of many men, we must be wary of an unlimited endorsement of them merely because they are "safe." Absolute safety at the cost of human intimacy may be too high a price for many, and that is an individual decision that must be respected.[7]

Chris, a man in his late twenties, came to me for psychotherapy after seeing two other psychotherapists briefly. He was on antidepressant medication prescribed by his general practitioner and although he reported that it helped limit his most severe slumps in mood, he still felt some periods of severe depression and experienced a "flatness" of emotion most of the time that he found disturbing. Chris had a lover for two years during his early twenties and had dated after that, but at the time I first saw him he had not had sex with another man for two years. His experience clarifies how much of our conceptualization, education, and public policy about HIV prevention in the narrowest sense fails to account for the total human concerns of gay men.

"Tell me something about your last therapy," I asked.

"Well, it was very short. I went to Dr. M because he was at Kaiser [a large California HMO] and he basically said, you know, 'You are what we call the *worried well*, and as long as I'm convinced that you are not suicidal, which I am, I've got to tell you that you don't need me, and I don't have time for you.' And this isn't exactly what he said, but it was more or less 'You've got to get your act together, keep yourself busy, and get on with things. You're healthy and you should be grateful for that.' "

"And how did you feel about this recommendation?" I asked.

"Well I was very upset, and I thought, 'Well, he hasn't listened to a thing I've said. He doesn't understand me.' "

"And what hadn't he listened to, or what didn't he understand?"

"He told me that if I wanted to have sex—I told him I hadn't had sex for two years, that is one of the first things I said—and he said, 'Well why don't you try a jack-off club? You're not going to catch anything if you don't touch other people.' " At this point Chris was silent for several minutes.

"Can you tell me what's going on—right now?" I asked him.

"I feel completely lost. I don't know what I'm doing. I've never really been comfortable with sex, it has never been easy for me. But AIDS has made it a *lot* worse. I really have a phobic reaction to people touching me, especially gay men. A guy I had a date with a few nights ago tried to kiss me and it was terrifying . . ."

"I can tell that it is painful for you," I said, "but it would help me if you could tell me more about that."

"I just went into some kind of unconscious flight. I don't know, we were in front of the restaurant saying goodbye and I went around the corner and just stood there and I was in a panic, and I thought, 'Well, *this is not right,* I shouldn't feel this way . . .' "

"This way?"

"This *frightened*—and *embarrassed*. Because I think he saw what happened. And I thought to myself, 'I'm just not interacting with other people very well.' I always think to myself it's the fear of getting AIDS. But it's also about getting close to people, especially because they might die. I felt that way when I was twenty. I've always been afraid of that, I guess, and I didn't even know anyone that had died. I always felt that, and now it's a lot worse because it's really happening. I mean, people are really dying, and this isn't just my thing."

Chris's intense feelings about the epidemic are important and troubling, and are intimately woven into his psychological history. The dismissal of these feelings as an expression of the "worried well," or as something that will be addressed through completely protected sex is an obvious simplification, but a common one. It is not unusual to see such feelings handled as they were in Chris's case. The gay therapist—often potentially overwhelmed by his own feelings about the epidemic—colludes with the psychotherapy patient in dissociating both his and the patient's feelings, in this instance by characterizing the feelings as expressions of the worried well and recommending that Chris "try a jack-off club." The dissociative implication is that Chris's—and perhaps the therapist's—distress is merely about contracting HIV, and with that problem solved through "100 percent safe sex," there is nothing else about life in the epidemic to feel bad about.

The Twelve-step Programs

Uncle Charley (my granduncle),
after a life of startling promiscuity,
received a Christian burial.
And all the family
is certain he has gone to heaven
(because in his last years
he achieved a glandular serenity
and a look of loss).
—Keith Waldrop, from Samsara[8]

The twelve-step programs have made tremendous constructive contributions to the lives of many in the gay communities. Substance abuse and addiction, and the compulsive use of sex have always been prominent responses to the inevitable developmental stresses of growing up gay. Today we have not only those traditional problems fueling addictive and compulsive behaviors, we have the AIDS epidemic itself. For many men, the danger of HIV has reduced the appeal of compulsive sexuality as a means of addressing anxiety, loneliness, or conflicts about intimacy. But the epidemic has exacerbated these very issues and thus exacerbated or created substance abuse problems for many. There is so much to forget about this epidemic, how could it be otherwise?

In this light, the ever increasing appeal of the twelve-step programs for gay men throughout the eighties and into the nineties is understandable. But the programs have also become a force in gay communities that is sometimes used to support emotional isolation and the abandonment of genuine intimacy and, unfortunately, new and subtle feelings of internalized homophobia. Regardless of where gay men perceive themselves politically, it is inescapable that many are heirs to the 1980s legacy of "just say no" asceticism. American society as a whole took a very hard turn away from artistic and sensual life during these years. The humanistic, often hedonistic, exploration of the sixties and, for gay communities especially, the seventies, seemed indefensible in the cold light of the Republican eighties. Before the election of Bill Clinton, it often seemed that anything not making a contribution to the gross national product was to be treated as an inebriate embarrassment.

It is remarkable that gay communities, so defiant in newfound freedoms during the seventies, have so broadly adopted this ascetic ethos. The epidemic has been a sobering event in many senses, contributing to literal sobriety and to a sobered approach to life in general, including sexual life. Much of this influence, unfortunately, has been unconscious and destructive. It includes the unconscious perception that the epidemic is retribution for the sexual energy and exploration of the seventies and that the new asceticism is a recognition of, and penance for, this transgression. This is not true, and we must make conscious and excise this destructive misperception from gay sensibilities and self-perceptions. Such feelings are nothing more than an—only marginally—new expression of both societal and internalized homophobia.[9]

Many men now appear to use twelve-step programs to assuage this reinvigorated homophobia and the shame and guilt it arouses. The coalition of pressures that brings men to the programs is understandable and compelling: a frightening epidemic; a broad societal asceticism that has been promoted during the very decade of the epidemic and has often seemed to imply the epidemic as motivation; and the reality, for many individuals, of a real problem with substances or compulsive sexuality.

But when the programs are used not only to change self-destructive behaviors but to pay retribution through abstinence for one's "irresponsibility," one's "failure," or one's "mistakes"—whether these be about substances or sex—then an element of self-punitiveness is introduced, which suggests underlying homophobia. The programs themselves do not speak of paying retribution, but this does not preclude a psychological interpretation about how some men appear to use them.

Related to the paying of retribution through abstinence is the use of abstinence, usually unconsciously, to avoid both long-standing and epidemic-reactive psychological issues. Abstinence may be used both indirectly and directly to avoid psychological conflict. For example, guilt and conflict about one's homosexuality may be addressed indirectly by adherence to the schedules, disciplines, and prescriptions of the program. In a general sense, the adherence serves to make one feel worthy and accomplished—despite being homosexual. Traditionally, this use of twelve-step programs has been accomplished through religious penitence.

In a more direct way of dealing with guilt and conflict about homosexuality, many gay men are now using twelve-step programs as a substitute for intimate relationships. Intimate relationships are replaced with social ones within the program (as, indeed, they often are in other gay institutions, such as the gym and bar), and free time is structured around meetings and other program-related events. In this case, homophobic feelings and self-doubt are assuaged directly by simply not being in a homosexual relationship; and long-standing conflicts about issues such as intimacy, as well as reactive problems such as anxiety about HIV, need not be addressed at all.

Like sex clubs, twelve-step programs provide many benefits, and are certainly not intrinsically destructive. However, the two share something important. Their utility and success lie partly in their appeal to the compulsive character trends of their clients—"addictive personalities," in the parlance of the programs. As a result, both sex clubs and twelve-step programs are themselves subject to compulsive use by members. Within the club or the program, compulsive behaviors attempt to accomplish what they always attempt: containment of anxiety and repression of psychological conflict. When sex clubs or twelve-step programs thus become an alternative to the examination of feelings and psychological conflict, an alternative to psychological growth, or an alternative to intimacy, then they are contributing to the personal isolation from which the gay communities now suffer so badly.

My experience with one psychotherapy patient, Kevin, will help illustrate some of these issues. Kevin had been gay since his teenage years. In therapy in his early thirties, he had three years before ended a four-year career of serious cocaine and alcohol abuse that never interfered with his work life but eliminated any important friendships or intimate relationships. For several years, Kevin went home after a competent day's work, locked himself in his apartment, and drank himself into unconsciousness. This substance abuse, largely absent earlier in Kevin's life, was partly a reaction to the huge stresses and painful feelings that came out of his life in the epidemic, but it was also about much longer-standing conflicts about homosexuality, intimacy with other men, and intimacy in general—all issues exacerbated by the epidemic.

Kevin came from a pious Catholic family, for which he had strong, positive feelings. He, his three sisters, and his parents were very close. Although he had come out to them as gay in the seventies, his homosexuality continued to be either denied or implicitly disparaged by all but one of his sisters. Partly through his own sense of feeling out of control with his substance abuse and partly through his parent's encouragement, Kevin went into recovery by joining Alcoholics Anonymous (AA). Kevin believed that his parents—having long ago given up on his Catholicism and its potential for containing his homosexuality—felt his participation in twelve-step programs would cure not only his substance abuse but his homosexuality as well. Though Kevin had no such conscious purposes himself, he was aware of exploiting their confusion in order to soften their antagonism about his life, and especially his sexuality. "If they ease off about my being gay because I'm in the program, that's fine with me." Kevin was also aware of his parents' perception of AA as a religiously structured, Christian organization.

Kevin, clean and sober for three years, came to therapy with a stated interest in working on long-standing issues in his life, including his difficulty with relationships. He had had no intimate relationships for the prior three years, nor had he had any sexual relationships other than an occasional anonymous encounter. Although Kevin considered himself "sexually addicted," the history and experience that he related to me did not suggest that he had ever used sex compulsively.[10] His practice of anonymous sex began in his teenage years when it was the only form of sexuality available for him. In later life, he continued having occasional anonymous sex, and I felt that Kevin's use of this form of sex had much more to do with conflicts about homosexuality and intimacy than it did with a compulsive process. In my understanding, anonymous sex represented a way of keeping sex out of his intimate relationships, and thus keeping those relationships "acceptable" because they were nonsexual. The integration of sexuality into a close, loving relationship would have raised considerable anxiety for Kevin.

After about six months of therapy, Kevin met another man, Tom, also an HIV-service provider, through a newspaper advertisement, and they started to date. I saw Kevin twice weekly in therapy, and the following session notes are a condensation of several week's sessions from around the beginning of this new relationship. The dialogue begins after Kevin and Tom had sex for the first time, a few weeks into their relationship.

"I'm really in an incredible state—I'm completely disorganized, confused, and I don't know what," Kevin told me. "It's unbelievable, but my head is spinning. Tom and I had sex on Friday night."

"And how did that go?" I asked.

"Well, this is the first time in years, and the first time since I've been clean and sober. It was very intense—I mean, it was incredible, it was wonderful, but it was very scary. I got up at six-thirty Saturday morning, went home and changed my clothes, and before my regular [AA] meeting I went to an SLAA [Sex and Love Addicts Anonymous] meeting."

"Why was that?"

"Why was what?"

"I'm wondering why you went to an SLAA meeting."

"I mean, you have no idea how I was feeling, I was feeling completely out of control," Kevin said in frustration with me. "I haven't felt like that in years, literally in years—since I was using."

"But when you say 'out of control'—can you tell me more about what you mean by that?"

"Well, it is the feeling that an addict has of being out of control. I was overwhelmed. Talking about it now makes me feel the same way all over again."

"Do you mean you feel sexual now?"

"No . . . but I feel just overwhelmed by the same feelings, out of control just thinking about it."

I tried to clarify my question. "What I am trying to get at is your equating having very strong feelings—mostly positive ones about Tom and sex with Tom, from what you say—your equating these strong feelings with being out of control, and being out of control with being addicted."

"I don't know what you're talking about," Kevin responded.

"Is it possible that you were just overwhelmed with positive feelings because of your *good* feelings about Tom, and because you haven't really had a relationship or sex with anyone you've cared about for several years? Doesn't it seem likely that would bring up very strong feelings?"

"But I don't want to have such strong feelings for Tom—I hardly know him. I don't want to *care* that much about him."

"Why not?"

"Because it's scary as hell, that's why."

"Because the feelings make you feel you've lost control?"

"Yes, of course."

"So having these very positive feelings about Tom you feel in danger?" I asked.

"Yes . . . I have stayed away from relationships for exactly these reasons."

"Let's come back to that and try to clarify the first idea for now. Feeling that you have let yourself care for someone, have feelings for someone, feel sexual with someone that you care about, you feel that you have lost control—and you did that because you are addicted."

"That's why I went to the SLAA meeting—I rely on my [AA] meetings to help me with my addiction, and I went to the SLAA meeting for the same reason. And, I'll tell you, it calmed me down and organized me. I felt much better. If I hadn't done that, I would have had to call you over the weekend."

"And why does the thought of calling me bother you?" I asked.

"First I'm out of control with Tom, and then you want me to call *you* on the weekend?"

"Is it that you would then feel even more out of control because you would be expressing feelings for me by relying on me?"

"Yes."

"So the SLAA meeting helped you bring your feelings not only about Tom, but about me, under control—feelings that you believe, since they signal danger, also signal addiction."

"I see from what you're getting at that I have some things mixed up here—although I am definitely addicted to sex."

"You've never convinced me of that," I said. "But I believe that you sometimes use the idea that you are addicted to sex as a way to avoid it, and to confuse and misinterpret frightening—and exciting—feelings about it."

"They're feelings I don't want to have," Kevin reasserted.

"I know they feel dangerous, but they include feelings about another man, about your relationship with him, about physical intimacy, and about the possibility of losing him. It seems natural to me that one would have such feelings, that you would have them about Tom, and be worried and confused by them. However, the idea that these feelings are simply signs of addiction, that you're 'out of control' with another addiction, eclipses all of your fears about intimacy with Tom—and relying on me—and you end up at an SLAA meeting."

"I see the confusions here, but I go back to the point where, if I hadn't gone to the meeting, I would have called you on a Saturday."

"You felt scared by needing me on a Saturday, and, it seems to me, calling would have been an acknowledgment—to both of us— that you value and depend on me."

"Well that's one of the reasons I didn't call."

Over the following weeks, Kevin continued to feel anxiety over both his feelings about Tom and me. He increased his AA meetings from three or four a week to nine or ten. I interpreted this as an effort to limit his time with Tom, who had already expressed feeling widowed by Kevin's meeting schedule. This schedule was also a way of pulling back from the therapy, and Kevin wondered what I thought of cutting our sessions back to once a week while he was doing so many meetings. I said that I thought he was trying to limit his involvement with me because of his worries about depending on me.

Kevin feared his growing sense of intimacy with both Tom and me, and used the meetings as a literal time consumer and a substitute social environment that might reduce his need for both of us. The meetings also served to structure his internal experience, providing a shared framework that organized his frightening feelings into relatively simplistic—and inaccurate—interpretations about addiction, which precluded having to examine conflict about relationships, sex, and intimacy. Because the inaccurate interpretations did not address the real anxiety about intimacy, the anxiety only worsened, and Kevin needed still more meetings. This cycle describes a compulsive behavioral solution to internal conflict. When the solutions involve sex or substances, rather than meetings, they are termed addictive. Feelings like "I need sex" or "I need a drink" are often inaccurate interpretations of other feelings, like loneliness, depression, or anxiety. Because the resulting behavior—sex or alcohol—fails to clarify or correct the real feelings, the behavior must be repeated, often compulsively.

For several weeks Kevin voiced frequent feelings that neither Tom nor I "approved" of his AA meetings, and that he expected more support for his effort to control self-destructive addictions. He felt endangered by Tom in other ways too, and talked about the difficulties they were having.

"Tom's drinking has been bothering me—but I'm beginning to see that it is connected to a lot of other things. For one thing, he's very intense . . ."

"Intense?"

"Intense about everything. He talks about the epidemic a lot, and his feelings are just right there—he just comes out with these surprising, intense things. He's very depressed about it—about AIDS—and I'm sometimes frightened by that."

"Frightened by his depression?" I asked.

"Well . . . I was thinking that it's not so much Tom I'm frightened of, his depression, or his drinking for that matter—it's *me*, it's myself. It's that I see myself in him and that he is so out front with it. And I sometimes feel when I'm with him that I have to get out of there, that I have to get away from him, because it's too much. And I don't trust myself or my feelings, I can't get them all over the carpet the way he does."

"That he makes you feel out of control . . ."

"Yes, that he makes me feel very out of control. And I can tell you when I realized this. We were making love one night—well, having sex, anyway. No, we were making love. You know, he's negative too—and this was the first time it came up, but he said that he would like to fuck. I said yes, though I didn't know who would be on top, and he asked me if I had condoms. Well, I realized that I wanted him to fuck me and I wanted him to do it without a condom, and I had this rationale that he was very conscientious about his health and has been tested a zillion times, so that it was most likely safe. When I asked him to do that, he said OK, he would do it however I wanted him to do, and that's what we did."

"I'm not clear. You asked him to do what?" I asked.

"I asked him to fuck me without a condom. And he did that, and I haven't done that in years and years. And it was wonderful. . . . But what I started to tell you was, the next day, when I was thinking about what we'd done—you know, it's so *forbidden*—and I had this sudden feeling of anger at him for luring me into unsafe sex and fucking me without a condom. And then I said, 'No, wait a minute—it's me that wanted to do that, it's me that it means so much to, it's not Tom.' It means a lot to me, and I am scared of wanting it so much, and it's Tom who was asking for condoms."

"So you were blaming Tom for *your* feelings?"

"I was blaming Tom for my feelings. Because I couldn't own up to them, because I'm scared of them. I'm scared of AIDS and what it's done to me, what it's taken from me, and I am more scared than ever to love anyone. All of this is my own stuff, my own feelings, and I realized that when Tom fucked me."

"And how do you associate having feelings about Tom and the epidemic? I'm not sure how you are connecting them."

"Well, partly it was the idea that I'm afraid of him dying. But it is really that I don't let myself have feelings, because I'm just afraid now that they will be too awful. This all started a long time before the epidemic—it started when my sister died [when Kevin was seven] and my parents never talked about it. They never said *one word,* and they haven't to this day, and it was very clear that none of us were supposed to have feelings about it. But now, there is AIDS, and there are so many people who have died, and I'm just afraid that all of this is going to catch up with me and be too much for me to deal with. We talk a lot at work when someone in the office dies about *letting the grief flow through you,* letting it pass through you, and I think I know what that means. But I also sometimes have the image that I have an appendix. . . . my real one was removed after it burst when I was a kid. I never told you about that."

"Why not?"

"I'm embarrassed by it. I feel responsible for it. I had awful pain, which I thought was a stomachache, and I was sitting at the dinner table in real agony—it was *killing* me—and no one noticed a thing. I think I was nine then, because we had just moved from the house where Melissa died. And I didn't say anything because I knew it wasn't OK to feel bad about *anything*. So I guess it burst and I started screaming and fell on the floor, and they took me to the hospital. And my parents were very angry at me."

"Angry about what?" I asked.

"Well, I started to say that they were angry about my not telling them sooner." Kevin suddenly started sobbing violently. "But I really thought they were angry at me for getting sick . . . I was talking about letting the grief flow through, and about the idea that I still had an appendix . . . and I'm sometimes afraid that every time someone dies, that the grief flows through. But some really bad part of it gets stuck in my appendix. And I can't admit that. But someday it's going to blow up. And I know that won't be Tom's doing either, it will be mine, and I can't admit it."

As I write, Kevin is still working in therapy. We have been able to focus increasingly on the central issue of feelings and their meanings, intimacy, Kevin's lifelong sense of loneliness, his fears of loss, and his use of substances to try to mitigate these feelings. Kevin came to the epidemic with most of these problems already well developed. But as the transcript makes clear, the realities—as well as the meanings—of the epidemic have badly exacerbated his pain and conflict, and have impeded his effort to clarify his feelings so that he is able to have the kind of intimacy he would like. In adopting explanations of addiction to explain his feelings, to contain anxiety, and to provide a plausible life without intimacy, Kevin borrows common solutions from the gay community as a whole. In Kevin's case, however, such efforts were of little use, for they controlled his anxiety only to the extent that he was willing to allow his participation in the program to monopolize his life—and even then, only if he was able to avoid the feelings of others.

At the beginning of this chapter, I asked what it meant for a man to say that he was "getting used to death." It must mean different things for different people at different times. What I hope it will not mean for the gay communities is that the decades we now call the AIDS epidemic have been so devastating that we will have to deny and repress our feelings about what happened, and that we will no longer have the capacity to know ourselves, to know others, or to love and be intimate. How we may avoid this unhappy solution is not simply answered. The best answers are likely to lie in insight about our feelings and our lives in the epidemic, rather than in their denial. Each individual must find his own best compromise between, on the one hand, a merely functional survival based in denial and repression, and, on the other, complete despair. Those compromises must embody an acknowledgment that we cannot ever again be who we were before this event began, for that would deny the truth and would leave us all living quite alone.

Chapter 7
Being Together: The Relations
of Positives and Negatives

Perhaps the distinction should not be made between people with AIDS, people with ARC, and HIV-positive people. Or even between those who test positive and those who test negative. Or between those with high T-cells and those with low T-cells. But between those who embrace life and those who fear death. Art versus AZT. Love, loving, and being loved, being the most important things . . . —Ron Henderson, a San Franciscan in AIDS services[1]

The AIDS epidemic has been an extraordinary event for the gay communities in the United States in so many ways that one can understand our overlooking one of its most unusual and powerful elements. Socially and psychologically, the epidemic is an event less about survivors and nonsurvivors than about the coexistence of presumed survivors and presumed nonsurvivors. This is historically unique. In the Holocaust, to which the AIDS epidemic is so often compared, the imprisoned were identified as nonsurvivors, and there was virtually no communication or contact between them and—potentially—surviving populations. In wars, both in battle and at home, all are survivors until the instant a bullet or a bomb makes one a survivor and another not. In earlier plagues, with unidentified causative organisms, all were survivors until one fell ill, and then the coexistence was generally of very limited duration. In the AIDS epidemic, survivors and nonsurvivors live together with knowledge of potential nonsurvivors—"the HIV positive"—a *decade* before their presumed deaths. Being HIV-positive, like being HIV-negative, has become as much an interpersonal, social, and psychological phenomenon as a medical one.

Imagine a new war, a war for the nineties and well into the next century. As the battle starts, half the citizenry are given a tiny, private tattoo, like a hallmark on precious metal, that marks them as presumed nonsurvivors of the war. These men can share the knowledge of their tattoos with others or not, and while the tattooed cannot rid themselves of the mark or the destiny, a presumed survivor of the war—a *tattoo-negative*—may become tattooed by engaging in ordinary human sex, even with someone he loves. The tattoo-negative and tattoo-positive must fight, work, live, and sleep side by side for lifetimes, united by old goals for their communities, and now by a new war. Joined by these commonalities, they must anticipate each others' loss, care for each other through staggering illness, and survive each others' deaths. How would the tattoo-negatives and tattoo-positives think and feel about each other? How would they relate as coworkers, citizens, and intimates? How would they negotiate common goals and purposes? How would such coexistence work? How could it? How could we clarify such a society, split down the middle by evident fate?

There is dispute in the gay communities—much of it still unspoken—about whether AIDS has finally united or fatally divided gay men. In different senses, at different times and places, and for different people, both seem true. *All* gay men live deeply in the AIDS epidemic in some way, and this condition is so pervasive and often destructive that it is sometimes surprising to remember that, in our most afflicted communities, only about half of us are actually infected with HIV. The common battle against AIDS, piggybacked onto older causes and purposes, has been a uniting force. But the predicted early death of half the troops—and all that means in *life*—has driven a painful wedge through the hearts of the gay communities.

Life in the AIDS epidemic often makes it difficult to know whether our perception of a given issue is alarmist and grossly exaggerated or a foolish denial of the obvious. The fact of HIV-antibody status—a *laboratory fact*—is central among such bewildering issues, and the common use of the word *status* is a measure of our need to hedge on its meanings. The fact implies so many different things. It suggests itself as a description of what one *is*—heard in the common expression "I am HIV," meaning HIV-positive—and it variably implies a prediction of long life ("living with HIV" *or* being HIV-negative), short life, assumed well-being, being at risk, wholeness, defectiveness, weakness, courage, personal and sexual acceptability, and privileged or disenfranchised status within the gay communities. Despite these complexities of meaning, in daily life antibody status is usually tacitly acknowledged as an important difference between positive and negative men, even when we do not quite know what it means—either medically or humanly. That a man's *status* is positive or negative hedges on the implication that he has or does not have, is or is not, something significant. His status may be unknown or may change—even positive men seem very occasionally to change—and we are free to attach to it what meaning we will. Never in history have the results of a blood test acquired such widely experienced, profound, and ambiguous social, interpersonal, and psychological meanings.

Chuck Frutchey, Director of Education for the San Francisco AIDS Foundation for the first decade of the epidemic, and HIV-positive himself, told me that he found both negative and, especially, positive gay men overly identified with HIV in general.[2] This is certainly true, and is evidenced by gay men's internalization of the larger society's homosexualization of AIDS and the reexpression of those internalized feelings as the AIDSification of homosexuality. The gay identity has become unrealistically entangled with AIDS to an extent not always apparent in the context of *realistic* involvement. But Frutchey went on to say that "negative men are sometimes uncomfortable with positive men's level of denial about the importance of HIV in their [positives'] lives." In his description, then, positive men are overidentified with HIV at the same time they deny the importance of their status (by the standards of uninfected men). Psychologically, this apparent contradiction is intelligible in the observation that we deny only things that are very important to us, and that this is a predictable—perhaps necessary—solution for many positive men. It is a solution, however, that complicates the relations of negative men with positive men. Woody Castrodale describes this idea:

> Being HIV-infected is a different thing for negatives and positives. For me, having HIV would be a death sentence. But when you talk to positives, they are living with a *challenge*. It's as if it were just another form of life, or a different career. "I'm just going to stay nonsymptomatic," is the approach. This difference is to me about a very big cognitive split in the gay community.[3]

AIDS prevention education has become a powerful, pervasive, social and cultural force in many gay communities, and this cognitive split, including its role in the relations of positives and negatives, is very clearly expressed in much of AIDS education. In the fields of medicine and public health, the terms *primary prevention* and *secondary prevention* have distinct, long-standing meanings. In the instance of HIV and the gay

communities, traditional use of the terms would define primary prevention as the effort to prevent currently uninfected men from contracting
HIV and secondary prevention as the effort to prevent men infected
with HIV from progressing to clinical disease. These clear concepts have
traditionally drawn useful distinctions.[4]

In discussing any form of prevention, the idea of "outcome population" must be clearly distinguished from "target population." Primary
prevention for the gay communities has, by both definition and reason, the purpose of keeping uninfected men uninfected. Uninfected men
are the only outcome population for primary prevention. Which target
populations primary prevention might address in pursuit of this purpose—for example, HIV-infected men, who necessarily participate in the
infection of uninfected men, although they are not part of the outcome
population—is an entirely independent issue. Decisions about including
or not including target populations are made by evaluating the potential
of their inclusion for changing the outcome for the outcome population.

The following excerpt from a primary prevention piece, *Asians and
AIDS: What's the Connection?*, is typical of our work since 1985:

> We must face the fact that Asians are at risk, and we must do some-
> thing about it. . . . We can find out the facts—how AIDS is trans-
> mitted and how it is not. We then have a choice—do nothing about
> it or use this information by translating it into safer sex behavior.
> The AIDS virus is often transmitted through having unsafe sex or
> sharing needles with an infected person. . . . Playing safer means
> knowing how to protect ourselves and our partners. . . . AIDS is not
> only a threat to you and your partners, but also to your friends.[5]

The ambiguity about the outcome population in this very typical "undifferentiated" educational piece is first suggested by use of the term *at
risk*. *At risk* is probably intended to *imply* a primary prevention intent
here, particularly because "doing something about [AIDS and Asians]"
is first defined as finding out "how AIDS is transmitted." But *at risk* is
commonly used for secondary prevention, as in the idea that an infected
man is *at risk* for opportunistic infections. The confusion is heightened
by the idea of "transmitting AIDS" (as opposed to HIV), because only
previously infected people are at risk *for AIDS*. A clear and unambiguous
primary prevention intent would have been conveyed simply by saying,
"at risk for HIV infection." The confusion, however, continues. While the
(presumably uninfected) reader is first told that HIV is transmitted by

having sex or sharing needles with "an infected person," he soon learns that *he* should "protect [his] partner" and that AIDS is a threat to "*your* partners . . . [and] *your* friends." Nowhere in the material is the term "uninfected" or "HIV-negative" used, and *nowhere is it simply stated that the purpose of the brochure is to help uninfected men remain uninfected.* In fact, the brochure displays a statement under the copyright notice reading, "The target audience of this brochure is the Gay/Bisexual community." Such confusions are virtually universal in our primary prevention today.

There are many reasons that this kind of undifferentiated prevention work has come about. Broadly speaking, the social and political climate in AIDS-wracked gay communities has made it almost impossible to direct resources to uninfected men—among the most important "others affected by HIV"—for any purpose. Prevention is no exception to this policy climate. In San Francisco, the U.S. leader in services for HIV-negative men, there are periodic outpourings of anger at the use of mental health or educational resources for men who "are in no way affected by HIV." Uninfected men know the prevention message, they are fortunate in not having HIV, and they should take care of themselves.

Underlying this emotional climate are specific historical developments dating back to 1985 and the release of the ELISA (Enzyme-linked Immunosorbent Assay) that made it increasingly difficult to acknowledge that HIV-negative men are the sole outcome population for primary prevention. Early in the epidemic, AIDS education was directed to all gay men, most of whom were presumed to be uninfected. Because we could not test for infection, the presumption was appropriate, and primary prevention spoke explicitly and unequivocally about not contracting HIV. But the introduction of the ELISA allowed us to actually test for HIV antibodies, and we discovered that many more men—tragically more— were infected with HIV than anyone had thought possible. As we learned that nearly 50 percent of gay men in San Francisco, New York, and Los Angeles were infected with HIV, the social and political identities of these larger gay communities began shifting from assumptions of HIV-negativity to assumptions of HIV-positivity. Ultimately individual identities followed suit, and most, if not all, gay men began to experience HIV and AIDS as important parts of what it meant to be gay. Newly known levels of HIV *prevalence* (the epidemiological term for levels of infection in a population) also escalated the number of services for those infected with HIV—more than 70 separate agencies in San Francisco alone by 1993. Education, historically a function of many of these agencies, came more and more to implicitly address the needs of positive men or to be confused about exactly whose needs it was addressing. By 1994, an educator at San Francisco's STOP AIDS Project told me that if HIV prevention were for uninfected men, rather than for "the gay community," he would leave his job; and another educator from New York's Gay Men's Health Crisis suggested that "primary" and "secondary" prevention were no longer useful ideas, and that we should begin to think in terms of a "continuum of prevention" that would span the needs of men from those who were uninfected to those in terminal stages of AIDS. Such feelings are, in fact, already implicit in too much of our education, including the 1994 campaign of the San Francisco AIDS Foundation, "Outliving Forecasts of Doom."

> *Gotta Believe*. Single Gay Man outliving the forecasts of doom. HERE WE ARE still pushing ahead. Positive or negative, we thought safe sex was just about surviving. There's more . . . *Keep it safe. Make a plan. See it through.*

Are we to believe that the single gay man, *infected or uninfected,* will experience safe sex, survival, the "more" in his life, and plans for the future similarly, regardless of antibody condition? Such doubtful assertions are rooted in the ideas that AIDS prevention is "for the gay community" and that primary and secondary prevention are no longer useful distinctions. They are assertions also rooted in the cognitive split of which Castrodale speaks. From the perspective of many HIV-negative men, these assertions deny the obvious, which is that HIV is a "death sentence." Indeed, it is since the popularization of the very useful idea (for positive men) of "living with AIDS"—rather than suffering or dying with it—that primary prevention has been unable to unequivocally assert its purpose on behalf of uninfected men—or, indeed, even call them "uninfected" rather than define them in terms of HIV by calling them "HIV-negative." A clear and distinct focus on primary prevention—regardless of how much secondary prevention is also done—feels as if it abandons the lives of HIV-positive men. If men are *living with AIDS,* indeed, *thriving* with AIDS, it becomes much more difficult to assert that it is very important to *not* have HIV. For an uninfected man to assert directly that *he does not want HIV* becomes a hurtful, invalidating, and abandoning experience for many *with* HIV. What is heard by positive men, already often feeling "defective" because of their infection, is "I do not want to be like you."

A continuum of prevention supports such blurring of distinctions between positives and negatives by suggesting that those with and without HIV represent a continuum of survival possibilities. For human and political reasons, most educators cannot assert clearly that, with regard to survival, those without HIV are *qualitatively* different from those with it. Although most public policy makers now privately acknowledge this qualitative difference—particularly since the public fall from grace of AZT at the 1993 International Conference on AIDS in Berlin—much of our education continues to belie or deny the idea that uninfected men have a *much* better chance of survival than HIV-positive men.

The cognitive split underlying these problems is by no means absolute. There are many positive men who are convinced they will progress from infection to death, and who resent the expectation that they experience their lives as "living or thriving with AIDS." Tom, a 29-year-old psychotherapy patient with AIDS and member of ACT UP (AIDS Coalition to Unleash Power), reflects such feelings.

"I resent the idea that I'm supposed to feel OK about having AIDS. A lot of people expect that of me, and they make it perfectly clear. I'm pissed off about it, I'm grumpy about it, and I'm going to complain about it. When Charles tells me he's 'living with AIDS,' I want to say to him, 'You know, you're an asshole. You're going to die just the way I am, and meanwhile you're sitting on your butt not doing anything about all the people who don't give a shit that we're dying.' When he talks about living with AIDS, I think he's really saying that this is the fate he deserves, that he feels like he deserves AIDS, and I think he feels like he deserves it because he's a fag, and fags get AIDS. He's just going to accept it like he accepts all the other abuse we've gotten from society."

"Are these things you say to Charles?"

"About getting angry—yeah, I say that to him. But about dying, no, because I know that would make him feel hopeless. His only sense of hope seems to come from thinking he's not going to die."

"And yours?"

"My sense of hope?"

"Yes, your sense of hope—because I often feel you have quite a bit."

"Hmm. I guess from feeling that I haven't lived in vain. Sounds like a cliché."

"What does it mean though?"

"It means that I've done something for other people and for my-self. That I can leave a slightly better world for other gay people—that means a lot to me. But this is making me think of part of Charles's feelings, about his wanting to feel that he's living with AIDS, and I suddenly realize that I agree with part of them. When you have HIV, people kind of let you go—you know, there goes another one. These are the people who can't stand it if they can't fix you—you're hopeless and if they can't fix you, they dismiss you because you're dying. They treat you as if you're *already* dead, [that] it's a foregone conclusion and we might as well get it over right now. And I resent that, and I think part of what Charles is saying is, 'Hey, I'm still here, I still want you to pay attention to me and love me.'"

"That this is what Charles means by 'living with AIDS.'"

"Yeah, that he wants people to know he's still here. I feel that too. But I can't stand his denial, and I would say to people that I'm dying, but while I'm doing that I'm real, I'm living, and meanwhile keep your fix-it mitts off me, but love me and treat me like a person."

Some HIV-negative men bridge the cognitive split so common between positives and negatives not by denying the dying of positives, but by feeling, and sometimes asserting, that they too are dying. Some negative men glibly deny their difference from positives by asserting that they could be "hit and killed by a bus tomorrow," a statistically implausible, if remotely *possible,* identification that is understandably irksome to positive men. But more profoundly, many uninfected men feel deeply, through realistic identifications, confused identifications, or guilt, that they *are* dying. Such feelings are often part of what allows an uninfected man to relate intimately to a positive man. Bolstered by the confusions of AIDS education, it is very easy for the uninfected man living in gay communities with high levels of infection—much less living with an infected partner—to feel that he is, indeed, on a continuum that spans the range from uninfected to terminally ill, and that progression along that continuum is an inevitability. That such identifications—especially when supported by AIDS prevention education itself—are contributing to new HIV infections is of serious concern. But prevention aside, such feelings have also been the source of profound human connections between negative and positive men, especially when they were in love before the difference of serostatus existed.

In the midst of this complexity of meanings of antibody status, one thing is certain: taken on the whole, negative and positive men *do* often attach different meanings to the issue, and those differences often make their relations difficult. The idea that this is a difference of meaning rather than fact bothers many, and in an attempt to reintroduce "reality," statistics are often marshalled to "correct" what one man perceives as another's inaccurate meaning. Statistics, however, predict only for groups, and have no value or utility in predicting for an individual. For someone looking at a group of positive men and wondering how *many* among them will survive, the statistics are a reasonable predictor. If the question is *who* among them will survive or what the odds are for a particular man, the statistics provide *no* information. If a positive man is among the minority percentage who survive over twelve years, that will be completely the case, not partially the case. To find oneself 100 percent alive in the year 2020, having spent the previous decades preparing for death would be paradoxical and disappointing, to say the least. Thus, even in this most concrete sense, it may be quite appropriate for negative and positive men to attach different meanings to HIV antibody status. Beyond that, meaning is not per se accountable to reality, and the different experiences of positives and negatives are also intelligible as one of perspective and purpose.

The very fact that positives and negatives do often attach different meanings to antibody status, has become, in itself, an important difference between the two. When we work through our denial about what the epidemic has meant for our communities, and when we separate "unity" politics from individual feelings, we must acknowledge that there are many differences between positive and negative men. That the differences are often felt to be important—and sometimes divisive—is described by a psychotherapy patient, Bill:

> There were seven of us who were at [an Eastern college] together, and we moved out here [to San Francisco] in '80 together because— well, we'd all sort of discovered about the same time that we were gay. As a matter of fact, we lived together for the first nine months or so, in a real heap on Fell Street. But about three years ago— I mean, we don't spend all of our time together anymore, but we are definitely best friends—Dennis, Mark, and I had a birthday party because we're all born within about a week of each other, and something happened that I guess we all sort of knew was going on. Except to Dennis, I had never talked about being [HIV] negative

and about what the other guys were. I knew Dennis was positive because we got tested together in '86. But I had always assumed—I was *assuming* that everyone else was negative. And no one *ever* talked about it. But at the party I started talking about Dennis and Mark and I being 30, and Bob said, "Well you know, most of us won't be here for the next decade." I was very shocked. And I found out that Bob, Ed, and Terry were positive too. And Dennis. The four of them had been positive for a long time, and none of us had talked about it. I was very shocked. And I realized that they had been living with this for years, and that in many ways we must have grown much more apart—at least more than I knew we had. They had just lived with this and, except for Dennis, I knew nothing about it and they never said anything.

That HIV test results are typically so hard to talk about, especially with those of opposite serostatus, is an important indicator of the profound sense of difference that HIV status can confer. The broader social implications of these individually and subjectively experienced differences are rarely discussed, although they are in the background of many men's thoughts. Most within the gay communities have maintained that there are no social consequences for communities divided almost precisely in half by antibody status in all its meanings, including life expectancy. But persistent claims of "viral apartheid" from some members of San Francisco's positive communities when services are provided for uninfected men belies this confidence. Tim, an uninfected San Franciscan in his late thirties working in AIDS service, reveals his conflict:

I have been thinking a lot about all the ads I see in the [San Francisco gay] papers: you know, "HIV-negative seeking same." And I wonder what this kind of thing is going to do to us. We all *have* AIDS, and we're definitely in this together. But I can also see why people try to avoid people with HIV. There's only so much a person can take. This is something about which I'm very, very ambivalent. I'm against it, and I understand it too, and I don't know where we, as a community, can go with this.[6]

*Why Do Uninfected Men Separate
Themselves from Positive Men?*

*I get telephone calls everyday from a friend who insists he is someone else; today he
called insisting he was me. Can you imagine that? Like the music we were married to,
that's a sad thing too.—Ippy Gizzi, from* Letters to Pauline [7]

At this point in the AIDS epidemic, one thing is certain about HIV-
positive and negative gay men: we are destined to decades of coexistence
in one form or another. Because there are differences, separation, and—
largely unspoken—conflict between us, it is important to try to clarify
the individual issues that underlie this situation. Realistic and unrealistic, these issues affect not only our political and social relations, but our
personal and intimate ones as well. In this effort at clarification, I will
discuss the separation between positives and negatives largely from the
point of view of negative men—although it is not uncommonly positive
men who feel these issues most strongly. The reasons that some negative
men maintain separation from positives may be usefully grouped into
three general areas: worldview, social, and psychological.

DIFFERENCES OF WORLDVIEW

Worldview differences, as I am using the idea, are about an individual's
most fundamental experiences of spirit and purpose in life, and his
assumptions of the scale and scope of life. The worldview of many positive men can be difficult for uninfected men to understand and even
more difficult to share. A psychotherapy patient in his mid-thirties with
middle-stage AIDS told me that before he knew he had HIV he was
interested in his work, career, and money.

> Those things mean nothing to me now, I have no idea anymore
> what they're even about. They're American ideas to me, and I—I'm
> somewhere else, I guess. The only things that mean anything to me
> are my friends, and love, and especially honesty about everything.
> And it is very important to me now to experience my sadness about
> things, to experience all of my feelings, which is something that I
> did not even know I was not doing before.

In contrast, uninfected men may live with more traditional values,
more conservatively, with more concern for the future, and with a
sense that the means—which is to say, one's life as it is lived in the

present—will be justified by the ends. This is a description of life based on teleological Aristotelian assumptions that are deeply enmeshed in Judeo-Christian values, and particularly in the contemporary American expression of them. Compared to the life of a man with HIV, the life of the uninfected man may be more restrained and pragmatic, and often emphasizes the external world and one's relationship to it, rather than the internal world of thoughts and feelings. This description of the life of a negative man is that of a "normal"—especially normal *male*—existence in late-twentieth-century, middle-class America with its particular values and form of life. But many HIV-positive men who think their death relatively imminent do not share such values—why would they?—and many uninfected men cannot breach this difference. Woody Castrodale conjectured about this issue in a personal communication:

> Maybe there is a direct and essentially unresolvable "conflict of interest" between HIV-negative gay men who must, by definition, think about going on, living on, denying death in the "healthy" sense, with no immediate exit in sight; and HIV-positive gay men who are forced to look death in the face and think about dying someday fairly soon. These two situations are not, after all, even remotely synonymous, and it could be that they conflict in some fairly important ways. And that HIV-negative gay men perhaps would like to deny that this conflict exists. And maybe HIV-positive gay men would like to deny the conflict also.[8]

In contrast to these feelings that there are fundamental and unbridgeable differences, some uninfected men find that the shift in values I have ascribed to positives may be conferred, not only by life with HIV in one's body, but by life with HIV in the broader sense. Many uninfected men find themselves more sympathetic to the values of positive men than to their own pre-epidemic values. Richard, a 26-year-old, uninfected psychotherapy patient expressed such feelings during a discussion of his mostly positive circle of friends:

> "You know the expression 'Home is where your heart is'? Well, HIV-positive men are where *my* heart is. I know that I'm generalizing, but positive men live a lot closer to their feelings. And this comes into the kind of things we talk about, what we do together, how we feel about each other—everything. Negative men are like my family: they have no feelings and they talk about nothing I care about.

"And what of the fact that you don't actually share HIV, itself, with positive men?" I asked Richard.

"Well, it's not the HIV, its how it makes positive men feel about their lives. In a way it's ironic—that the people who know how to live best are the ones most likely to die. Maybe I don't have to do that. Maybe I can survive and still be connected to everything."

I thought about Richard's uncertainty for a moment. "What do you think about your possibilities of surviving HIV?" I asked him.

"I don't know. I've thought about it a lot. It would be so easy to get. And sometimes I think that's destiny for me. Other times I think, 'Oh shit, this is the last thing in the world I want.' What I know for sure is that I *am* going to follow my heart, and I think it's leading me to the understanding that having HIV gives a person. I don't think that means you have to have HIV or die. But I am definitely going to follow my heart."

As a group, positive men more often contemplate the real possibility of death than uninfected men, and this often creates a capacity to *be* in the present rather than merely existing in it, and leads to lives lived more intensely and fully. These lives, in turn, change those who live them. The psychological intimacy that Richard finds in his relationships with positive men is based in such differences, and for him it is compelling.

SOCIAL DIFFERENCES SEPARATING NEGATIVE AND POSITIVE MEN

The worldview differences between positive and negative men quite naturally generate social differences. A society reflects the sense of life, values, and purposes of its members, and it is understandable that there would be social differences between positive and negative men reflecting underlying differences in values about life. People united by common values spend time together, eat together, and have sex together.

Having HIV can represent a lot in common between two people. Positive men may share health and nutritional concerns; political or organizational activity; a mutual desire for normal, unprotected sex; relief at not having to fear infecting negative partners; as well as innumerable practical issues, such as medical treatment and medication. These commonalities are partly exclusive of those without HIV, and the exclusion of negatives from the lives of positives is part of how the positive and negative communities have come upon their rift. Additionally, many positive men with a conscious or unconscious sense of "defectiveness"

about having HIV—not uncommonly entangled in unresolved homophobia that blames HIV infection on homosexuality—feel most comfortable with other positive men, because their relationships are equalized
by the shared condition. When based in feelings of defectiveness about
HIV or homophobia, this self-ghettoing of positive men is not unlike the
self-ghettoing of many gay men from heterosexual society.

The rift between positives and negatives also comes from uninfected
men sharing certain values. In gay communities with high levels of HIV
infection, being uninfected can be a lot to have in common too. Negative
men have many needs that they cannot appropriately rely on positive
men for, not the least of which is to talk about the complex experience of
apparently surviving the epidemic. On reflection, it is clear that a refined
protocol has developed between many negatives and positives in gay
communities. This protocol is largely the responsibility of uninfected
men to honor, and the prerogative of positive men to waive. Topics often
avoided by negatives in the presence of positives may include any but the
most serious health concerns; psychological issues or being in psychotherapy, especially to do with HIV-negative issues; thoughts, plans, or
actions that make an assumption of a moderately long-term future or a
normal life span; thoughts about death or cavalierness about the value of
life; fears about loss; and many of the beliefs negatives hold about AIDS
and its treatment.

Negative men often feel the discussion of such issues will be experienced by a positive man as petty, insensitive, provocative, burdensome,
hurtful, or upsetting. Indeed, this is sometimes the case, and certainly
empathy for the perspective of a man anticipating or experiencing a
debilitating or fatal illness is appropriate. Negatives thus need negatives
for some kinds of conversation, friendship, and support. Charlie, an uninfected psychotherapy patient in his late twenties, discussed this issue
in a therapy hour shortly after he and his positive lover, David, had
attended two memorial services for friends in a single day.

> It's amazing when I think about my age and what's been going on.
> I had two memorials on Friday, one for Neil and one for John. We
> were at Neil's and talking to his parents, and his mother, who was
> crying most of the time, said to us, "You know I'm so happy to see
> you two young men so happy and healthy" and all that stuff, and
> I thought, well, first of all she has no idea who has HIV, because
> she's talking to David too, and most of the people in the room have
> HIV. But I was also thinking about how lousy I was feeling—about

Neil, and especially John—and about every half hour it was coming over me like a panic attack, and I would think, "Oh my God, John is *actually dead*." I couldn't say anything to Neil's mother, of course. I didn't even want to tell her why we had to leave, which was to go to John's house. I was really upset about both of them, and David, you know, is so anxious about himself at this point, that when someone dies it's very hard for him, so I don't tell him if I'm very upset. Finally, when we got home after John's, David just went to bed because he was exhausted. I called Leslie on the phone to tell her about what had happened, and I just started to cry the minute she picked up the phone. I was so relieved she was there and would listen to me, and that I knew she would be OK with whatever I needed to say. She was the only one I had been able to talk to all day about any of it.

PSYCHOLOGICAL ISSUES

To the extent that it becomes a broad trend within gay communities, the isolation of negative men from positives will be destructive and impoverishing for everyone. Avoiding others' feelings is often an effort to avoid our own feelings, because our feelings are stimulated by the feelings of others. Thus separating ourselves from others is partly an effort to separate from parts of ourselves. The worst probable result of this psychological operation is discussed in chapter 6: men leading lives that rely on suppressing, encapsulating, containing, denying, or splitting off feelings. Ultimately, such men may consciously deny an internal life of feelings; rely on a fragmentation of self and others rather than on a capacity for the complexity and ambivalence of feelings; be limited to relationships that do not account for the other as a whole human being; and lack empathy and a capacity for guilt. Compulsive behaviors and the attribution of hated parts of oneself to others (*projection*) are also characteristic of such lives. Many uninfected men, living under the extraordinary burden of the epidemic, are experiencing such problems. This suggests an unhappy psychological prognosis for the gay male communities, which had shown so much social, personal, and psychological growth in the decade or two before the epidemic made itself known.

There are four psychological "constellations" especially pertinent to the separation of negative men from positives. These are fear and anxiety about HIV-positive people in men with compulsive character trends

(*obsessive-compulsive trends*);[9] the rejection of HIV-positive people because they raise anxiety by threatening one's own self-esteem (*narcissistic anxiety*); the redirection of—usually homophobic—self-hatred
toward those who have the virus (*projective defenses*); and the indiscriminate use of denial to avoid those with HIV, in an effort to limit
painful feelings.

Fear and anxiety about HIV and HIV-positive men are voiced by many,
not all of whom possess obsessive-compulsive character styles. At the
end of this section I will talk about psychologically "uncomplicated" fear
and anxiety as distinct from my subject here. The man with genuine
obsessive-compulsive trends is much more likely to act on his fear than
the man with uncomplicated fear. He is also more likely to assiduously
avoid *any* physical contact with men who might carry HIV, and to ru-
minate unrealistically and obsessively about possible exposure. The man
thus maintains isolation from all others, for he is not sure who has HIV
and who does not. This isolation is likely to be an extension of isolation
and difficulty with emotional and physical intimacy that existed before
the epidemic, but the feelings are now focused on a new, external object
of fear.

When compared to men with uncomplicated fear and anxiety, the
most obvious characteristics of truly obsessive men include a history of
similar feelings and problems, the unrealistic nature of their fear (about,
for example, an incident that possibly exposed them to HIV), and a truly
obsessive, ruminative approach to the issues. Such men are also likely
to engage in isolated, impulsive incidents of dangerous unprotected sex.
This may be a "counterphobic" gesture aimed at denying or mastering
the limiting and painful anxiety, or it may be a breakthrough of needs
and feelings normally hidden behind the obsessive defenses. These may
include masochistic impulses or the desire for emotional and physical
intimacy.

It is my observation that deficiencies of self-esteem are more common in gay men than in the population at large. Although these deficiencies (or *narcissistic character trends*) have been used to explain the
origins, or clarify the nature, of homosexuality by some developmental
psychologists, it seems obvious that poor self-esteem is often simply a
consequence of the treatment one receives growing up homosexual—
despised by much of society, and often by one's family. Additionally, gay
children have had few public gay role models during adolescent development; their education is often disrupted by conflict with or withdrawal

from peers; and opportunities to learn social and interpersonal skills are often completely unavailable.

Unfortunately, the AIDS epidemic is likely to engage and exacerbate whatever deficiencies of self-esteem a gay man comes to the epidemic with. Homosexuality and HIV have become so entangled in the American mind—including the gay American mind—that for many being gay is synonymous with pioneering the worst plague in twentieth-century American history. Often unconsciously, many gay men feel accused by the very fact of AIDS. For these men, the prevalence of HIV in gay communities confirms suspicions and fears that what they were doing was wrong, that they would receive retribution for it, and that AIDS is the retribution. The epidemic is thus experienced as another—huge—injury to already limited reservoirs of self-esteem.

The man with poor self-esteem, unable to gain insight into his feelings, tries to protect himself from the injury by not being associated with those who have HIV, those who work with it, or even those who acknowledge it as a central issue in the gay communities. This dissociation from the apparent sources of injury to self-esteem entails a dissociation from aspects of self. The man becomes dissociated from his sense of personal deficiency or self-contempt, which are now felt, perhaps unconsciously, about those who have HIV, are involved with it, or affected by it. He begins to lose whatever empathy he once had for others and, unfortunately, his capacity for intimacy with anyone, HIV-infected or otherwise.

At best, men whose poor self-esteem guides their response to the epidemic express a persistent indifference to HIV issues and, perhaps only unconsciously, avoid significant personal contact with those thought to be HIV-infected. At worst, deficiencies of self-esteem lead a man to harbor anger at those who are HIV-infected. Those with HIV threaten, simply by association, to contaminate or weaken him by "draining" self-esteem. Sometimes accompanied by paranoid elements, this more severe response is founded in a global lack of empathy that may be supported by an unformulated position about why positives deserve no empathy: people with HIV want too much, are monopolizing the attention and resources of the gay community, and they got what they deserved for what they did. Though very rarely voiced openly, such feelings are not infrequently felt privately. Men with such feelings often possess a capacity for only superficial relationships. These are often focused on physical beauty—a criterion that makes little allowance for HIV-positive men because they are experienced as physically defective. A lack of capacity for guilt, and paranoid or obsessive character styles are also common among men with severe deficiencies of self-esteem.

A psychotherapy patient in his early twenties, Frank, described an incident with David, a man whom he had been dating for a brief period of time. David's feelings of poor self-esteem had become entangled in feelings about disease and sexuality, and his narcissistic anxiety had taken on a particularly literal and primitive form.

> David and I have been doing fine, but when I went over to his house on Thursday night, he was very cold—he didn't touch me when I came in, and he was very formal. I said, "What's going on?" and he said, "You've given me something that I *did not need or want.*" It turned out that he had this tiny sore on his penis, and he had the idea that he got it from me—but I don't have anything like that. So I said, "Why do you think this is from me?" and he said, "Well, it's certainly not *mine.*"

David also announced that he would not be seeing Frank anymore and that he had made a decision to move to Europe. Frank was inexperienced in relationships, but we were able to discuss his feelings of being accused and rejected, and his sense that he was being assigned all of David's bad feelings about himself ("He's got this incredible, gorgeous body and he thinks he's fat and out of shape."). I interpreted David's attributing the sore to Frank as a projection of his own sense of defectiveness onto Frank to protect his own self-esteem. Although he knew it was implausible, Frank identified with the defectiveness David attributed to him because of his own shaky, if relatively healthy, self-esteem. Frank concluded, I thought correctly, that David had decided to live in Europe to "get away from the corruption and contamination in the Bay Area gay community." David was a man whose poor self-esteem demanded a defection from the gay community and the illness and death that it now represented.

Sometimes men with very poor self-esteem create an internal confusion of homophobic feelings with feelings about HIV, and project that confused self-hatred onto those who have the virus. Deficiencies of self-esteem may be broadly based in a person's experience of himself, though for the gay man, they will almost certainly include, as one important element, feelings about his homosexuality. The projection of homophobia, in itself, is almost exclusively about homophobic self-hatred. When the projection is directed at men with HIV, the process involves the internal transformation of homophobic feelings into feelings ostensibly about HIV, which are then projected onto those with HIV. This internal transformation of *homo*phobia into *AIDS*phobia is one aspect of the process I referred to earlier as the "AIDSification" of AIDS.

Gay men often reject other gay men for being too different from themselves, and there are, indeed, many varieties of identification among gay men. These differences are partly the result of polarization motivated by self-hatred, which is projected into others and their differences. For example, the disdain or hatred a "straight-looking, straight-acting" gay man may feel for an effeminate man can be understood as a displacement of his homophobic feelings (for himself and others) into hatred of effeminate men, who are then despised. This common displacement is often rooted in an unconscious confusion of effeminacy with homosexuality, and, although this may be partly a result of social stereotypes, psychologically the very purpose of the confusion is to allow the displacement. Once homophobia is displaced onto effeminacy, self-hatred may be directed away from oneself and toward others.

This sort of psychological projection often provides the "benefit" of not only directing self-hatred elsewhere, but of disguising or denying the hated condition—for example, homosexuality—in oneself. The irrational, unconscious entanglement of AIDS and homosexuality allows the displacement of self-hatred onto HIV-positive men. Having accomplished this displacement, other gay men are avoided not because they are gay, but because gay men have HIV.[10]

Denial is often used indiscriminately to avoid HIV-positive men and the painful or anxious feelings associated with them. Noah, an uninfected psychotherapy patient, had been on a date recently with a man whose lover and business partner had both died of AIDS within the last year. Noah told me about their date, and said he had been quite attracted to the man, although he doubted that they would pursue a relationship further.

> "What reservations do you have about taking it further?" I asked.
> "I'm not sure," Noah responded. "I'm not sure he's interested in me. And I guess I'm not completely sure what I think about him."
> "Is HIV an issue?"
> "No. I don't know his HIV status anyway."
> "Well, you're not naive about HIV. Given this man's history, it might have occurred to you that he might have HIV."
> "I didn't even think of it," Noah said, "I didn't think about his

HIV status one way or the other. I'm not sure I want to right now."

"Do you want me to drop this?"

"No."

"Well, then I wonder why you hadn't thought about it one way or the other. You know that his lover and business partner have both died in the last year, and, in fact, you expressed concern about getting involved with someone who was in that kind of transition, the 'end' of a relationship, as you put it. I wonder why the possibility of his having HIV didn't even come to mind."

Noah was thoughtful for a moment.

"Well, I didn't think of it, and I didn't think of the significance of his being positive. It scares me, now that I am thinking about it, to fall in love with someone who might die. But I can't treat him any differently just because he has HIV. He isn't any different, he's the same person whether he has HIV or not."

"Is that so?" I asked.

"Do you mean is he *bad* because he has HIV? I mean, you sound like my grandmother."

"Is that what you think I meant? Or is that idea somewhere in the back of your mind?"

"I suppose I do have that feeling, and I'm not sure if I mean that in the sense that it would be dangerous to get too involved with him because he would die. Or maybe I actually have the feeling that he's bad—he's gay, he got fucked, and now he has AIDS. Probably all of the above. It's pathetic, but I'm sure that I still have unconscious stuff like that. The difference is my grandmother says it out loud—and she believes it too."

"So those really are feelings about his being different?"

"Yes, except, of course, that it isn't true, because he couldn't have done anything that I haven't done."

"So in that sense the differences aren't realistic, and not thinking about the whole issue is a way of not wanting to acknowledge that you have any feelings like your grandmother."

"Yes, I'd rather *not.*"

"But I wonder, along a more realistic vein, if having HIV doesn't make some people different, change the way they think about things, their values, their way of life?"

Noah responded.

"I feel uncomfortable even talking about this. I feel morally inadequate because I'm even thinking about it. None of this had occurred to me, and I'm wondering how that was possible. I don't want to feel that there are these things between us, that we are going to have all this new prejudice in the gay community."

We sat silently for a few moments and I continued.

"I imagine that none of this occurred to you because the feelings are altogether troubling—that just having to think about someone's HIV status is troubling, brings up your conflict, and what you feel are prejudicial feelings, feelings that are wrong to you. But what will come of keeping all of this unconscious?"

"Well it occurs to me," Noah responded, "that I've kept it unconscious, and I've done it by dating men who are negative, or who I've been pretty sure are negative."

"Was this selection intentional?"

"No, it wasn't. As a matter of fact, if anyone had asked me, 'Who do you date, do you seriously date men who are positive?' I would have said 'Oh, sure.' Except that I just wasn't doing it and I never noticed that. It just didn't actually happen."

"And your Friday night date, were you pretty sure he was negative?"

"No, I wasn't, and there has been something nagging at me about the whole idea of dating him, something, you know, that just had me uneasy about the whole thing, and this was it. By going out with him and thinking about him seriously, I was letting all these issues come up, the whole issue of falling in love with positive men. The whole thing has just popped out of the closet."

PSYCHOLOGICALLY UNCOMPLICATED FEAR AND ANXIETY

He was probably sloppy drunk. I think he hated
concrete. I hardly knew him and couldn't quite take
his gushings on friendship. He probably
hated us all on occasion, figuring us
cowards not to be dissolved with him. And we were.
One has to draw the line somewhere.
—Keith Waldrop, *from* For Two Different Deaths [11]

As already described, fear and anxiety about HIV is sometimes unrealistic, in the sense that it is transferred from other conscious and unconscious psychological issues. There is also relatively realistic, psychologically uncomplicated fear and anxiety. These feelings are not always without unconscious complications, nor are they necessarily entirely free of problematic psychological issues; but they are based in conscious perceptions and decisions that may be a realistic and sensible response to the AIDS epidemic.

Many men, although they have had no experience with loss from HIV, anticipate and fear the loss of a potential positive partner, or fear contracting HIV from a positive partner because they appreciate the complexity and anomalies of the biology and epidemiology of HIV, or because they cannot or do not want to confine themselves to protected sex. Some of these issues may provide a psychologically uncomplicated basis for not choosing a partner who is HIV-positive.

For most people living outside the gay communities and the epidemic, that choice seems obvious. Indeed, many who do not comprehend the form of life the epidemic has created for gay men would question a man pursuing a relationship with another man known to be infected with a fatal virus. "If I started a relationship with a man I knew had lymphatic cancer," a heterosexual woman friend asked me, "wouldn't you wonder about my motivations?" This is an obvious perception, but one that fails to account for the nature of interpersonal and social issues in communities that often have 50 percent of the population dealing with fatal disease. For the gay man, my friend's assumption of relationships limited to "healthy" men would be difficult to conduct in practice—too many gay men have HIV and it is not always possible to know who does— and it would entail social and psychological costs that would not occur in middle-class American society. To reject HIV-positive gay men as a group, or a particular man because he carries HIV, raises serious psychological conflict in many men. It is a decision that necessarily entails the rejection or denial of positive feelings and identifications with both one's community and with innumerable individuals. This fact, obvious to most gay men, is by mainstream American standards both radical and almost incomprehensible.

In addition to the anticipation of loss or infection, many gay men have *already* had huge losses in the epidemic. Many uninfected men—and many positive men—feel they cannot risk more. Several of my psychotherapy patients have lost two lovers to AIDS, one has lost three, and innumerable men have lost ten or twenty close friends. Given such experience, a man's decision to attempt avoiding important relationships with positive men may be an appropriate and adaptive measure, psychologically speaking. Nevertheless, the categorical exclusion of so many from one's life—and the loss of access to feelings connected to those being excluded—is necessarily psychologically costly. A man making this decision has already paid tremendous psychological costs and is attempting to reduce further psychological damage, rather than avoid it. The human costs of the epidemic are always determined by a—not always voluntary—balance between life-affirming connections and isolating safety.

The Correspondence of Mark

I do not need to know your real name.
This much seems obvious, that as we move along the path, slowly but certainly the path
replaces us. And also, just as strands in the vitreous humour cloud the visual field, words
stray, making our thought opaque.—Keith Waldrop, from Potential Random [12]

In 1987 I had been seeing a psychotherapy patient, Mark, for about two years. He was a working journalist in his mid-thirties, and at this point in the therapy he met Tom, a social worker in his late twenties. They became involved in a relationship that occupied much of our time in therapy hours. A year after they met, Tom decided to have an ELISA to obtain a travel visa and, expecting to be uninfected, had the results come back positive. Feeling that this could not be true because earlier testing had given negative results, Tom retested, and Mark, who had never been tested, was tested at the same time. Though they had engaged for the past year in relatively protected sex, Mark seemed convinced that he was positive too, and wanted to confirm that. Tom's test came back positive again, but Mark's was negative.

The two men continued to live together for about another three months. Tom seemed to be in a serious depression and Mark discussed this, as well as his own feelings, session after session. At the end of the three months, Tom seemed to suddenly mobilize his energy and announced to Mark that he was moving out. He was returning to a previous lover. This decision was discussed between them for only a few days, and Tom left, essentially cutting off contact with Mark for nearly a year, although they did occasionally meet, and had sex on a few occasions. During that time, Mark continued to write Tom, but his letters were virtually unanswered. Mark asked if I would read copies of the letters, and doing so provided me much insight into his feelings and experience. Our discussions, in turn, provided Mark a way to clarify feelings about Tom as well as someone to respond to his powerful correspondence. Feeling the material was very important, I asked Mark (a pseudonym) for permission to use it here, substantially edited and shortened. The correspondence reveals and clarifies many of the complicated and painful issues that HIV has brought to "mixed antibody" relationships, and to the broader social and political issues that now exist between the positive and negative "communities."

September 11
Ever since you had the HIV test, I have tried not to burden you with my feelings and my problems. Obviously you had enough of your own. But there are certain things I feel I must say, and I do not mean them to be hurtful. When I said on Monday that you have never made me angry, that was the truth, and your doubting my statement is about your confusion between my being hurt and getting angry. You have hurt me plenty, and though I have tried not to burden you with that in the past months, that is the truth. But I have not gotten angry at you for hurting me because I think I know why you have done it, and I think that you have mostly done your best with an awful situation.

What I want to say is this: You cannot get rid of the HIV by getting rid of me. Though you found out about it while we were together, it is not my fault in any sense of that idea, and you can't blame me for it. It won't go away if you go to live with someone you lived with before you had it, and it won't go away if you try to get rid of the feelings you have about it. When you said to me that you couldn't be with someone who looked sad every time he looked at you, you were talking about yourself too, not just me. I love you enough that I would go for whatever helped you, even if it meant your leaving me. I really mean that. I send my love.

There were many feelings and thoughts, during this period of grief in the months after they separated, that Mark could not express directly to Tom. We realized that Mark confused the loss of the relationship with Tom's death. This confusion considerably complicated his grief, and it also inhibited the expression of many feelings toward Tom, including anger at Tom's abandonment of the relationship. There were other complications and confusions that we were able to distinguish and clarify only over time. They included Mark's identification with Tom, and the confusions that it brought to his sense of himself, his own health, and his expectations of his life.

Thursday, September 17

I am still amazed at how implausible it seems that you are gone. I just didn't think it could happen, and I know now that part of the reason is that your having HIV has made me feel even closer to you than I did before. I know that this is exactly what you couldn't tolerate, but your fear and depression made you so much more open. This sometimes made me feel love for you that seemed so large that it was as if I could actually feel my heart swelling to some huge size inside me. If I could take the HIV into myself, and that would get rid of it for you, I would do that. I really mean that. And I also fear that the more I tell you that, the more you will run from me, for I know that the whole thing just makes you feel too vulnerable. You were always afraid that I would try to take care of you, and the possibility of your getting sick makes that seem like a realistic possibility.

I have talked a lot with Walt [the author] about why I was so sure that I had HIV because you had it. Part of it was just fear because we have been physically so close and had so much sex together. Whether it was safe or not, I've had a lot of irrational feelings about that. I think you were feeling the same thing when you said that you now felt like you were nothing but a danger to the people you loved. I have not really been afraid of getting HIV from you, and you know that I haven't done anything differently since you got the test, which is what I wanted to do. If you feel like you are a danger, I hope you will separate that out from your ideas that I think that. I don't and I don't care. I have the idea that Alan [the lover to whom Tom had returned, also HIV-negative] really is afraid of HIV and I hope part of your comfort with him isn't that he confirms your feelings of being a pariah and a danger.

Mark had discussed with me feeling "on guard" while having sex with Tom in a way he had not been before the HIV test. He also had several moments of fear while making love to Tom, felt they were irrational, and expressed a conscious commitment not to act on them. He realized that Tom was experiencing a sense of personal failure about having HIV, and now perceived himself as defective. He was determined not to support those feelings by treating Tom as if there were something wrong with him. But Mark also conjectured that Tom might be picking up his fear, and wondered if he should talk about it directly. We discussed people having all kinds of feelings and fantasies about partners that might be hurtful if known, and the importance of exercising judgment about whether more damage came to the relationship as a result of talking about them or not talking about them. Mark decided that his intimate physical expression had been adequate proof of his desires and that he did not need to talk about this with Tom. The letter continues:

But there are lots of other reasons I thought I was positive too, and I'm just beginning to understand them. And they are things which are about feelings, but are a lot more important than ideas about transmitting HIV. If I had to sum them up, I'd say that it just seemed impossible to me that something so important could be different between us. We couldn't be this different about anything that mattered so much. I often think back on those first days after the test. And what occurred to me then was that we were in it together, and that meant much more to me in a positive way than having HIV meant in a negative way. I thought, we're in it together, and we'll just do it, whatever that is, but being together is the most important thing.

We were real idiots about this test. We should have done the whole thing together, we should have talked about what it might mean, we should have gone down there together, or decided not to get tested together, and when I think back on it, the casualness that we approached it with was built on nothing but ignorance and denial about the potential and our feelings. It was as if you were going to get your teeth X-rayed. But instead of having to get a filling, you find out that your path in life has just completely diverged from the path of the person you love most. This test has fucked everything up and we didn't account for any of this possibility. I don't know about our destinies and how much different they are. I know that you feel they are more different than I do, but I don't know what that feeling is and I'm not sure you do either. I know that you feel I don't understand your situation, and I know some of that must be true. I want to say more about this. I didn't think we could be this different about something so important, and I don't want to be that different. I don't want HIV, but I don't want to be this different either, I don't want to be separated from you by this. I feel like my destiny is for it to relate to your destiny, and that has nothing to do with our *ending up* differently. We're not ending up now, we're living and we can still do that. You're healthy and so am I and the difference between us is information, just information that we don't even completely know the importance of. Please, please think about the meaning that HIV has taken on for us, and about whether we have control over that meaning. Love.

Mark began talking in therapy about still other feelings. These included the sense of being abandoned by Tom, both when he was depressed and now during his "manic rally with Alan," as Mark called it. He said in one session, "I feel as if Tom has run off with someone named HIV." At the same time, Mark began to realize that he felt some relief at Tom's leaving, for he feared Tom's getting sick, and wondered if Tom had been able to stay with the relationship whether he could have tolerated his own fearful feelings. Unlike Tom, Mark could get rid of HIV, at least for the time being, quite literally by "getting rid" of Tom. Like Tom, this rid him of none of his feelings. Mark also wondered if Tom were able to come back to the relationship whether he would be able to respond, or would feel like running from it.

In discussing this important ambivalence, Mark came to feel that he had expressed it to Tom in several ways over the past several months. He felt that he had sometimes supported Tom's withdrawal, and that when Tom first started discussing his intent to leave the relationship, he had presented himself as too objective and magnanimous. Mark said to me during this session,

> You know, I don't think I ever said to him, "I don't care what you want, I want you to stay with me. This means everything to me." I just wasn't that strong, although part of me felt that way. It's as if I was always giving him the out to do what he wanted to do, which was to leave, and I was—part of me was—secretly hoping that he would take it. When I think about it now, he might have been testing me, testing how much I still loved him even though he had this "defect," and although I kept giving him the right answers, my fear never let me say them loudly enough. I feel cowardly when I think of this now, that I never really held on to him so tightly that he could have no doubt how I felt. It's since he left that I've felt so strongly.

I commented that the prospect of Tom getting AIDS was daunting, and although one might love a person enough to live with that possibility, it seemed to me that ambivalence was understandable and appropriate. Mark needed to recognize his ambivalence and make decisions that at least acknowledged it. Mark started to cry at this point.

> "You know, Tom had no choices at all in this—he *had* it, he had HIV whether he went or stayed. When I think how frightened he was, how hopeless it all seemed, it just overwhelms me. He is stuck with that, and if I love him, I'm stuck with it too. His feeling like he has to leave me just denies my feelings for him."
>
> I wondered if Mark felt that because Tom did not have choices about HIV, he felt that he could not have choices.
>
> "About what?" he wondered.
>
> "For one thing about having HIV or not. I think this is part of the source of your sense that you have HIV. If Tom has it, I must have it."
>
> "I think that's true." Mark hesitated a moment. "I don't feel like I deserve any choices Tom doesn't have."
>
> "Why?"
>
> "I didn't tell you this when it happened, but about a week after Tom got the first test, he woke me up in the middle of the night, and he said, 'I'm sorry to wake you up, but I'm really scared.' And I said, you know, 'What's going on?' He said he'd been thinking a lot and realized he wasn't afraid to die, but that he was afraid of suffering a lot. I told him that he didn't have to. And do you know what he said to me? He said, 'But I realized that I don't know how to kill myself. And I wonder if you will help me with that.' And I started crying because I realized he was just trapped in himself with these awful feelings, that he couldn't get out, and that these feelings were just rolling over and over inside of him with no way out. He was lying there looking frightened and trapped in the most awful reality I can think of. And I thought to myself, I will never leave him alone in this. I will do anything for him, and I will never, never leave him alone to feel this bad by himself."
>
> "What did you say to him?" I asked.
>
> "I said I will help you with this whenever you want. We'll figure all of this out. I promise."

Over the following weeks, we explored the guilt that contributed to Mark's feelings that he was positive and deserved no choices Tom did not have. The guilt seemed to come partly out of Mark's feeling completely helpless with Tom's situation. We also agreed that the feelings of helplessness also contributed to his "objectivity" about Tom leaving the relationship. Unconsciously, Mark felt that if there was nothing he could do for Tom, he was unworthy of the relationship, and perhaps someone else *could* help. We also agreed that Tom had probably sensed Mark's ambivalence about allowing the relationship to end, and that this was an instance where it would be less destructive to discuss potentially hurtful things—Mark's ambivalence—than to not discuss them. This seemed particularly important because Mark felt that Tom had ambivalence of his own about leaving. He was leaving, Mark conjectured, not only because of the differences the positive ELISA had created, but also to protect Mark from a future burdened with illness and death.

Other clarifications helped Mark sort out the relationship and his feelings about it. Tom's return to Alan, who was uninfected, seemed another indication of Tom's ambivalence and confusion. While Tom wanted someone with whom he could share his HIV status, he also wanted to deny HIV, and he was returning to Alan, with whom he had been in a relationship before he knew of his HIV infection. Alan, unlike Mark, was a man who had great difficulty talking about feelings, and Tom must have felt some safety in this.

October 2

I have—of course—been thinking about us a lot and about how HIV has been so destructive for us. I know that my feelings are complicated. But there is a bottom line to all this, and that is that we love each other very much and we will just go along, day by day, and deal with whatever happens, with HIV or anything else. You know that I'm not looking forward to your getting sick any more than you are, and of course I've thought about that. But we will simply deal with it. I want you to know that I love you and want you back. That I have reservations about HIV and all the possibilities is aside from the point. I have no reservations about you and wanting you. Please do think about what I'm saying here. Love.

Tom did not respond to this letter except to say in a return note that he appreciated Mark's love and that at another time this might all have worked out.

In sessions through the following year, Mark was able to work on a wide range of conflicts that had arisen in his relationship to Tom. One of these was his occasional but repeated engagements in unprotected sex. We attempted to clarify the feelings of identification, guilt, and self-destructive depression that motivated this potentially danger-ous activity. These were difficult times for Mark, for he was working not only on feelings of love, loss, and guilt about Tom, but also their con-nection to feelings about his childhood and family relationships. Mark was also dealing with his experience of being a potential survivor of the epidemic. He volunteered a great deal of time for gay political activities and thought actively about coexisting with positive men in the epidemic and the sometimes considerable differences in experience, purpose, and meaning that he perceived between himself and men with HIV. Mark also continued to identify with Tom and other positive men, and discov-ered that there were reasons other than guilt for this. In addition to his intimate relationship with Tom, Mark volunteered for the Shanti Project as an "emotional support" volunteer for men with AIDS. Contrary to his sense of differences with positive men, he began to develop an intensity of feeling, an urgency about life, and an ability to live more fully, which he attributed to sharing with many positive men the feeling that death seemed only a step away. Mark felt strongly that he did not fear death, and that his acceptance of it was a release from the fear of life. Yet, it nagged at him that he did not actually have HIV, and might actually live another fifty years. About two years after their separation, Mark and Tom were once again spending time together. Mark said the following in a therapy hour:

> "I know that when you really understand that life isn't *necessary,* then you can live it. When I was afraid of death, when I didn't think about it, I was clinging to life, and it's like hanging on to the steer-ing wheel to keep yourself from sliding out of your seat—you can't steer the car at the same time. I feel very freed up by not fearing death."

"You have also expressed some concern about these feelings," I reminded him.

> "Well, me, I'm really caught in the middle. Tom has an oppor-tunity to work through his life that I don't feel like I have. When he decided to stop taking Prozac, he said to me that it was just resigning from really feeling things, and that he could just work through the stuff and come out on the other side. I admired that, but I thought, well, he also doesn't have to be a survivor, he can cut to the core of it and be done with it. Having to live as a survivor

with the losses—including his at some point—I just think, bring on the Prozac and turn up the music. *I can't deal with it.* I've got to account for a future of some kind. I go back and forth on this constantly."

"So the short life provides the opportunity, and the long life the dead end," I commented.

"That's how it feels. Though I know that I couldn't say that to Tom—tell him about all the advantages he has."

"Why not?"

"This is like telling him what an opportunity the epidemic has been for me, how much he and the epidemic have helped me make sense of my life. For someone who has HIV it's hard to see the opportunity in all this—and it's very odd, but while I think of this insight as something I share with HIV-positive people, they are usually very alienated about it. I mean, they don't want to hear it for the most part, at least from someone who's negative. . . . I'm on the outside and it's, like, 'Who is this negative guy trying to tell people with HIV what they're feeling, or trying to tell them he's feeling what they're feeling?' It's lonely in the middle, but the only way I could be on Tom's side would be to have HIV, which I really don't think I want—we both know I'm ambivalent about *that.* And to be on the other side, oh well—I'd have to give up everything I've learned, I'd have to pretend that I felt I had a future."

"Pretend that you felt you had a future?"

"Well, I really don't feel that way. Partly it's the feeling that eventually—somehow—I'll actually get AIDS. But aside from that, I just find *right now* so intense, who *wants* a future? Who could think about it? It's like being lost in the trees, you just have no sense of the forest, and who wants to. I don't plan anything, and I guess I'm sometimes not sure if that's from insight or stupidity. But that's the way it actually is, and I don't think I could change it if I wanted to."

"Well, the intensity of the life you've been leading, it has something to do with living in a protracted emergency—a war—and with the change of insight that people experience doing that."

"I know. There are days, you know, when the whole epidemic is so exhausting, I'm amazed when I drive by a gas station and people are in there pumping gas and I think, 'God it's amazing, but people still put gas in their cars, and these other ordinary things you see them doing all over the place.' I wonder what's motivating them—

it seems impossibly hard. Other days I am just knocked out by
how wonderful life seems, like every minute of it is very, very precious. I am talking about *intensity*. It's incredibly intense, and I'm
so thankful to Tom that I can feel that."

Conclusions

I'd like an inclusive mind, where nothing could
possibly be out of the question. . . .
Thinking like this made Brueghel paint
a windmill near Calvary. When Adam, as it
fell out, got too old to know Eve, he sat
his inspired carcass down by his hoe, watching
his sweaty children screw up generation
after generation.
—Keith Waldrop, *from* Angel to Love, Man to World [13]

The separations and conflicts that the HIV-antibody test and AIDS have
wrought in the gay communities are profoundly and painfully felt by
many gay men, negative and positive alike. These problems are too
complex for simple prescriptions. Although negative and positive men
continue to have much in common, there *are* often real and important differences in the feelings and lives of negatives and positives, and
the gay communities must acknowledge this. We must explore—and
struggle with—what those differences mean to us, and how those meanings affect our relations.

With regard to biological survival, uninfected men must be supported
in the feeling that there is sufficient advantage in not having HIV that
it is worth the considerable trouble of trying to stay that way. With regard to *human* survival, we must distinguish the rejection of HIV per se
from the rejection of HIV-positive men because of irrational fear, threatened self-esteem, or the projection of self-hatred. If, in turn, positive
men feel invalidated, discounted, or displaced because negative men in-
vest significant value in not having HIV, they must examine their own
confusions of meaning about homosexuality and HIV, and their own
self-hatred—a self-hatred too often reprojected onto negative men, and
too often confused with the indigenous hatred that sometimes seems to
envelop the world like a second, sad troposphere of human making.

The distrust, resentment, and anger that negative and positive men sometimes feel for each other is nothing more than the relentless work of homophobia—the same homophobia that we have always allowed to put our lives at risk, both biologically and humanly. In deeply understanding that, we will regain whole communities, and we will regain a sense of humanity as happier, more honest men capable of intimacy substantially unfettered by our own malicious ghosts. Being gay has always been about the acceptance of feeling different, but differences, in themselves, are neither accusations nor betrayal. The differences we now experience among ourselves—*being* negative and *being* positive—are deeply rooted in the complexity and ambivalence of human feelings, and in the changed values and expectations of life that come with wartime. We cannot be who we were before the epidemic, and to hope that our relations can remain unchanged is an impossible hope that can be sustained only by denial, dishonesty, and the impoverishment of our authentic feelings. A personal advertisement appeared in the *San Francisco Sentinel*:

> Box 3121: Cute, early thirties activist, two years widowed, and HIV+, wants to find someone who knows the special importance of love when mortality is in sight.

For this man, HIV status is not the final distinction between gay men. The final distinction is between those who are able to embrace life, even in the face of death, and those who are entangled in death even as they appear to live.

Chapter 8
Being Sexual: The Politics
and Humanity of Gay Sex
in the Epidemic

As far as I can tell, the worst thing is not dying—the worst thing is not living. All those people who say they're afraid of dying? I think what they really mean is they're afraid of living. That's the big thing I've learned from AIDS.—A psychotherapy patient to the author

For uninfected gay men, protected sex is central to biological—if not psychological and human—survival of the AIDS epidemic. Yet, among all the problems affecting men in the epidemic, unprotected sex has been the one most prohibited for discussion. It was only after the first decade of the epidemic was well past that an uninfected man could say publicly that he was "having problems" with safer sex and hope to escape ridicule from uninfected and infected men alike. Safer sex had become a moral posture in the gay communities, and this has made the topic of unprotected sex, or one's feelings about it, a taboo.

This situation has developed partly out of concern for the reduction of HIV transmission. But the moral posture is also rooted in complex politics—both between the gay communities and the heterosexual mainstream, and between negative and positive men within the gay communities—that badly obscure the psychological and human issues of gay sex in the epidemic. Unfortunately, these politics collude with the denial of guilt, shame, homophobia, and conflicts about intimacy that inform many gay men's experience of sexuality in the epidemic. Such feelings fly in the face of the moral, public posture. Our public talk about gay sex too often has not been about the real human issues, but about assuring HIV funding, the respectability of homosexuality and the gay communities, and the continuing, sometimes strained relations of negative and positive gay men.

For much of heterosexual society, completely unfamiliar with the realities of being gay in the age of AIDS, the common practice of *protected* sex between positive and negative men is often met with complete disbelief. The admission to unprotected sex among gay men "who know better" is felt by many in the gay communities—perhaps quite correctly—to be a sure way of destroying all the new acceptance garnered by gay men for their handling of the epidemic. The worst possibility is that through continued unprotected sex, gay men will finally confirm the widely held, usually unvoiced suspicion that they *did,* after all, bring AIDS upon themselves—or are doing so now—and deserve neither political nor economic support for their self-induced woes. These homophobic public pressures, and the internalized psychological conflict that gives them credibility, are now convincing too many gay men that the only *good* homosexual is the celibate one, or the one who pretends he is. The Pope said that, and internalized homophobia, guilt, and fear are giving his words new voices in gay communities.

The complex experience of many gay men regarding sex, and the prohibitions against feeling or discussing it openly, are described in Woody Castrodale's description of a meeting of the HIV-negative support group he facilitates:

> Chuck had been talking—and it was the first time in the history of the group that anyone had been willing to bring it up—that he was often feeling like having unsafe sex. After he talked for a few moments, Craig blurted out, "I can't believe you're talking like this. I don't know about you, but I intend to stay alive, and you're going to commit suicide."
>
> Another member of the group, George, then said, "You know, Craig, I don't think I heard Charles say he wanted to commit suicide, I don't think that's a good analogy. I don't think Charles is talking about committing suicide. He's talking about wanting to *have sex,* and I think that's what's making you so agitated.
>
> I was sitting listening to this, and my mind went into a sort of free fall. The more I've been facilitating this group, the more I realize that I don't want to live without risk—that would not be living. And sometimes the group makes me think that we're hiding behind these prohibitions about talking about one thing or another as a way to hide out against life. I realized, with regard to this issue of sex, how *complicated* it is. What it comes right down to is life, and death,

and sex, and these things mixed up together make quite a brew. At that moment with the group, I couldn't talk about it because my feelings on this subject are just too complex. I couldn't keep my personal sensibilities out of my responsibility as a facilitator.[1]

The External Politics of Sex

The observations of a psychologist are likely to find the roots of politics in individual feelings. But before discussing the psychological and human matters of sex in the epidemic, I believe it important to try to clarify some of the politics that obscure them. The politics that have kept gay men from feeling, thinking, and talking honestly about their sex are of two types. The first is the exhausting political effort directed at the pernicious homophobia of the heterosexual mainstream at a time when the gay communities could well use both hands for dealing with the epidemic. The second is the political situation within the gay communities between negative and positive men. This *is* a situation—if a quiet, often denied one—that is largely about the intensely conflicted and painful issue of how to address the needs of uninfected men without seeming to dismiss or invalidate the lives of positive men.

Much of the political effort about gay sex directed at the heterosexual communities is a displacement from what were previously gay political issues. For many gay men, for so long on the outside of mainstream values, "safer sex" provided a pious position that has virtually replaced traditional gay political activism. For many men, safer sex—indeed, AIDS in general—has provided the first opportunity to experience a respectable position in the world that does not rest on concealment or denial of one's homosexuality. That piety and newfound respectability is expressed in numerous ways. Gay men can now have *good* sex by having safer sex, and *do* good and *be* good by not caving into "relapse." Such feelings arguably attained their most refined expression in the 1993 campaign of the San Francisco AIDS Foundation, which stated that "The Moral Majority [of gay men] is made up of . . . men who express their sexuality in a healthy way." Unfortunately, our attachment to such piety and respectability—given substance and credibility by genuine concerns about unprotected sex—has often led to the exploitation of shame and guilt to keep men "safe." This approach is particularly noteworthy, and particularly destructive, when directed at a group that has always been burdened with shame and guilt about sex because it was *gay* sex.

If unprotected sex is moral anathema, being a "late converter"—contracting HIV after you should have known better—is a cardinal sin. The obvious ethical issue of protecting *others* from HIV aside, unprotected sex that puts oneself at risk has been publicly characterized as a betrayal of one's social and ethical responsibilities as a gay man. Frank, a psychotherapy patient in his mid-forties and worker in AIDS education, voiced a popular public position in gay communities after speaking with a friend about his recent episode of unprotected sex:

> I find it unbelievable that people still have unsafe sex. It's stupid
> and irresponsible—*period.* For me it's an open and shut case. We
> have been educating people for eight years now, and the message
> should have gotten through: put on a rubber or get your dick out
> of my bed. The idea that people are still even thinking about unsafe
> sex is just irresponsible. And this responsibility goes way beyond
> responsibility to the *individual's* health. It is an issue of responsi-
> bility to the entire gay community. Personally and professionally,
> unsafe sex is something which is not a part of my life and will *not*
> be again.

What is so strident in Frank's words is his insistence that there is *nothing to talk about,* despite the issue of unprotected sex being prominent enough for Frank to have developed a position on it. Such positions exploit shame and guilt, and threaten ostracism, and in so doing ignore both social and psychological experience. Such an approach has never worked to make a homosexual man feel heterosexual—and only rarely worked to make him *behave* heterosexually—and it will not work to make a man who values unprotected sex, for whatever reasons, feel differently. Unfortunately, shame and guilt *have* worked in keeping gay men closeted and quiet about their homosexuality; and, finally, with the 1991 public disclosure of the "third wave" of the AIDS epidemic among gay men,[2] it became widely apparent that shame and guilt had been working on a large scale to keep gay men in the closet about unprotected sex. This silence, sustained against three or four years of unequivocal epidemiological evidence, was immensely destructive. Unprotected sex is *commonplace* among gay men, and unless it can be talked about rather than merely prohibited, there will be no opportunity for making relatively clear, conscious decisions about it. Unprotected sex will remain impulsive and covert among gay men in bed, but no less destructive for its public invisibility.

Will, a psychotherapy patient in his early thirties, came to a session filled with alarm about being sexually "completely out of control." He and his boyfriend had been "experimenting with unsafe sex," and Will said he felt "untethered by reason for the first time in my life." He seemed to want me to dictate limits on his sexual behavior for him, and I wondered if this was one reason he had brought the subject up.

> "Yeah, I think I'd like that," he said.
> "But what would that do?" I wondered.
> "Nothing, I suppose. I suppose it would mean nothing."
> "But it would certainly circumvent our looking at the feelings behind your very much wanting to have unprotected sex."
> "It certainly would," responded Will. "I'm very upset because I'm suddenly finding something I thought impossible incredibly easy. If you just told me not to do it, I wouldn't have to think about any of it."

He left the session exhausted and without feeling much resolution.

With two intervening sessions, Will suddenly brought up the subject again. He told me that since our conversation about unprotected sex, he and his boyfriend had not been doing it. I asked why.

> "I don't know. I just haven't felt like it. I think that just talking about it changed it. It was something about just saying it *out loud*. It made it real, and then, you know, these two contradictory worlds couldn't coexist: the dream world in which it seemed irresistible and a good idea—and the real world in which it seemed like a really bad idea. And there's something else I thought about—before we talked about it, unsafe sex seemed to symbolize something for me. Intimacy, or just letting myself go out of control. But when we talked about it, I thought, 'Well, I can find some other symbols for those things—I don't need this.' "
> "You said the 'real' world, in which unprotected sex seemed like a really bad idea. Is that how you feel? That unprotected sex is desirable in a 'dream' world and a really bad idea in the 'real' world?"
> "What else would I think about it?"
> "I'm wondering more about how you *feel* about it."
> "Hmm. I *feel* like it's important in a lot of ways. I still *feel* that. It's just that it doesn't make any sense."
> "But I doubt you're having sex of *any* kind because it makes a lot of sense."

"No," responded Will with obvious rapture on his face. "It has nothing to do with sense. The things that I want Mike to do to me definitely have nothing to do with sense."

"But they are very important to you."

"Very. I'm just going to have to think a lot about this. I can see that. Because—I've been avoiding saying it, but what I want to say is that it is very important to me for Mike to come inside of me. I *want* that very much. God, I don't know if this makes any sense to you, but sometimes that is incredibly important to me. But I'm going to have to sort this all out. We've been talking about getting PCRs [polymerase chain reactions to detect HIV DNA in the blood]. My doctor suggested that. It's all incredibly complicated and I'm going to have to think a lot about this."

The Internal Politics of Sex

The political situation *within* many gay communities—that surrounding the sometimes apparently conflicting interests of negative and positive men—has obscured complex feelings about sexuality in different ways than the politics concerned with external homophobia. Just as HIV-negative issues in general have been difficult to assert, the complexity of feeling that many uninfected men feel about protected and unprotected sex has not been a subject readily acknowledged as important to the gay agenda—despite its self-evident, critical importance to the course of the epidemic within gay communities. At the simplest level, the internal politics about sexuality are expressed in the sometimes explicit and sometimes only conjectured feelings of positive men that if *they* can deal with HIV, uninfected men can learn to deal with condoms.

Beneath this simple and not altogether unreasonable expectation lie an extraordinary number of much more complicated and largely unclarified feelings. Positive men have all the sexual feelings, needs, and conflicts that uninfected men have, but experience them with the additional complexity of also often feeling that they have contracted HIV as retribution for their sexuality, and that they are now also burdened with the responsibility for not transmitting it to other gay men who "deserve" it as much as they do. Though usually unconscious, such feelings are common, if not so common as the guilty feeling of many uninfected men that they, too, deserve HIV.

The resentment of many positive men and guilt of many negative men have colluded with the common, homophobically-rooted feeling that positive men should limit their sexuality—in the name of "responsibility," the name of health, or, at worst, in the name of decency and repentance—to curb the sexuality of uninfected men too. If the feeling is that positive men should limit their sexuality—although hardly the practice, especially in larger gay communities where positive men are not as isolated—then the uninfected, the fortunate ones in an underdog community, feel guilt about flaunting the "benefits" of their good fortune. If positive men are paying sexual penance for having HIV, negative men must pay sexual penance for *not* having it; and, of course, *all* gay men have some motivation to pay sexual penance simply for being gay. Negative men are thus paying penance not only to the external homophobe, but to positive gay men as well. This observation makes some sense of the familiar but unthinking *expectation* that two uninfected men limit themselves to protected sex, and the willingness of so many men—publicly at least—to honor the expectation. As members of minority communities exquisitely sensitive to inequity, gay men seem to have landed on the "democratic" idea that the only permissible sex is the kind that *anyone* could have with *anyone*.

Such internal "politics," as well as the external politics directed at homophobia, foreclose on most of the potential discussion of complex issues that demand clarification if gay communities are to survive in a biological or any worthwhile human sense. The politics have also created an astonishing double bind for the sexual and interpersonal lives of uninfected men and those who would help spare them the fate of contracting HIV. Uninfected men—in one specific and important sense unaffected by the epidemic—are being instructed to behave *as if* they were infected. The instruction is simply this: get tested, and if you are negative, go home and behave as if you were positive, by using condoms, every time for the rest of your life. This directive is supported by the possibility that the man *might* otherwise contract HIV; by the homophobic desire—external and internal—that gay men have "good" and approved sex; and by the complex interactions of guilt, resentment, and equity that exist between negative and positive men. The cost of assuaging these feelings is that uninfected men are being given little incentive to remain uninfected and are supported in the common unconscious feelings that contracting HIV is an inevitability. "If neither of us *really* has HIV, why are we using condoms?" a psychotherapy patient, himself a physician, asked me. "Is it because I might *really have* HIV? Or Steven might?"

Psychological Approaches to Education

My discussion of the politics of gay sex in the epidemic is not intended to discredit the frequent importance of protected sex. Rather, it is aimed at lifting the political burden from the realities and psychology of the issue. The facts about new seroconversions are alarming—and they are not new. By 1988, studies of gay men in urban centers were being conducted that would be replicated all over the U.S. About one-third of gay men would *self-report* the practice of unprotected anal sex,[3] a behavior in itself always heavily stigmatized and now also bearing the considerable onus of HIV transmission. We know from considerable psychological experience with the anonymous self-reporting of severely stigmatized behaviors, that they are underreported by as much as 30 to 50 percent, regardless of how information is collected. Thus the real figures about unprotected anal sex are certainly higher than reported, and are likely to be about 45 to 53 percent. Besides the potential for HIV transmission, there is something else very important about these figures. In terms of the percentages of gay men practicing anal sex (though probably not in terms of *numbers of occurrences*) they are astonishingly close to the self-report figures we had about the practice of anal intercourse—50 to 60 percent of gay men—before the epidemic. This leaves the possibility that our education may be of little or no value at all in motivating change in the behavior that all gay men, and their grandmothers, know to be the most dangerous for transmitting HIV.

Despite the overwhelming evidence that gay men are already HIV-smart, prevention efforts continue to be based on the model used in the earliest years of the epidemic. This is a public health, social marketing model that espouses information and education as the foundation of behavior change, and the establishment of "community standards of behavior"—sometimes "diffused" through selected community leaders —to motivate implementation of the new behaviors. Psychologically described, this has been an effort to provide people with sensible information and, for those not persuaded by good sense alone, to coerce behavior change through the power of social influence or compliance.

While the social marketing model probably has utility, its expression in AIDS education has been largely simplistic and—according to some experts in social marketing itself—incompetent. It is not a model traditionally brimming with psychological insight about sexuality, and, despite its relative successes with smoking, seat belts, and cholesterol, it has yet to prove its worth in changing *any* sexual behaviors. Furthermore, the complex psychological and psychosocial issues that have arisen as a result of the epidemic itself continue to be almost completely unmentioned and unexplored.

Typical among AIDS service agencies is the San Francisco AIDS Foundation, by far the largest agency in the Bay Area responsible for HIV prevention, and the third largest in the nation. Not a single staff mental health professional is involved in the conceptualization or validation testing of AIDS education. Rather, prevention programs are managed by non-mental-health personnel—those with backgrounds in public health and "media specialists."

In a June 1993 interagency meeting of San Francisco AIDS providers to address HIV-negative issues—not the least of which is HIV transmission—an educator from the San Francisco AIDS Foundation discussed a series of focus groups conducted by media analysts to evaluate a new campaign on oral sex. He reported that the "tag line" of the campaign was "Enjoy Oral Sex," but, to the consternation of the analysts, the men in the focus groups almost universally objected to the line, despite all "admitting" to the personal practice of unprotected oral sex. I commented that it seemed late in the epidemic to feel consternation over the discrepancies between public statement and private behavior, and that those educated to doubt the safety of oral sex but practicing it anyway would quite naturally experience anxiety about the idea of enjoying it and saying so publicly. The educator, little interested in this observation, replied that they had in any case solved the problem by changing the tag line to "Enjoy Sex" and this less specific statement was much more acceptable to the group. I responded they had not solved the problem of how these men felt, but skirted it. His reply was that acceptance of the new tag line increased readership of the campaign, and in increasing "positive response, we get more bang for the buck. *That* is what AIDS education is all about."

"Do you ever use psychological opinion when doing such campaign analysis?" I wondered.

"For what?" he asked.

"To help clarify people's feelings about sex and death."

"That is *not* what we're talking about. You seem to want us to do psychotherapy from billboards. We're doing *education*."

I relate this story, not because I think this man or the San Francisco AIDS Foundation uniquely deficient, but rather because they are typical of how we have addressed these issues in the United States.[4] A 1992 survey of the educational materials of the Gay Men's Health Crisis, the nation's largest AIDS service agency, reveals approaches that are similarly literal in their conceptualization of the issues leading to unprotected sex. A 1991 publication purports that "Safer Sex is Just Common Sense," and we are told to memorize the three important facts about HIV: "AIDS is preventable, AIDS is not easy to get, and a few simple precautions will keep you protected."[5] Clearly, if safer sex were only a matter of common sense, and involved only a few simple precautions, seroconversions would not be as prevalent as they are. It is more or less true that the execution of safer sex *techniques* is simple; but the conscious and unconscious feelings and thoughts that motivate one to employ safer techniques—or not to employ them—are a complex issue that is not only ignored but *denied* by such simple prescriptions. That "safer sex is just common sense," implies that anyone who does not practice it is simply a fool. Even such a subtle and coercive use of shame colludes with the individual's own homophobia, doubt, and anxiety, and maintains the repression of feelings that are necessarily and appropriately associated with issues of sex and death.

Public education is *not* a forum for conducting psychological treatment. But AIDS education must incorporate psychological understandings into its conceptualization of the problem if it is to become effective with a problem as complex as a lifelong epidemic. Education must eschew an exclusive belief in relatively simplistic schemes of behavioral change that persist in ignoring the role of feelings in human sexuality—sexuality that now also holds fatal potential. The idea that psychology has no role in *explicating* the educational demands of the epidemic makes as little sense as the idea that X rays have no role in the diagnosis of gallstones because the treatment will ultimately be surgical. This misperception is in part an expression of disciplinary territorialism; but in this epidemic among gay men, it is also because many in educational work are having feelings we are afraid to examine in ourselves: homophobic feelings, feelings about death and loss, and feelings about the old and new dangers of intimacy. We are thus understandably reluctant to examine them in others or to acknowledge their relevance to our work. AIDS education is significantly tied to psychological issues, because human life is filled with them. No denial of this fact will eliminate the need to acknowledge complex, not easily addressed feelings when the issues are intimacy, sex, and death. When, as educators, we understand this, we will not continue to pretend or to teach that protected sex is a matter of "common sense" and that anyone not practicing it is a fool or member of a "clinical" population.

In the sphere of clinical psychology, when possibly dangerous unprotected sexual activity—that between serodiscordant partners or partners of unknown serostatus—is known to be occurring, we have an opportunity to help clarify the meaning and possible consequences of the behavior. Unprotected sex is one obvious way of not remaining a survivor of the epidemic. A psychological description of unprotected sex will reveal that while its potential lethality is sometimes a deterrent, it is sometimes also a significant, often unconscious, motivation to practice it. In other words, while our education and public policy continue to assume that unprotected sex is practiced despite its dangers, some men engage in it for precisely that reason. Other self-destructive behaviors, such as extreme substance abuse, are also common among survivors of the AIDS epidemic, and they too should be tacitly considered part of the following discussion.

From a psychological perspective, when educated gay men engage in unprotected anal intercourse with serodiscordant or sero-unknown partners, we must assume that the behavior has *meaning* that should be understood. When protected sex would be appropriate, ambivalence about it or the failure to practice it suggests *in part* that a man is experiencing ambivalence about surviving the epidemic and his identity as HIV-negative. The knowing exposure of oneself to HIV suggests *in part* the desire, usually ambivalent and unconscious, not to survive.

Ordinary Sex and Its Meanings

While it is important that we recognize these meanings, they may constitute only part of the meaning for many men. Our homophobia, and our narrow, intense focus on reducing HIV transmission has made it difficult to recognize the most obvious thing about "unsafe" sex: it is simply ordinary human sex. It is often motivated by what would be, in nonepidemic times, positive human values.[6] That such ordinary, well-motivated, human behaviors may now so easily transmit a deadly, untreatable virus—in the age of medical science and proliferating antimicrobials—is an important source of the real psychological complexity of our situation. The very words now used to describe sex—*safe, unsafe,* and *relapse*—profoundly prejudice our thinking, and banish to the netherlands the entire subject of the complex meanings of ordinary human sex. While the term *unsafe*—meaning *unprotected*—is *often* also accurate, its very absoluteness, its lack of regard to context and circumstance, raises unconscious conflict and doubt. It categorically dismisses an entire class of important behaviors because they are dangerous. In truth, unprotected sex is not unsafe in the act itself, but becomes unsafe in the presence of HIV in one of two serodiscordant partners.

Our primary educational instruction, as categorical as the idea of unsafe sex itself, has told gay men to "use a condom every time," and "If you don't like condoms, don't fuck." The recommendation is based in a desire to curb HIV transmission and the belief that serostatus cannot be adequately determined by the average gay man—itself a problematic and sometimes doubtful proposition. But the indiscriminateness of the recommendation also frequently expresses homophobic disgust for the idea, or a homophobic dismissal of its importance, as if it had no comparability whatsoever to the court's favorite prince, heterosexual vaginal sex. But what *is* so important about having a penis in your rectum—or putting yours in someone else's—that millions of gay men continue to do it even at the risk of death?

Anal sex has interpersonal and psychological *meaning* for many gay men—in other words, for many men it is comparable to vaginal sex between heterosexuals or lesbians. At the most superficial—and homophobic—level, anal intercourse may seem nothing more than a necessity for men having sex with men, for excepting the mouth, the anus is the only (likely) sexually receptive orifice of the male body. But the significance of anal intercourse among men has real significance aside from its anatomical convenience, and that significance is partly suggested in both the work of Freud, in his connection of paranoia to homosexual anxiety, and the work of Erikson, who describes paranoia as being about "protecting the rear."

Anal penetration, which for resolutely heterosexual men could only be the outcome of rape, is one of the most sensitive and inflammatory topics associated with homosexuality. Though the term *sodomy* properly refers to any of the "unnatural" sexual acts, including bestiality, it has come to mean anal intercourse in popular parlance. It is anal intercourse that the heterosexual male generally thinks of when he thinks about homosexual sex at all, and it is a possibility that arouses nearly universal feelings of fear, anger, shame, humiliation, and degradation in heterosexual men. Many gay men as well have similar feelings about receptive anal intercourse, and, contrary to popular ideas, there are many gay men who have never had—especially receptive—anal intercourse and have no intention of ever doing so. The issue is so significant among gay men that most, whether consciously or not, have self-identifications and ideas about others that create one of the most pervasive and powerful divisions in gay communities—that between "tops" (insertive partners) and "bottoms" (anal receptive partners).

The distinctions between tops and bottoms is not simply about sexual behaviors, but also important psychological issues. The man who is a receptive anal partner explores aspects of human experience that have largely been reserved—perhaps *relegated* is more accurate—to women. Women have been expected to be, sexually and otherwise, all that men are *not* supposed to be: passive, receptive, vulnerable, compliant, trusting, and giving. In gay male sex such psychological experience may be nurtured, if only privately and perhaps unconsciously, in the receptive partner, who is often less physically active, receives the semen of his partner, is vulnerable by virtue of being entered from behind, is likely to demonstrate compliance with his partner's wishes, and must trust that he will not be hurt or abused. These are all reasons—almost completely ignored by education—that it is often difficult for the receptive partner to be assertive about the use of condoms. Assertiveness may be contrary to the whole emotional timbre of the experience.

While feelings of vulnerability and trust during the sexual act is expected routinely of women (including women engaging in anal intercourse), they are feelings that arouse anxiety and dread in most men, including many gay men. Within gay communities we see a range of acceptance of such feelings by men. The least acceptance is expressed by men who are "exclusive tops," and from there the differences are graded in the ways that anal intercourse is accomplished. As with heterosexual sex, the receptive partner may sit on top of the insertive partner who is lying on his back. This is perhaps the least "vulnerable" form of receptive sex, because the receptive partner is literally "on top," giving him much more physical control than is possible in any other position. The insertive partner, often physically passive during such sex, becomes the one "being fucked."

Other positions arouse varying degrees of vulnerability in the receptive partner, each with emotional significance for many men: lying on the back with legs in the air, standing, kneeling, or, at the most vulnerable end of the spectrum, lying on the stomach. This last renders a man relatively compliant and physically passive during sex, and is likely to elicit the strongest feelings of vulnerability and trust—or distrust—of the insertive partner. It is, not coincidentally, the gay equivalent of the much male-favored "missionary" position in heterosexual sex. In both cases the "top" has maximal control over the act, including the important issue of depth of penetration.

Why the vulnerability experienced in receptive sex is so repugnant to most heterosexual men—who routinely expect women to engage in it—is essentially the question women have started to ask in pursuit of their liberation from male domination. The answer with regard to heterosexual men is much the same as with homosexual men: they fear the feelings. These include feelings of vulnerability, helplessness, and trust in another. It is an extraordinary, if familiar, fact that women have come to so routinely allow such feelings and men to so routinely abhor them. The sexual act and how it is conducted reflect our interpersonal, social, and psychological roles, and traditional heterosexual sex expresses the difference between the traditional acculturation of boys and girls in most Western societies. Boys are taught to *act out* their feelings in the world competitively, directively, aggressively, and often violently; girls are taught to internalize their feelings and live quietly, contemplatively, and receptively. Men give and women receive, men are external and women internal, men *fuck* and women *get* fucked.

What is most distressing about this dichotomy is the contempt so many cultures—perhaps particularly the American—feel for the "feminine" position and, by implication, for homosexuality. Men who routinely penetrate women vaginally (or anally) and ejaculate within them so often harbor a deprecatory sense of precisely the feminine position they rely upon to fulfill their sexuality: women are weak, helpless, soiled receptacles of men's externalized semen. For a man to experience the feminine position psychologically or enact it sexually arouses contempt in other men, often in women, and, often, profound shame in the homosexual man himself. Tom, a psychotherapy patient in his early twenties, had, through developmental good fortune, circumvented such shame.

"I have never had anyone come inside of me, because by the time I got into sex—well, it was all over, it was all just safe sex. I've thought a lot about it with Bobby, because someday I'd like to make love with him, and have him come in me—you know, like a prize, like something to take home with me. Sunday morning we went to breakfast, and I fantasized that he had come in me the night before. And I was just sitting there, like nothing was going on, but I knew there was still this part of him inside of me from the night before. I felt very close to him because of that, and the idea just made me feel very warm and special and close to him. I felt very privileged, I'd say. I felt like I could feel it inside of me. I don't even know. Can you *feel* it when someone's cum is inside of you?

"I think it's more important to understand your fantasy about what it would be like than for me to just try to answer the question," I responded.

"Well, it's my idea that you could feel it—like a warm lump that was part of Bobby, that he had left behind for me. I bet that's what women have too, when men come in them. I don't know if this is realistic or not, but that's what I think. I think women would know this."

"And women have babies inside too, and that's something the man leaves behind in a manner of speaking," I said. Tom thought about this for a moment and continued.

"So I guess having someone's cum inside of you is as close as we get to being pregnant. That's sort of a joke, you know. You say to a man you really love, "I want to have your baby." But this is really what we're talking about now, the joke is really about this feeling. *Wow!* I never thought of that, but it's the same thing. At breakfast it was like I was very proud to be carrying around Bobby's baby, and it was that pride that made me feel like I was almost gloating."

Much of the cruel retaliation reported against homosexual men is against precisely the kinds of human and humane feelings Tom expresses. In sixteenth- and seventeenth-century Europe, homosexual men were often put to death by torture: red-hot fire pokers were inserted in their rectums until, one can only imagine, they died of shock or bled to death. In a more recent example, described by a colleague about a high school friend in Texas during the 1950s, a young homosexual man was anally raped by four classmates and left bound in his garage with a live soldering iron inserted in his rectum. Such torture is an attempt by men to literally obliterate in others what they most fear in themselves, which is receptivity, understood concretely in the form of the receptive orifice. The most well-adjusted homosexual man cannot help but feel terror at the recounting of such violence, for it colludes with his own shame, and with his feelings that perhaps he should, after all, be more careful about "covering his rear," for trust and openness are not always reciprocated.

The homosexual experience, when it is not too limited or damaged by the immense developmental pressures working against it, offers the possibility of a richness of human experience that the rigidly heterosexual man is denied. This was the meaning of a 36-year-old psychotherapy patient, Barry, when he said to me after his first experience with receptive anal intercourse:

> I know that I've always had a lot of feelings about it [anal intercourse as the receptive partner]—one way or the other. When I was coming out, it was the thing I was most afraid of, and I didn't know why. It just seemed very *dangerous*. But what was dangerous, I realize, was my feeling that I really wanted to trust someone, and the feeling that I couldn't. I am so knocked out by how powerful it [his recent experience] was. It is the first time in my life that I have felt like a person, that I accept myself and my feelings, that I feel *real*—and *whole*. In some strange way, all the fear I've had in my life was about *this*. It was about getting fucked! But it was all transformed into other things—fear about running out of money, and especially fear of other people. I don't know what. But I feel so unafraid now, because I feel too whole within myself to fear things the way I used to. It's as if I finally just looked the whole thing in the face. I feel very—*authentic*. I trust myself now, is what I guess I'm saying.

It is, of course, not only anal sex that carries such profound human meanings—it is all the sucking, rubbing, licking, and pumping that we do lying together naked. But our society's erotophobic prescriptions against *all* of this—its denial of the meaning and importance of sex and physical intimacy, and especially its prescriptions against any of this happening in unapproved forms—spawns deep and troubling doubt in the minds of gay men whose experience tells them otherwise. The AIDS epidemic seems almost irresistibly to support the doubt, and too many gay men are now feeling that gay sex, itself, is dangerous. A young psychotherapy patient, first dealing with his homosexuality in the age of AIDS, told me:

> "I was eleven when I first heard about AIDS, and it terrified me and I knew that I could never be gay. I just couldn't do that to my-

self or my family. When I was sixteen, I decided I had to come out, but that I wouldn't have any sex. I told my mom I was gay, and I said to her, 'But don't worry because I'm never going to have sex. You don't have to worry about that.' That was the only way I could see that it would be safe to be gay.

"And was it just AIDS that made you want to tell her you wouldn't have sex?"

"Well, it was partly that. But it was also because I thought that would just make the whole thing more acceptable to her. You know, she wouldn't have to imagine her son with someone else's dick in his mouth—much less up his butt. And I thought if she could not think about that, it would go over with her a lot better."

Categorical advice about protected sex, and its often destructive consequences, is moored in the assumption that people do not have the judgment or the information to behave noncategorically. While that is sometimes true, we must carefully examine the almost universal assumption among educators that if we give men "too much information"—which is to say, something like *the whole truth* to the best of our knowledge—they will abuse it, exercise faulty judgment, or otherwise come up with unintended results. "Directive education is necessary because men need to be told *what to do,*" an educator at the San Francisco AIDS Foundation told me. The most sacrosanct expression of this approach is seen in the absolute prohibition against saying that it is *sometimes* acceptable to have anal sex without a condom, which is when no one really has HIV. We all know—or ought to know—this is true. Yet the nearly universal response to this assertion is that such an "admission" would encourage men to do dangerous things. Part of the answer to this objection is obvious. Some men *are* making such obvious decisions within like-antibody relationships; and, unfortunately, others *are* doing dangerous things. One of the reasons for the dangerous behaviors is our prohibition against discussing obvious possibilities. Our prohibition does not allow men to have the information or develop the judgment to discern when a particular desired behavior is likely to transmit HIV and when it is not. Our practice of simply instructing men in behaviors—"a condom every time"—actively obstructs the development of a capacity for informed judgment and perpetuates society's homophobic desire to simply dictate behaviors to gay men. People thus disempowered by directive instruction that contradicts their instincts—and often the truth—behave secretly, unthinkingly, and often self-destructively. We cannot use *these* results to predict the behavior of an informed, educated, and respected population.

It is my experience that unprotected sex certainly occurs in recreational or anonymous sexual encounters, but it is most often discussed by psychotherapy patients as a part of ongoing relationships.

> Recent research studies have found relationship status to be significant: men in mutually monogamous relationships had unprotected anal intercourse more frequently than men in any other relationship category, including nonmonogamous relationships and men outside a primary relationship. In general, men in any kind of relationship were more likely to have engaged in unsafe sexual behavior than men who were not.[7]

Furthermore, there appear to be differences in the practice of unprotected sex according to serostatus. In general, uninfected men seem most likely to practice unprotected sex within relationships—"negotiated safety," in the parlance of Australian psychologist Ron Gold—and protected sex outside of them.[8] HIV-positive men, as a group, appear to conform more to the converse. In either case, the common idea that HIV is transmitted primarily through recreational or anonymous sex is partly the product of homophobic public assumptions. Some AIDS educators appear to acknowledge this, as in the San Francisco AIDS Foundation campaigns "Rubbers are for lovers" and "A man protects the one he loves." But on the whole, our education seems to portray the majority of sex occurring in sex clubs or public toilets, and there are remarkably few campaign "visuals" that appear to portray men in relationships—for example, having sex in a domestic setting, which is where a lot of it really takes place. This practice not only confirms homophobic assumptions about gay sex and "promiscuity," but implies that the human meanings of gay sex are minimal or dispensable.

Within gay male relationships the exchange of semen, anally or orally, is often experienced as an important expression of intimacy, just as it is vaginally, anally, or orally within heterosexual relationships. Within gay male relationships, this exchange often holds an especially important position, for it not only leaves behind tangible evidence of powerful intimacy, it stands in defiance of prohibitions against homosexuality: we put our semen where we want to. Our promotion of protected sex—which by definition cannot include semen exchange—has caused us to deny its human importance and the importance of many other positive aspects of the "exchange of body fluids."

It is not only homophobia but our limited capacity to talk about human emotional life in general that has allowed important feelings like Tom's to become obscured and ignored in our response to the epidemic. Clearly, even many of those who *are* able to think about the meanings of vaginal sex have not been able to translate that understanding to gay sex. The promotion of condoms as an alternative to abstention from vaginal sex would have been seen immediately as nothing more than a marginally acceptable, *short-term* solution to the problem of HIV transmission. This would have been the case because condoms are a substantial intrusion on intimacy for many men, and vaginal sex is recognized—if sometimes only reluctantly by conservative forces—as an essential part of human life. Aside from the irresponsibility of men, who do not risk pregnancy, why have we spent billions of dollars researching alternative methods of contraception, all of which prove to be more expensive and less effective than condoms? *Had* the epidemic first occurred among heterosexuals, it seems very likely that unprotected vaginal sex would have come to be considered a calculated risk necessary to live ordinary human life as we expect to lead it, very much like driving an automobile. Bruce, a psychotherapy patient, comments on his experience of condoms. His words express the feelings of many gay, as well as heterosexual, men:

> When I was a kid, my uncle—who was elected by my parents to do the sex education—told me that using a condom was like taking a shower with your raincoat on. That's my experience with them precisely. Of course, my uncle was talking about straight sex, and his solution was that the woman should take care of the contraception. But I do find condoms a complete breach of intimacy, and if they remind me of anything, it's sticking a dildo up someone's ass. You're not in there, your dick is there—with its raincoat on. In sex, touch is the most important thing to me, and that means skin. That's how I connect to another person. I find this whether I'm getting fucked or doing the fucking. It's almost the same thing to me: no skin, no connection. It just changes the whole experience.

Certainly many gay men, particularly when engaged in casual sex, have adapted to non-anal sex or the use of condoms. This is because some men are insensitive to the differences; because some men find anal sex with condoms more "hygienic," as a physician psychotherapy patient explained it to me; because some sex is really just about recreation and the intrusion of the condom is thus less significant; and because internalized homophobia and guilt conspire to make many gay men feel that if they are going to have prohibited sex, the least they can do is be good by conducting it in socially approved ways. The homophobia and guilt are only exacerbated by education that not only makes an appeal for the minimal intrusion of the condom, but actually touts its positive appeal. A supervisor of "safe sex workshops" at San Francisco's AIDS Health Project reported to me in 1990 that she felt they had accomplished widespread acceptance of condoms by promoting their erotic potential. "In fact," she continued, "we find that most men who take our workshops end up preferring sex *with* condoms to sex without them." David, a psychotherapy patient in his thirties, speaks from a different perspective.

> I was one of those people who said very early on that if oral sex transmitted HIV, then the guys from San Francisco General [Hospital] could come and haul me away right now. Oral sex was all I had left, and so far as I'm concerned, it's not enough. Fucking meant a lot to me, and it's been almost impossible since the epidemic started. I usually can't stay hard with a condom, and I know a lot of guys like that. The whole thing is incredibly frustrating and disappointing. I can't stand the things. I'm *really* angry about all this talk we get about how condoms aren't so bad. I've never met anyone who thought that. They've been a disaster for me, and I know I'm not the only one. The only thing I can say for them is, *they're better than being dead.* And that's not much to say for something that used to be so important in my relationships. That's the *booby* prize.

David's feelings are certainly stronger than those of many gay men. His physical difficulties with condoms, however, are common, and are partly the product of education's neglect of the details of condom selection. Political and economic constraints, as well as the erotophobic and homophobic dismissal of the importance of the tactile experience in anal intercourse, have kept most educators from discussing condoms in anything but the most generic way. In fact, there are tremendous differences among brands and types of condoms that affect the sexual experience. Form, size, thickness, hysteresis (a measure of the "springiness" of the latex), odor, color, and packaging may all contribute idiosyncratically to satisfaction with a given product. While men are free to experiment on their own, if we cared about the issue, we would be discussing it in detail and teaching men how to make these discriminations.[9]

The easy dismissal that many readers are likely to feel about David's anger and disappointment discounts not only the significant physical problems many men experience with condoms, but the psychological ones as well. The condom has been strutted as a focal symbol in many gay communities: a symbol of an *age* in gay life, of hope, of survival, of possibilities, and of gay men being good, being accepted, and behaving responsibly. This once unmentionable object is now seen on T-shirts, earrings, and keyrings. But in the bedroom itself, the condom has other meanings. It introduces disturbing, often unconscious associations every time it appears in lovemaking: associations of pleasure and violence, sex and punishment, intimacy and injury, love and killing—or being killed. Lovemaking done, it lies filled with lethal fluid, a concrete reminder of entangled feelings about homosexuality, sin, punishment, suffering, and death.

At the center of the internal homophobia of gay men is a kernel of hopelessness invariably first experienced by the gay adolescent: my life will be impossible because of *what* I am. The epidemic so often feels as if it has brought that hopeless future to adult fruition. Gay sex will be punished, and AIDS is the punishment. Gay men have made their beds and now must lie in them. In other words, AIDS has provided new unconscious motivations—as if more were needed in these communities—for gay men and their AIDS educators to further introject the projected self-hatred of homophobes. For communities finally recovering from centuries of stigmatization for their sexual practices to now have many of those practices actually become "unsafe"—potentially lethal—has created treacherous psychological waters for gay men. As adolescents caught in confusing webs of sexual drive, hopelessness, and societal prohibition, many men found sex itself the only completely convincing, natural, and conflict-free aspect of being gay. The gay man's first homosexual experience is often powerful enough to make his course in life seem a destiny—despite the overwhelming prohibition. But for many, sex has now become as problematic and conflict-ridden as the social complications of being gay.

Despite the prohibitions and external and internal politics that have enshrouded ordinary, unprotected sex, and complex feelings about it, many men are privately making choices between their experience of sexual and emotional needs on the one hand and biological survival on the other. An uninfected psychotherapy patient, Will, told me the story of meeting another man while on a week's vacation. Vacationing alone, Will met Kevin in a bar, and the two spent several days together, including hours of discussion about their lives, families, work, and the epidemic. Knowing that Will was negative, Kevin finally hesitatingly revealed that he was positive and was very lonely living in a gay community that largely shunned people with HIV. A few days later, Kevin invited Will to his home for dinner, and after "the worst spaghetti I've ever eaten," the two began making love on the living room floor.

> "After we'd been on the floor for a couple of hours, I rolled Kevin over on his side—I mean, we didn't have any condoms—and I went into him. He was obviously very pleased, but he was startled too, and he said, 'Why are you doing this?' And I said to him, 'Because it's important.'"
>
> "And why, reflecting now, do you think you did this despite your appreciation of the risks," I asked.
>
> "Because it was important." Will sat quietly for a moment. "It was really a remarkable time. Though I haven't seen him for a year now, I think about him and his life a lot. He is an amazing person, and it was very important."

Our denial of such feelings—and incidents—cannot help clarify the issues. While there is no doubt about the statistical dangers of unprotected sex today, such sex often includes the desire to be intimate and to love another human being in ways that feel meaningful and powerful. These issues and the nature of the choices being made must be made more conscious and clear. Is it true, a man like Will must ask himself, that this expression of intimacy, love, and connection is as important or more important than survival itself? For a man whose experience is that condoms are not satisfactory, or that mutual masturbation and oral sex are not good substitutes for anal intercourse, the social and political pressures to accept these substitutes merely forecloses on a real effort to think and talk about the issues and make decisions consciously and clearly. Feelings are not resolved or dissipated by denial or repression. For the man forced to pretend that his real feelings do not exist, the alternative is often acting out those feelings in unconscious, impulsive, and therefore dangerous ways. This is precisely what happens when a man suppresses and represses homosexual feelings in an effort to comply with what he has been told he ought to feel. Every homosexual man has at one time been forced to pretend to others, as well as to himself, that his homosexual feelings did not exist. Can we now expect gay men to pretend that the way their homosexuality is physically expressed, something so deeply rooted in personal experience, has changed, or that successfully changing it will be done with a simple decision and no emotional consequences? Robert, an uninfected psychotherapy patient in his middle thirties, spoke about his relationship with Mark, an HIV-positive lover of three years.

> "The subject of unsafe sex, I know, is not something you talk about with anyone," Robert told me one day. "I mean, I've had the worst reactions, and mostly I don't talk about what Mark and I do."
>
> "You have alluded to having unprotected sex with Mark before. But you seem to be asking right now for permission to talk about it."
>
> "Well, I know that you don't approve of it."
>
> "Why do you say that?" I wondered.
>
> "Well, you couldn't. You've never told me what to do. But you wouldn't. You're a psychologist, among other things."
>
> "Well, these other things and my attitudes aside, *you* seem reluctant to talk about your sex with Mark. Maybe we should look at your reluctance to talk to me about this."
>
> "Well, Mark and I mostly have safe sex and sometimes we don't. I am more into fucking without condoms than he is—he is trying to protect me mostly—and when we do it, it is so powerful and important for us."
>
> "And you believe I disapprove of this?"
>
> "Oh, I'm sure you do."
>
> "But tell me why you're sure."
>
> "Because it's not good for me—not good for my health."
>
> "You seem to be implying a distinction between what's good for you and what's good for your health. When you're doing it, are you cognizant of the possible consequences—in terms of your health?"
>
> "Of course," Robert responded with irritation. "I think about it before, and sometimes during, and after. But, you know, *Mark* is not going to kill me, and I'm not going to kill myself. If I get it, AIDS is going to kill me, and I have no expectations of how long anyone is going to live anymore anyway. I used to wake up in the

middle of the night worrying about it, and I had the dream about the gargoyles over and over [Robert had dreamed that he walked up roads, and gargoyles were lined up along the shoulders. 'They stared at me, but they never blocked my way,' he told me]. But most people have no idea what it's like to be gay now, and my answer to them is that if I lived my life now worrying about how long Mark or I were going to live, I would just go crazy, because almost no one I know is going to live very long by all odds."

"But you are disturbed by others' lack of support," I said.

"But I *love* Mark. I already felt that way two months after I met him. That seems more important to me."

"More important than what?" I asked.

"Than worrying about how long I will be able to love him before he's dead— or before I'm dead, for that matter. I don't know how long I'll be around either. If there were another way, if we could be in another life, I wouldn't want to go through this. I have to. I won't be the kind of person who would run away from this."

"What is the connection," I wondered, "between loving him and contracting HIV from him?"

"Well, if you mean do I have to get AIDS from him to show him I love him, I know the answer is *no*. But it's different—and that is that the way we express our love to each other, I might get it from him. I do think it's important for us to express our love to each other in certain ways, but I think that's different."

"From what?"

"From getting AIDS *because* I love him. I know you're not supposed to get AIDS from people because you love them. Everyone has told me that. They have that on the Muni signs. I love him, and I may also get his HIV, and that is a different thing. I'm not trying to prove to him I love him, because I know he knows that. Our sex is incredibly intense, and it's part of what makes our relationship so important. Sex for me is about—I'm talking about sex with someone I love—is about holding back nothing, about being completely into your feelings and into the other person and his feelings. We can do that. I can't imagine what it would be like without him."

"Though at some point that may happen."

"Oh, it will probably happen. But right now is where I exist, and I don't have to imagine it right now because we've got it."

"Can you imagine a relationship after Mark?"

"After he's dead?"

"After he's dead or after your feelings about each other change, if that should happen," I clarified.

"I could imagine that, I guess. I was in love once before Mark [with Jerry, a previous lover who had died of AIDS about five years before this session]. What I didn't say because I was embarrassed was—I'm talking about what our sex means again—is that being inside of him, or his being inside of me, is the most wonderful thing I can imagine. Jerry taught me what that meant, and it was the most wonderful discovery to me that you could have someone else inside of you and that could mean so much. At the time, of course, I thought this was an original discovery, like I'd discovered The New World. But it has never left me, how wonderful a thing that is. Does this make sense to you?"

"If you're asking me about the importance of sex, the answer is *yes*. But I have the sense that you're asking me about the total decision about Mark, and about having unprotected sex with him, and I have to point out again that I think you ask this because of your own doubts—that you seem to want my support to dispel those doubts."

Robert thought about my statement for a moment.

"I know you don't have the answer. I don't—nobody does. I have doubts, but I also know that I've spent too much of my life in the past and the future and in something that was going on somewhere else in the present. I don't want to live that way anymore. I don't see the sense in it."

"It is surely obvious, but I should say it: You are making a choice between your relationship to Mark—I should say, expressing your relationship in certain ways—and survival—in all probability."

"Yes, of course, I know that," Robert responded with irritation again, and again he was silent for several moments.

"Are you angry with me for saying that?" I asked him.

"I feel an obligation to stick around for other people, not for myself—except for Mark. My mother is hysterical with the idea that Mark is positive, and of course I wouldn't think of telling her about what kind of sex we have. But I spent my first two years here [in therapy] figuring out how I'd spent my first 33 years living for other people—and especially for my mother and sister. I won't do that anymore."

"Do you think I suggested that you do that?"

"No, I felt that. People are saying that to me all the time, 'Oh I hope you won't get sick because we don't know what we'd do without you.' I love my friends, and they have been very good friends to me, especially when Jerry was sick, but they can't come over in the middle of the night and get in bed with me when I feel like shit, and I'm wondering what we're doing here—what I'm doing here. My commitment to Mark comes from *my heart* and most of the rest of this comes from my guilt. I won't live that out anymore."

"Won't live what out?"

"My guilt. *My guilt.* And I meant I won't *live* that out, like, I won't survive because my mother needs that. I will live in my heart, not my guilt. It is other people who want me to survive, and it's only part of me. The other part wants to live in my heart."

"Society," I observed, "places a lot of value on survival. If everyone lived in their heart, there's a whole lot that wouldn't get done."

"Like what?" Robert asked.

"Like, at the most mundane end of things, picking up the garbage and delivering letters. But this isn't the whole story, or I think it isn't. Because some people, within themselves—I don't know if within their hearts—but within themselves, very much want to survive."

"Well, I have no objection to that if that's what someone wants. People are welcome to live as long as they want so far as I'm concerned." Robert sat quietly for several minutes, and then suddenly started up again, practically shouting.

"*Be Here for the Cure!* [an educational campaign of the San Francisco AIDS Foundation]. Now what the fuck does that mean? That they won't invite me to their party if I die too soon? That they won't invite Mark to the party if he doesn't take all the pills and shit they feed him? What do they know about a cure? *What* cure? I really resent that. That's not an invitation, it's a threat. Jerry's death and Mark—they have taught me so much that I sometimes look at what people live for and I think it's pathetic. Are we supposed to hide under the bed while we wait for the cure party? What they should have said, what I would have said is, "Get out from under the bed and *be here for life.*" And that means *right now,* because that's when it happens. All of the fear within me, the fear which takes me out of my heart, I will just pick it out piece by piece until it's gone. I can't go back on this. I won't. I lived in fear with Jerry, I lived in fear of getting it from him, in fear of dying, in fear of his dying, in fear of everything. I won't do it again. I will live in my heart as much as I can. And when I can't, when I'm too afraid—well, that will be too bad for me."

Some Problematic Reasons People Have Unprotected Sex

At least one poet [Traherne] thanked the Lord for giving him
desire, in a general sense of course. For a time
one of my brothers slept eighteen hours a day, having
nothing to rise for. Leonardo thought the world would end
by a gradual diminution of desire, in, obviously,
the narrower sense. . . .
The farther our desire extends, the more we know of
the void.
—*Keith Waldrop, from* Windmill [10]

Why people are motivated to unprotected sex that may expose them to HIV is a complex question. Educators and others frustrated with continuing unprotected sex between gay men often refer to a "pathological fringe" that is unreachable by education. The idea of *psychological* pathology should be clarified, because it is an idea borrowed from medicine, in which the term describes an anatomic or functional manifestation of a disease process. Some psychological problems are the result of organic (physiologically based) problems that are manifested in behavior. A brain tumor resulting in character changes or a mood disorder is an example, and in such a case the idea of *psychopathology* has validity in the ordinary, medical sense of the term. But depression in response to a life event is not "pathological" in the same sense that tumor growth is pathological in cancer—even though depression is considered psychopathology.

An important reason to draw a distinction between the two very different uses of the term *pathology* is that medical pathology is universal in the human species, while "pathology" in a psychological sense is culturally relative. Tumor growth in the brain is pathological in all cultures, while suicidal feelings, as an example, are not. In Native American and many Asian cultures, suicide is an option in life that people exercise routinely, and, within culturally specified circumstances, it is not pathological at all. Even in American culture, in times of war or in the case of terminal illness, suicidal impulses are widely accepted. Thus the idea of psychopathology is more about an individual's deviation from cultural and social expectations than about an intrinsic property of a mental state.

A recognition of the cultural relativity of psychopathology is important to the examination of psychological motivations to engage in unprotected sex, because these motivations—conscious and unconscious—conflict with cultural values about survival. Some of the motivation to survive is instinctual, rather than cultural. In Darwinian theory of natural selection, those members of a species with the strongest instinctual or inborn survival *behaviors* are most likely to survive and reproduce. Survival is thus simply the consequence of behaviors that *happen to result* in survival, and this is very different from the popularized version of Darwin's hypothesis that we have survival instinct *in order* to survive.

The abstract mental experience that takes place in the cerebral cortex of humans is complex, and it often suppresses or supplants more purely instinctual behavior and feelings. Thus we engage in much behavior, including life-threatening and life-promoting behaviors, that are *not* instinctually based, but are developed through cortically mediated acculturation. What we often describe as the "instinct to survive" is partly a product of culture, not instinct, and the cultural relativity of survival-motivation demonstrates this. All human cultures seem to define some acceptable life-threatening behaviors; and all seem to define *un*acceptable life-threatening behavior.

If biological survival is considered the essential purpose of human life, then motivations to engage in unprotected sex—which assuredly offers the possibility of shortened life—will be understood as pathological. If the possibility of other essential values and purposes are accepted, values that are not about longevity but about the content or quality of life, then unprotected sex might not be considered pathological. In a personal way, this is partly the point that Will and Robert make in the preceding quotations. The question about such "decisions" is whether or not they are really decisions, or are substantially the expression of unconscious or confused feelings.

THE DESIRE NOT TO SURVIVE

He can never manage to distinguish death's three weapons: a song, a dance, and whatever is absolutely pointless.—Keith Waldrop, from Potential Random.[11]

Because AIDS is such an available and psychologically meaningful way for a gay man to not survive, it is surprising how difficult it has been for us to acknowledge that some men engage in unprotected sex for precisely that purpose. There are many psychologically intelligible reasons men might not wish to survive the AIDS epidemic. They include depression, anxiety, and guilt, including guilt about surviving; lives emptied by loss, isolation, and loneliness; the loss of social affiliation and psychological identity; and anticipation of a future that holds more of the same.

Despite the incredible physical and psychological toll of the epidemic, many doubt that such problems could be sufficient for a man—not otherwise depressed or suicidal for "personal" reasons or without a history of depression or suicidality—to want to not survive. Such doubt is rooted at least partly in the denial of what AIDS has wrought for its survivors, a denial similar to that experienced by a man after his first positive HIV test or AIDS diagnosis: It seems *impossible* that AIDS could end his life. But doubt is also bolstered by our assumptions about survival as a cardinal purpose in human life and about psychopathology as the foundation for any acceptance or pursuit of death, regardless of circumstances.

Popular assumptions about survival and pathology are reinforced by the emotional significance of the "self-destructive" individual for others. The desire of some to not survive implicitly threatens the powerful, shared, social description of reality that allows us the optimism to entertain a personal and communal future—even in the midst of a plague. The entertainment of the possibility of death or death itself is experienced as an act of betrayal that nettles our own unconscious doubts about our lives and about our own, also unconscious, "treasonous" feelings about the communal future. We turn each death into a communal event with social meaning—the funeral—and then we all go home.

Human disasters with other men, microbes, or other forces of nature always produce a number of potential survivors so distressed by the event and so identified with nonsurvivors that they sacrifice themselves to the needs or causes of the nonsurvivors. As one example, there are those who sacrifice their lives during a fatal, communicable plague by nursing or doctoring the ill. Because we need and approve of these actions, we experience them as social contributions rather than as socially depleting self-destructiveness. To the extent that the self-destructiveness of the act is acknowledged at all, we describe it as altruistic, rather than as reckless or the suicidal expression of psychopathology. Such men and women are perceived not as a threat to the social fabric, but as heroes and champions of the society.

The fact remains that the nurse or doctor is often making a conscious or unconscious decision to end his or her "normal" life, and society does not define that as pathological. The nurse or doctor is often more personally or socially identified with the patient than with other potential survivors, and that identification is an important motivation for the sacrifice. In the AIDS epidemic we find not only gay men identified with people with HIV. We also find lesbians and large numbers of heterosexual health care providers whose personal sacrifices are so great that we must assume some psychological identification, perhaps unconscious, with gay men. In the personal histories of these people, I have often found important experiences of loss or survivor guilt, both of which certainly contribute to the identification.

In many other instances of culturally sanctioned self-sacrifice, there may be no material contribution to society, or the material contribution may be followed by a final, premature gesture of death. One's death makes a statement that affirms one's social, political, and ideological identification and allegiance. Every country and party has such heroes. The captain who goes down with his ship, and the soldier who runs headlong into enemy fire are among them. The death need not, aside from its personal and social meanings, contribute anything. That the gay man, profoundly identified with his community, often feels such allegiance and identification is understandable. The experience of a loving partner with HIV powerfully interacts with the social identification in this regard and intensifies the importance of feelings of identification and allegiance. To the extent that AIDS remains substantially within gay communities and that the communities or individuals within them are unable to develop lives and identities that include more than AIDS, gay identities will remain entangled—both appropriately and needlessly— with AIDS. As long as that is the case, for some gay men a death by AIDS will continue to serve as an important and meaningful expression of identity and allegiance.

THE FEELING THAT ONE WILL NOT SURVIVE

Here is what will happen: the lamps will flicker, past the lightest brown, going out. Cog after cog will find its gravest position.—Keith Waldrop, from The Quest For Mount Misery[12]

There is a phenomenon commonly experienced by survivors of the epidemic that is rarely discussed, and that is the sense of inevitability that so many gay men feel about their futures and HIV. Many men with consistent negative test histories and safer sex behavior to match do not believe they will survive. Patients often say they *know* they are uninfected but *feel like* or *believe* they are positive—or will, somehow, inevitably become so. The belief may be inconsistent over time and rationally unconvincing, but it can be persistent and compelling. Michael, a 22-year-old, uninfected psychotherapy patient, had been suffering from an undiagnosed genital dermatitis (that seemed unlike an HIV-related problem) for several weeks. He talked about his feelings shortly after finding out that a man whom he had been dating, and with whom he had had one sexual experience, "safely" conducted, was positive. This was his first personal encounter with HIV.

> When I found out that Peter was positive, it freaked me out—not for myself, but just the whole thing. I don't know how to live with this, because I feel afraid to kiss him, even if I *know* that's OK, because it just plays into my whole fear about HIV. Over the weekend I wanted to call my mom and talk to her, but I thought, you can't talk to her about this because she's going to tell you that you're going to get AIDS because you're gay. I feel like all this is stacked up against me. I mean, I had enough trouble with sex and being gay without this—and now I find myself feeling just like my mother. And in my rational mind I know this isn't true, but I keep feeling, *you are going to get AIDS because you're gay.* And Peter confirms that. I know how people get AIDS, but I also have this feeling that it's out there—that my life is already written and out there—and that I will get AIDS because I'm gay, that if you're gay, *you get AIDS.* When I went to the dermatologist last week, he told me not to sit on anything because he didn't know what I had and he didn't want to get it all over the place, and I just felt like he was saying to me, 'You're a homosexual, and God knows what you filthy people have, but I don't want it.' When he did that, my first thought was, well he's probably right—I'm dirty, I'm a queer, and I have AIDS, and I

don't want to contaminate his other patients. Then I got mad."

"What did you do?" I asked.

"I told him to cram it and left."

Such feelings of destiny within gay men are supported logically, as opposed to psychologically, by the idea that one is already infected and does not know it, or that one will unavoidably become infected through future behaviors. Such logical concerns are not without basis or merit. There are certainly numerous anomalies in the biology and medicine of HIV that might well make a man doubt his HIV-negative status as reported by an ELISA; and, with regard to future behaviors, there is widespread dispute over what is safer sex and what is not. This ambiguity arises because information is based on epidemiology (compiled by self-report) rather than biological experimentation; and because a homophobic society has put little time and money into determining what is safe and what is not, because it does not place positive value on *any* homosexual activity.

> At GMHC's [Gay Men's Health Crisis] workshops, the goal has shifted from rigid rules to giving men the information they need to make their own decisions about sexual behavior. "Risk exists along a continuum," explains Reinfeld [GMHC Director of Education]. "We try to give people an understanding that their willingness to accept risk also lies along a continuum." But that men are still asking questions—about [activities] which are very low-risk, at least for HIV transmission—indicates that a lot of the specialized but necessary information needed to make informed choices is still not easily available.[13]

Unlike the feelings of inevitability about contracting HIV that are rooted in more or less rational issues, many such feelings—perhaps most—are rooted in irrational feelings. A man's feeling that he has, or will eventually have, HIV or AIDS involves complex psychological processes that go much deeper than rational—or rationalized—doubts about the ELISA or modes of transmission. Such processes often arise out of largely unconscious processes, and often have serious consequences. In her study of HIV-negative gay men, psychologist Rachel Schochet concluded that

> highly significant relationships were found between post-traumatic stress symptoms and experiencing many deaths of acquaintances, *not really believing one is HIV-negative, and having unsafe sex in the*

past year. . . . Experiencing many losses of lovers, friends, roommates, and acquaintances also correlated with not really believing one's sero-status [emphasis added].[14]

We see in Michael's story about his visit to the dermatologist that feelings of inevitability about contracting HIV regardless of behavior often involve an internalization of others' homophobia. In this case it is the homophobia of the dermatologist, and Michael, aware of the process, was ultimately able to temporarily externalize and redirect the homophobic feelings to their source by telling the dermatologist to "cram it." The physician's homophobia supports the prediction that if you are gay, you get AIDS, or something else that is awful, unmanageable, and unforgivable. The prediction harbors a covert or unconscious hope that the gay patient will and ought to be punished to pay for his transgressions, and a gay man internalizing the homophobia also internalizes the unconscious, projected prediction and hope as a sense of personal destiny. The sense of destiny is all too easily self-fulfilling by means of unprotected sex, especially for the man whose negative identity is precarious precisely because he is not sure he is, or can stay, uninfected. Nagging doubts about serostatus, and the internalized homophobic sense of a destiny that includes HIV, are experienced by many gay men living in the epidemic.

Many men who are convinced that they must *already* have HIV base their conscious feelings in an appraisal of their sexual histories. These men commonly also voice nearly magical explanations for their negative status, and, finally, a deeper, more unconscious sense that they *ought* to be positive. The ought is ostensibly about sexual history; but beneath that often lies a sense of *deserving* to be positive because they are gay: "I did all the [bad and prohibited] things my positive friends did." These are, of course, expressions of homophobia. In contrast, when the *ought* in men's feelings expresses a sense that they *should* be positive—or simply *are*—it is not only homophobia, but internalization and identification, guilt, and depression that may play a role in their feelings.

Internalization and identification. The death of a friend or partner, and the feelings of loss, grief, and emptiness that accompany it, are often fended off by a psychological "internalization" of the dead man, an idea discussed more fully in chapter 4. The fending off of loss by internalization—taking in parts of the dead person—is something we see most concretely in those who take over a dead loved one's home, clothing, and possessions, living in the house like its former tenant, and often taking over his mannerisms, habits, attitudes, and activities. Though often psychologically primitive (in the sense that the dead person is taken in whole and unassimilated, rather than integrated), this kind of internalization is often necessary to ward off unmanageable grief. Internalizing fantasies are also a normal part of healthy adult experience. For example, they are one aspect of the power and emotional significance of oral, vaginal, and anal intercourse, in which fantasies of internalization are made quite literal.

Identification is considered a more mature, developmentally integrated form of internalization. In actual practice, however, internalization and identification are not always separate and discrete processes. Rarely is one or the other the sole approach to grief to the exclusion of the other. Both work in fending off feelings of separation and loss by making a man feel he has *taken in,* is *like,* or simply *is* the man he has lost. When the person identified with or internalized has HIV, is dying, or is dead, both internalization and identification may make the survivor feel that he too has HIV or is dying or dead. This is a particularly likely consequence of internalization, because of its primitiveness and indiscriminateness, and because it is often an early, instinctive, and unconsidered response to an overwhelming loss. A man, immediately after a lover's death, may feel *consciously* that he is sick and dying, even if he lacks a rational explanation for how that could be. The internalization may be so complete that it may not even occur to him that he is not. A man experiencing such feelings may easily expose himself to unprotected sex. What difference would it make for someone already infected and dying? A psychotherapy patient, Manuel, talks about the weeks following his lover's positive HIV test result. At that time Manuel had not yet been tested.

> "It was about a month ago, right after Rick got his HIV test— you know, that's when we started having unsafe sex. When I think back on it, it was just that—I guess, if *Rick* was positive then *I* was positive. I just never thought otherwise about it. Our sex then was very powerful—it was my way of holding on to him, saying that AIDS could not have him, it was how we stayed together. We were in it together."

I asked Manuel what he meant by their being "in it together": "Were you trying to contract HIV from Rick to stay together? Because when you talk about holding onto him, not letting AIDS have him, it sounds as if you knew you didn't have it."

"It was that we had HIV together, we had everything together, that HIV couldn't separate us, that it couldn't break us apart. It wasn't that I was trying to get it. Maybe I was trying to get it, but I didn't know it. I knew I was positive. But a couple of weeks later when things had cooled off a little bit, Carol asked me if I was worried about myself. I couldn't think for a minute what she meant, and then she said, 'Well, are you worried that you might have gotten it from Rick?' Well, I was completely amazed. It was the first time that I thought that I might not have it. Then I went to get tested, and when the nurse read me the results [which were negative] on Tuesday, this awful thing just went through me, and I thought, oh my God, this can't be true, because Rick has it, and it can't be that I'm negative. I just felt like this awful thing had happened, like someone had cut us in half."

In the sense that they lacked any reasonable basis, Manuel's early feelings that he had HIV were the result of an internalization or primitive identification with Rick. As we continued in therapy over the following months, a more complex identification with Rick developed and Manuel began experiencing, more and more consciously, a desire to have HIV as an expression of his devotion to Rick and commitment to supporting him.

So far, I have described quite natural sources of internalization and identification. In disenfranchised, minority gay communities, men with particular personal losses, as well as men identifying with their communities in a broader sense, will experience such feelings, and these feelings will sometimes lead to contracting HIV. Unfortunately, feelings of internalization and identification are also severely exacerbated by our conceptualization of the epidemic and our current AIDS education. This is accomplished largely by the implicit homophobia of much education—and its implication that gay men have sinned together—and by the apparently intentional *reinforcement* of identification between positive and negative men. These are both immensely destructive forces. If our education blurs or obscures differences between positive and negative men, we should not be surprised that many uninfected men develop identifications with positive men and no longer see real purpose in trying to avoid HIV.

In 1991 the San Francisco AIDS Foundation released a campaign that invited gay men to "Be Here for the Cure." Though widely borrowed by other prevention agencies, many gay men expressed confusion about whom the campaign was for. Were positive men being encouraged to hang on medically, or were uninfected men being told to stay negative, both waiting for "the cure"?

"I don't want the AIDS cure to be the focus of my life," Charles, an HIV-negative psychotherapy patient told me. "Sure, if I were positive, I'd be waiting for the cure. And I'd like that for all my positive friends, because then I'd know they're going to be OK. But I can't sit around with them making that the big hope in my life. I don't want to. I don't think it's going to happen and I feel like I've got to *get on* with my life. If I wait for the epidemic to be over, that might never happen."

"Is '*Be here for the cure*' asking you to organize your life around the cure?"

"I don't know what it's about. But I mean, I found myself in the Candlelight March [in remembrance of those who have died of AIDS] with Bruce, and the next thing I know I'm carrying one of those signs with the globe on it [the image of the campaign]. I'm there, Bruce is there, Jim is there—almost everyone I know was there—and we're marching down the street like we were all in it together—waiting for the cure. And it seemed so natural, and then afterwards I thought to myself, 'Well, you know we're really *not* all in it together, because Bruce is positive and Jim and I aren't.' And I've got a sign, Bruce has a sign, Jim has a sign, and I'm feeling like we're all the same. *Bruce* is waiting for the cure—I mean he thinks it's going to happen. I don't think so, and I don't want to be walking down the street feeling like I've got HIV and I've got to organize my whole life around it. I remember Douglas [who died of AIDS] *all the time*. I mean, I never stop thinking about him, and I don't have to show that by marching around with a sign about the cure as if I've got it too. Afterwards, I felt like I just got sucked into something that wasn't mine."

Guilt. To this point, I have described internalization and identification as processes for "holding onto" the HIV-positive, dying, or dead by making the potential survivor feel like the person with HIV. While fending off loss is almost always an important objective of internalization and identification, *feeling like* the person with HIV may also be an objective of these processes, rather than simply a by-product. In coming to feel like the man with HIV, the survivor also reduces the differences between himself and the person with HIV. It is precisely the difference between the survivor and the person with HIV that forms the basis of guilt, including guilt about survival: "The greater the discrepancy between one's own fate and the fate of the loved person one failed to help, the greater the empathic distress and the more poignant one's guilt [about surviving]".[15] As one becomes more like the person with HIV, the basis for any guilt is reduced: infected men rarely feel generalized guilt about other infected men. Thus internalization and identification may serve unconsciously to reduce guilt by making the survivor like those he is guilty about, especially when the internalization or identification includes a negative man's "taking on" another's HIV.

Additionally, there are ways in which guilt about surviving—which so often includes feelings that one is not worthy of surviving—leads more directly to the feeling that one is somehow fated not to survive *anyway* (and therefore must have or will have HIV). This sense of destiny about AIDS may fulfill the wish not to survive, but is often experienced as the feeling that one will not be *allowed* to survive because of one's unworthiness. Such feelings rest on largely unconscious, primitive, magical thought, sometimes associated with conscious or unconscious beliefs in an omnipotent being—God or parent—who sees to it that people get what they deserve. Such magical thinking is a common result of the hopelessness, helplessness, and passivity experienced by those living in an unmanaged epidemic. No longer feeling in control of one's life, one is tempted to assign control, in fact or in fantasy, to someone else. Unfortunately, such passivity may well become a self-fulfilling prophecy of HIV infection. In later psychotherapy sessions with Manuel, it became clear that such complex feelings were part of his experience in the months following Rick's positive ELISA:

> "Rick has never said anything like this, but I know that I had the feeling after his test that if I were negative, he might be mad at me. I never thought that consciously, but I can see it now when I think back on it. And I didn't want to be negative either. So, if I thought he might be mad at me, I must have had the idea that I might be negative. But there was something else about our [unprotected] sex then, and it was like, oh, what the fuck—if Rick is positive, then

everything's out of control, our lives are completely fucked up, and what difference does it make if I have it or not?"

"So your sex was a combination of thinking you had HIV and wanting it in order to stay with Rick," I commented. "But it was also a way of making sure you had it so that Rick wouldn't resent you."

"It was all those things, but you forgot the other part—that everything seemed so fucked up, that I was thinking, there's nothing you can do about anything anymore, this is just all out of your hands—if you get it, you get it, and there's nothing you're going to do about that or anything else. I mean, we weren't doing anything about anything. One morning we went into the kitchen, and the garbage was really stinking, and Rick, who is usually so clean about everything, said to me, 'Somehow I thought if we waited long enough the garbage would disappear on its own.' We had been living with that for days, and I don't think either one of us thought we could do anything about it. By June, all of his plants had died too, and when I would ask him if I should water them, he would just say, 'Oh, forget it.' It was, like, if the garbage is in here stinking, or the plants are dropping dead, well those are just the things you have to put up with in life."

Depression. The hopelessness, helplessness, and passivity experienced by Manuel and Rick is characteristic of depression. When depression is chronic, these feelings can easily make life seem impossible. Because they have had the good fortune to escape HIV, many uninfected men are unable to feel privately or talk openly about the unhappiness of their survival. Such men may begin consciously or unconsciously to feel their difficult life experience is a result of their own unconsciously imagined "AIDS." This may serve two purposes. For the uninfected man, himself, the unconscious belief that he really has HIV helps make sense of his depression, and it allows him to experience a shared, publicly acknowledged source of unhappiness. This is a process related, in some senses, to other displacements of psychological conflicts into physical conditions: a lonely, neglected child cries *because his arm hurts.* Physical symptoms are often more acceptable than psychological symptoms, and this is particularly true during an epidemic.

In addition to his own need to make sense of his unhappiness, the uninfected man may feel that his condition will have more plausibility for other people—particularly infected men—if he has, or is thought to have, HIV or AIDS. This can motivate a man to consciously misrepresent his HIV condition or, less consciously, to slide into the feelings and behaviors—indeed, the form of life—of a positive man. The conscious, if impulsive, misrepresentation of HIV status is described in the story of Bill, a depressed, HIV-negative psychotherapy patient having dinner with three positive friends:

> "We were in a booth by the window in the New York Deli, and all these guys were going by on Market Street, and every now and then someone would go by, and you'd say to yourself, 'Well, he really has it bad—you know, AIDS. He looks terrible. I wonder what the poor guy's got.'"

"*Who* would say to himself?" I interrupted.

> "Well, *I* would. I'm sure everyone was doing it. You know, 'Maybe he's got CMV [cytomegalovirus],' or 'I guess that's K.S. [Kaposi's sarcoma] on his neck.' You know, you notice those kinds of things. But what I wanted to tell you was, this guy goes by and Steve waves at him and he waves back, and then Steve says to us, 'That guy and I are in the same [medication] trial at General [San Francisco General Hospital].' And Ricardo says, 'Oh yeah, what are you on?' The next thing I know, we're sort of going around the table talking about who's taking what, and I'm thinking, 'What the fuck am I going to say when it comes to me?' I was going to get up and go to the toilet, and just as I started to stand up, Ricardo says, 'Bill, what are you taking?' And I said, 'Oh me? Just AZT.'"

Bill started to laugh at this point. "Just AZT?" I queried, too surprised to laugh.

"Right. *Just AZT.*"

"And then what did you do?"

"I went to the toilet."

"That doesn't seem like a complete resolution to me."

"To say the least. In fact, they all think I'm positive now. I sat down in the toilet—it's so small in there you can hardly breathe—and I didn't know if I was going to start crying or laughing. I kept thinking, 'Just AZT? What the fuck did you say that for? Just AZT?' I went over this again and again, and I knew I was going to have to go back out and sit down and look at them, and I didn't know if I could do it."

"What were the feelings that made that seem so difficult?"

"I was embarrassed. And ashamed."

"Why ashamed?" I asked.

"Because I've been so depressed—about the epidemic—and I don't have a good reason to be depressed. I don't have AIDS, and people I know who *do* aren't as depressed as I am."

"And did you feel some guilt at that moment?"

"Yeah, I was very guilty. It was like I was . . . I started to say *bragging,* but that doesn't seem right."

"What about the feeling though? The feeling that it was bragging?"

"I was claiming that I was part of things when I wasn't. I couldn't come out to them as negative. It wouldn't have made any sense. In some ways I realized that I've been pretending—I realized this while I was sitting in the bathroom—I've been pretending that I'm positive. Not by saying anything, but by little things. By being *affected* by the epidemic. I mean, Ricardo, who *is* positive, is taking the epidemic a lot better than I am. And I could just see myself saying, 'Oh well, I'm not taking anything. I'm negative.' I know Ricardo's mouth would just have fallen right on the floor, and he'd be thinking, 'Well, then what the hell is he so depressed about all the time!?' I'd have to say, 'Well, I know I'm not as affected as you guys, but I'm upset about it too.' I couldn't see myself saying that."

Over the following weeks, we were able to further explore the meaning of "the deli incident," as it came to be known in therapy hours. Bill's guilt was about his grief. Not having HIV, he felt it inappropriate to have any important feelings about the epidemic unless they were on behalf of, or about, someone with HIV. For himself—about his own life—he felt his grief unjustified and unsupported, and in some senses, a betrayal of those with HIV. In addition to those feelings, Bill felt guilt about his grief because he felt it *was* justified and realistic, and that Ricardo and other friends with HIV were simply denying their feelings. Bill often felt that his own—often inescapably apparent—feelings confronted Ricardo's denial and made Ricardo uncomfortable. Bill thus often suppressed his feelings and colluded with Ricardo, and felt a great deal of unconscious anger at Ricardo for being "compelled" to collude with Ricardo's denial. He felt guilt about that anger, too, for it was, after all, Ricardo who was actually dealing with having HIV. Amidst this muddle of feelings, one was quite clear: the clearest resolution, said Bill, would be accomplished by contracting HIV himself.

Bill's incident at dinner expresses both conscious and unconscious processes. Though misrepresentations of HIV status, in my experience, are most often made unconsciously, both are expressed by uninfected men who live as a dying man does, without a belief in or sense of responsibility to the future, existing within the scope and scale of a life that may end any day. This form of life often feels plausible and defensible only if the man actually has HIV, and the "incentive" to have it may be enhanced by the sometimes liberating nature of such lives. "Sometimes Ricardo is so *right now* in a way that I can't be because I'm going to have a normal life span," said Bill. Some of Bill's depression would be ameliorated by this liberation, he thought. But he also feared—and hoped—that the liberation might make the complex burden of an expected normal life span unacceptable. Another uninfected psychotherapy patient, Earl, talked about "toying" with unprotected sex with his positive lover, Les. He describes some of the psychological "gains" for negatives in "being" HIV-positive.

> "I'd rather be alive today and really living my life, and dead next month than be dead and walking around for the next forty years. HIV has taught me how to live too, especially because I can see the changes in Les. When I had the burn mark on my leg [initially mistakenly misdiagnosed as Kaposi's sarcoma, often a first symptom of AIDS], for that week that I thought it was K.S., it was very liberating. I felt *very free*. Finally, I didn't have to think about my whole life, especially after Les died. I thought, 'Well, now we can just live it to the hilt, and get it over with, and I'm not going to be doing tax returns and cleaning the goddam house for the next forty years.' There's a lot to be said for that so far as I'm concerned. And I'll tell you something else—during that week is the only time that Les has treated me as an equal since he got diagnosed. He treated me very differently. He would ask about my feelings, and if I wanted to do something, that counted again. It wasn't just Les, because it was the first time since he got diagnosed that *I* thought it was OK to get what I wanted. And when we found out it wasn't K.S. after all, that all stopped. I wouldn't ask and he wouldn't offer, and this creates a lot of resentment on my part."
>
> "And a lot of guilt too," I commented.

"Yeah, and a lot of guilt too; because I won't even ask to watch something on the TV. I figure he should choose, and I let him. The guilt started first, but the more resentment I feel, the more guilty I get about it and everything else."

SUBSTANCE USE AND ABUSE

Substance use and abuse is one of the most often cited reasons for unprotected sex. In some populations of gay men, research has established a *correlation* between substance use and unprotected sex, which is to say that substance use and unprotected sex are seen together in enough individuals that the coincidence is more than statistical chance. Correlations, however, provide no inferences or information in themselves about how or why the two are related—beyond simply appearing in the same individuals—but AIDS educators have usually interpreted the correlation as a *causal* relationship. The correlation between substance use and unprotected sex is generally interpreted to mean that people have unprotected sex *because* they use substances. Thus, the reasoning goes, we can reduce unprotected sex by reducing substance use.

Alternative explanations for this correlation—ones that make more psychological sense—are much more useful to understanding reasons people have unprotected sex. These include the insight that often people are not having unprotected sex because they have been drinking, but rather they have been drinking in order to have unprotected sex. This explanation acknowledges that unprotected sex is often important and compelling, and that the disinhibition provided by substances is often necessary to act out the desire. People are also using substances in order to have *protected* sex, either because they have long-standing anxiety or conflict about sex or—quite commonly—because as a society we have failed to validate the human importance of sex, especially gay sex. Our current AIDS education often reflects this societal failure by reiterating societal homophobia, moralism, directiveness, and erotophobia. These are important contributions to many men's need to use substances to engage in sex of any sort.

Poor self-esteem is another common underlying motivator for both excessive substance use and unprotected sex, and depression may underlie and motivate both. Such explanations include the rudimentary psychological idea that substance use is not simply the source of behaviors but also the consequence of feelings. This insight has been obscured by medical models of substance abuse because such models define abuse as the primary problem, thus eclipsing psychological meaning. It is *feelings* that are responsible for unprotected sex, feelings evidenced not at the substance-impaired moment that the sex occurs, but at the moment the man decides to use the substance. Thus the response of men who report having unprotected sex "because I was drunk," does not provide adequate understanding. The real question is, "Why did you get drunk?"

In summary, substance abuse and unprotected sex are related in a number of different, complex ways, but perhaps least commonly by a simple causal relationship. I suspect that men who have unprotected sex *simply because they are substance impaired* are relatively rare. The appeal of this simplistic causal explanation certainly lies partly in the fact that we disapprove of both substance abuse and unprotected sex, and it has often seemed to provide a way of containing two sins with one directive.

DENIAL IN YOUNGER MEN

Denial, in both the psychological and ordinary senses of the term, describes an attempt to simply disavow the existence of unpleasant reality, despite the apparent evidence. The AIDS epidemic has spawned an epidemic of denial. Denial is exercised against perceiving the psychological impact of HIV on the infected, the uninfected, and gay communities as a whole; against fears about the projected course of the epidemic; and against useful approaches to prevention. It is thus hardly a surprise to find denial playing a multifaceted role in unprotected sex.

Simple denial is often operative in men of all ages, although it seems to hold a special developmental position in the lives of the young. Men in their teens and early twenties often ride a familiar postadolescent wave of omnipotence and invulnerability that, among other things, allows them to embark on life without being overwhelmed by it. How else could a 20-year-old venture out of the house into the next fifty years of his life? Although sexually active only after the discovery of HIV and its probable routes of transmission, an astonishing number of young men are seroconverting: one-third of gay 20-year-old men will be infected or dead of AIDS by age 30.[16] In "Boys," William Hayes relates the ominous story of Ethan, a bartender at San Francisco's Stud, a well-known dance bar.

> Contradicting the widespread distrust of gay men older than themselves, most boys [whom Ethan] meets just want to get fucked.

"I've got rubbers in my room and I hardly ever use them anymore. But they don't ask," Ethan adds. "They don't seem to think about it."

They think they don't have to. That the children are safe is one of the dreams of the infected city. Some boys believe that—perhaps because they just turned twenty-one, or they are only twenty-six, and AIDS has always been around, or they are HIV-negative, or, less clinically, they are simply too young and strong to become sick, like older gay men. Even if we are unsafe, these boys think, we are safe together.

"We all just keep on thinking that they will have a cure for it by the time we get it," one boy says, trustfully. "Of course, it will happen," he insists. "I mean, what the hell, we can send a man to space. How complex can this be?"[17]

When such young men reflect in psychotherapy about the behaviors that likely infected them, they are often bewildered by their naïveté and denial. But the denial of the young is an important part of what it means to be young, and even when buried in remorse about contracting HIV, many young men feel deeply that it could not have been otherwise. A young man seems to lead his life as he leads it, and he cannot be told that some paths are more difficult than others until he treads them himself. To formulate a sense of oneself as gay, and to begin to live that self in the world, is complex enough without having to worry that the whole thing might kill you before you are out of your twenties.

Although there is a popular idea that the young deny the possibility of contracting AIDS because it is "a disease of older gay men," I find many young men not only recognizing the *possibility* of AIDS for themselves, but accepting it as a destiny about which they can do very little. Pedro Zamora, a young, HIV-positive gay man and AIDS educator, first came to national notoriety as the HIV-positive member of seven young people portrayed in the MTV broadcast *The Real World.* As an educator, he points out, "My generation doesn't know of a time when AIDS didn't factor into a decision about sex," and draws the conclusion that young men have "no excuse . . . for not wanting to protect themselves."[18]

Contrary to Zamora's conclusion, there are many social and psychological reasons that young men contract HIV. It is often precisely the fact that young men were born into the epidemic that creates a seamless integration of AIDS and HIV into their lives and makes them lackadaisical about protected sex. Unlike older men, they often cannot even *imagine* a gay life without AIDS as, at the very least, a possibility. Thus denial in the young is psychologically enmeshed with the common sense of inevitability about contracting HIV. The result of this enmeshing is the surprising denial of many young men that *not* contracting HIV is a possibility in life, quite opposite to simple denial of the reality that contracting HIV *is* possible. Sean, an uninfected psychotherapy patient in his early twenties, felt an easygoing destiny about contracting HIV, and we spoke about it often.

> "People your age," Sean said, "are always talking about the epidemic as something that's *happened* to them. For me—I mean, it was just *there* when I grew up and became gay."
>
> "So you feel that you have more acceptance of it than older people."
>
> "You could call it that. If it weren't for AIDS, I couldn't tell you what being gay would be all about."
>
> "And how does that leave you feeling about contracting HIV yourself? Is it important *not* to?" Sean thought about my question for a moment.
>
> "Yeah. I guess it's fairly important."

This mix of denial with feelings of inevitability in young people is, as with older men, exacerbated by the identification of negative men with positive men. It was Sean who first called my attention to Pedro Zamora, and his appearance on the cover of *POZ* magazine, a glossy "lifestyle" magazine that appears to be aimed largely at an audience of well-educated, middle-class gay men with HIV.

> "He's incredibly *hot,*" Sean told me, "and I understand he's going to be the leader of the Q Action [a prevention program of San Francisco's STOP AIDS Project]. They're going to have a lot of guys going to *those* meetings even though he's positive."
>
> "You say 'even though' he's positive?"
>
> "Yeah. That's why they put him on the cover. They try to show in *POZ* that positive men are hot too—you know, that they have sex and are attractive and that they shouldn't be dismissed just because they're positive. I agree with that."
>
> "But you said 'even though he's positive' in referring to Zamora. Do you have other feelings about him as well?"
>
> "Hmm. Yeah, I did say that. I guess what I was thinking is, if you think about it, it's kind of weird. They say he's a good AIDS educator though."

"And what's kind of weird?"

"Well, I probably shouldn't be saying this—but here's this guy who's *got* AIDS, and he's going to tell the rest of us how to not get it."

"Is he contributing his experience with the problem?"

"Like, what he did wrong, and how we shouldn't do it?"

"Something like that."

"Yeah, I guess he could do that. But what I was thinking about is that Matt and I were sitting around reading the [*POZ*] interview with him, and talking about how hot he is. And Matt said to me, 'I'd like to be exactly like him—he's got everything a queer queen could want. He's got it made.' And I said, 'Yeah, but he's got AIDS too.' And Matt said, 'So what? A lot of guys have AIDS. I mean, he wouldn't be where he is if he didn't have AIDS. He'd be hot, but that's a dime a dozen. Guys who have AIDS get a lot more attention.'"

Such identifications—regardless of their factual accuracy—are common, and contribute to both the sense of inevitability about contracting HIV and the denial that a life without HIV is possible. They are particularly powerful for the young because their identifications with HIV are so seamlessly integrated into their development as gay men, and because, in general, young HIV positive men *do* receive more attention, support, and social service within developed gay communities than their uninfected counterparts. While many positive men have made important contributions to education, Zamora is not only an educator but a spokesperson and symbol for gay men with whom many young men seem to be identifying. The intelligence, clarity, and commitment he reveals in the *POZ* interview offer an admirable model for young gay men trying to make sense of their lives—especially those who are HIV-positive. But in the interview he shows little psychological insight about the complex feelings people have about HIV and sex, and why a man might have conflicted feelings about Zamora's having HIV or have difficulty raising the subject: "If you're that concerned about it [my being HIV-positive] now, you should have been that concerned about it when you were all over me in the bar. I have no patience for it."[19] The question about Zamora in relation to issues of denial, identification, and the sense of inevitability is whether he should serve as *the* spokesman and symbol for an HIV *prevention* program—which is to say, a program for men who *do not* have HIV. This question, of course, goes straight to the heart of the political tensions between positive and negative men within the gay communities. But if denial, confused identifications, and authentically humane political and personal sensitivities cause young men to experience HIV as seamlessly inevitable—much less *desirable*—the fates of the gay communities are sealed.

DENIAL IN OLDER MEN

Older men also exercise simple denial, but it is commonly about denying that they *might* contract HIV with unprotected sex. Older men, often holding Zamora's assumption that those born into the epidemic are—or ought to be—more conscientious about protected sex, frequently assume that younger men are uninfected. They thus sometimes expose themselves, or their younger partners to HIV because of denial rationalized by such assumptions. A man's simple denial may not only be about his partners, but about himself.

> Ethan, who belongs to the group of men in their thirties that comprises nearly 50 percent of the AIDS cases here [in San Francisco], is certainly not alone in practicing unsafe sex. Many of Ethan's friends, in fact, are HIV-positive, and a close friend recently died of AIDS. But Ethan is afraid to take the test. "I know what I'm doing is wrong," he says, but he doesn't want to think about it. "I guess I've just gotten to the point where I feel like, maybe I'm just on borrowed time or something. It should matter, but all I know is, I'd rather be having fun than not having fun, and all of a sudden I've got spots all over me and nobody's gonna look at me, and nobody wants me, or I'm not going to be able to do anything." [20]

Finally, among simple forms of denial leading to unprotected sex is the denial of gay identity. Men, young and old, who are not self-identified as gay—or who are consciously self-identified as heterosexuals—often do not consider themselves members of a "high-risk group" likely to contract HIV. Many of these are very young men whose gay identity is only in formation, older men who are also coming out, or older men who are leading established, covert homosexual lives. All three groups are very difficult to reach with public education for gay men. While the actual behaviors of such men may entail very high risks for HIV transmission, denial obscures this with the rationalization that identity is the risk factor. Fortunately, many educators have abandoned the misleading idea of "risk groups," but not before the popular press and public perception had fully absorbed it. The idea that one gets AIDS because of a particular psychological and social identification is obviously specious; but it is an idea powerfully driven not only by early mistakes in AIDS education but by self-hatred and hatred of others, homophobia and internalized homophobia, and the projection and internalization of all that is hated. When a gay man states, as have a handful of my psychotherapy patients, that he feels regret for being gay because it will or has already given him HIV, it becomes clear that the confusions and self-hatred of others may be internalized and unleashed on the self in profoundly destructive ways.

COMPLEX DENIAL

In contrast to straightforward uses of denial, denial appears to be involved in unprotected sexual activity in an entirely different way. In an effort to encourage protected sex, our education has usually tried to discourage men's recognition of their anxiety about it: "I suck with abandon, knowing that the rubber keeps both of us protected."[21] In fact, few men have complete confidence in safer sex, especially if unconscious, often irrational fears are included in the consideration. The very fact of protected sex is at least an unconscious reminder of the *potential* lethality of the act, and although unconscious and irrational fears might be dissipated by acknowledgment and clarification, the politics of protected sex rarely permit that. Safer sex is, after all, the gay man's expression of social and personal responsibility. To mention even unconscious feelings of doubt causes unpsychological thinkers to assume that the inviolate code of safer sex is being questioned. In general, the psychological (as opposed to intellectual) confidence in protected sex is extremely low. Public disputes about what is safer and what is not, particularly with regard to oral sex; the clinical observations of anomalous seroconversion frequently reported by medical personnel working in HIV services; and the complexity of biological and epidemiological models, all conspire to raise doubts about *any* kind of sex, much less homosexual sex—which raised more than enough conscious and unconscious conflict even when a lethal virus was not in question. Thus plausible, as well as completely irrational and unconscious, sources of fear and anxiety belie one of the truly grand fallacies of the epidemic: Gay men are doing just fine with safer sex, thank you very much. Dave, in general a not particularly anxious, 30-year-old psychotherapy patient, describes such feelings succinctly:

"People say that they're OK with safe sex, but I'm not one of them—not if I really look at my feelings. If you asked me how I *felt,* I'd say that I sometimes feel that you'd have to get dressed up in a *space suit* to have really safe sex. And then the obvious question is 'What's the point?' I'm sure as hell not going to wear rubber gloves, but on the other hand, I have just had so many doubts about it— every little scrape and cut on your hand, and worrying that some cum is going to get on it. I ignore these things most of the time, and then suddenly I notice myself thinking about it. 'Gee, look at this cut on my finger. I wonder if any cum got in it. Hmm, let's see. I was lying on my right side when Greg [Dave's boyfriend, who was HIV-positive] came on my arm, and then I reached over with my left hand to pick up the towel, and then . . .'—I mean, this kind of shit can go on and on, and it can drive you crazy."

"Do you think these are *reasonable* fears?" I wondered.

"I doubt it. I don't even know anymore. I once had scraped the side of my thigh while I was gardening—I mean, just kind of rough, red skin, but no real blood or anything. Maybe a day or so after I got this scrape, Greg came on me and it got on this area and I noticed it was stinging. Burning. So I thought, 'Shit, now you've done it,' and I called up Les [Dave's internist] the next day and told him the story to see if I should come in. And he said to me, 'I really wouldn't worry about it, Dave.' I said, 'You don't think I could have gotten HIV that way?' And do you know what he said? He said, 'I don't know if you could have gotten HIV that way, I haven't even seen the scrape. But in any case there's nothing much to do about it now. We'll do an ELISA anyway at your next checkup. In the mean time, put some antiseptic on it and don't let it get infected.' Does that inspire confidence or what?"

Despite the likelihood that the risks of even loosely defined protected sex are no greater than those of many well- accepted daily activities like automobile travel, Dave's feelings are not uncommon. They are, however, uncommonly *admitted* to. Most gay men have been encouraged in their natural tendency to deny conflicted feelings about protected sex, and to some extent must invoke denial every time they have sex. Denial is necessary to counter the intrusion of unconscious feelings into consciousness so that sexual feelings of intimacy, trust, and enjoyment may be experienced—and, for the particularly anxious, to even allow erection or orgasm.

Unfortunately, denial habitually invoked to quell fears about *protected* sex is easily mustered to allow unprotected sex. The psychological tendency is to produce an internal *climate* of denial around sexuality that as easily inhibits feelings about unprotected sex as those about protected sex. Perhaps this is partially an inevitability during a sexually vectored epidemic in minority communities traditionally abused because of their sexuality. But, if there are significant motivations to engage in unprotected sex, then denial—among the most global and indiscriminate of psychological defenses—serves admirably, for it is among the few psychological defenses with enough primitive, reality-distorting muscle to allow unprotected sex in the life of a man who has his eye on biological survival.

Particularly among men who are unusually anxious in general, there is a significant correlation in my psychotherapy patients between the fear of protected sex and the practice of unprotected sex. Men who express conscious anxiety and reticence about protected sex seem often the most likely to engage in sporadic, impulsive episodes of unprotected sex. Paul, a psychotherapy patient in his late thirties, was an intelligent and well-educated man who worked in a technical field. He had a long, pre-epidemic history of anxiety problems, including anxiety about his homosexuality, sex in general, and emotional intimacy. Fears about HIV had badly aggravated these problems, and he sometimes shunned even casual kissing because of fear of HIV transmission. For several years he had been unable to have an orgasm unless involved in solitary masturbation. He came to a therapy session following a weekend in Los Angeles, where he had stayed in a gay hotel.

> "Saturday night I got fucked," he announced quite flatly as he sat down for the hour.
> "Really?" I said.
> "Not only that, but without a rubber."
> "Do you know why?" I asked.
> "Well, of course, I've replayed it a thousand times. I can tell you the facts, and they are pretty straightforward. I met this very attractive guy by the pool, we talked for a while, he asked me if I wanted to come back to his room, and I agreed. We went to his room, and though I was a little anxious at first, at some point he asked me if I would like him to fuck me—and at that moment, I clearly just switched into some altered state of consciousness. I was there for almost two hours, and it felt like ten minutes. It was as

if I'd become someone else, as if I were watching us in the room, rather than being in the middle of it. Unfortunately—I—got fucked without a condom, and I've been obsessing over it ever since. I roll it over and over and over in my mind, and I have the idea that if I just go through it one more time, I'll realize that it never happened, that my memory has played a trick on me."

"But it sounds as if it happened—and to *you*."

"No doubt about it."

"And do you understand what this 'altered state of consciousness' was, what it is that was going on?" I asked.

"I can tell you that being in L.A. had something to do with it— that I felt far away from home, and from myself, and that it all had the quality of a dream, very timeless and a world in itself in some way. It was that feeling that I was not in my real life that let me do it. And probably not in my real body. Shit, I hardly . . ."

"Hardly what?"

"I started to say that I've hardly let anyone kiss me in six years. And here I am getting fucked on a hotel bed without a condom— it's really unbelievable."

"The invitation at the pool," I wondered, "he wasn't inviting you up to the room to watch TV. What did you imagine, down at the pool, might happen if you went to his room?"

"I've gone over that with all the rest, of course, and I had two thoughts about it. One is that I pretended to myself that I didn't know, that I just spaced out and followed him up to the room, and I wasn't consciously thinking about what we would do. But the other part, which I have trouble verbalizing, is that I was ushered along by some sense of destiny. This was a setup, of course, because I chose to stay in a gay hotel with a pool. But it was as if I'd gone there, even gone to L.A., for this purpose. I was there to do something that I have not been able to do for years."

"To get fucked without a condom?" I asked.

"No, the destiny was about getting fucked, about just having sex and letting myself be in it. And the condom—what can I say?—if *I'd* been there, I would have seen that he used a condom."

"But the hitch is, I think, that you couldn't be there because you're too concerned about HIV, and that has made you mostly deny an interest in sex. That part of you couldn't be there—the worried part. You had to be in Los Angeles, and you had to be in an altered state of consciousness in order to allow it at all."

Paul was pensive for a moment and then responded.

"Well, what you're talking about now is related to what I've been thinking of as the sense of destiny. Because what it was, is that I turned myself over, so to speak, to the part of me that wanted the sexual intimacy we've been talking about [in therapy]. And I just followed along behind, the part of me that has avoided all of this, just trailed along behind and sat there watching."

"This splitting yourself into these two people you talk about seems a way of overcoming the fear that you've had about sex."

"Yes, I'm feeling as we're talking right now," Paul said, "that I just had to get out of that—I have felt constantly like a prisoner in myself in some way, and it was as if I had to shut my eyes and leap out the window to get out."

"Instead of using the elevator."

"The elevator?"

"Instead of getting together with both sides of yourself, and thinking your feelings through, and making a decision to be sexually intimate with someone in a reasonably safe way—or unsafe way, for that matter."

"Yes, I had to jump. It was like being in a burning building. It finally gets too hot, and then you jump. Later you figure out if they've got the nets out or you're going to land in the middle of the street. It was a very extreme move."

"And the extremeness comes," I tried to clarify, "from the sexual feelings having been unacceptable for so long, your denying them even as they churned around unconsciously. When you're able to make feelings like that conscious, then you can better reckon with them in the context of your life. Otherwise they're something that just pops out in L.A."

Paul's description of his experience in Los Angeles has a dissociative, *fugue-like* quality. His experience of being outside his body, watching himself on the bed, in an altered state of consciousness, and behaving very uncharacteristically all convey this. Such dissociative defenses are often an effort to control fear about an involuntary situation, or a voluntary one that expresses unconscious motivations. Without the dissociation—"if *I'd* been there," as Paul put it—the anxiety and fear would have been prohibitive. Denial, in a special sense of the term, is an aspect of dissociative behavior such as Paul's. Paul had kept his sexual desires largely unconscious because of the anxiety they produced, and he needed to deny, in a dissociative sense, what was going on in the hotel room.

When impulsive, uncharacteristic behavior like Paul's is less severely dissociative, it may be an expression of denial in the form of *counterphobia*. It is not uncommon for men feeling immobilized by anxiety, fear, hopelessness, or depression to impulsively engage in precisely the activity that gives rise to their feelings. Such counterphobic behavior is not only by nature impulsive—for it is the product of a sudden "breakthrough" of suppressed feelings—it tends to be reckless and compulsive, which raises the risks of the behavior considerably beyond what they might have been had the activity been conducted more consciously.

In part, counterphobic behavior is an attempt to counter feelings of anxiety and helplessness by "mastering" the feared activity. It also often vents tension and anger about feelings of helplessness and the situation that produced it. It certainly motivates some unprotected sex, and it is an idea that provides some insight into Paul's dissociative experience, as well as more common, less fugue-like experiences of other men. There is often a correlation between fears about sex in general or protected sex and the counterphobic and impulsive engagement in unprotected sex.

SELF-ESTEEM

Self-esteem problems are usually developmental in origin, and in the lives of many gay men they certainly predate the AIDS epidemic. But in addition to a developmental accumulation of deficits of self-esteem, some gay men experience the epidemic itself as an injury to self-esteem. Particularly for gay men whose self-esteem has derived heavily from their identity as members of a gay community, the epidemic may make that membership a liability. The gay communities are now plagued by disease and death, and are subjected to much of society's wrath for the very existence of HIV. Positive—and negative—men commonly experience their HIV-status as a defect that garners rejection by men in the other group, and positive men often experience their HIV-status as the concrete expression of a broad and profound sense of being defective, contagious, dirty, or undesirable. Additionally, illness, disfigurement, death, depression, and the lack of broad social acknowledgment and support for what the gay communities are experiencing all contribute to injured self-esteem.

Regardless of the sources, poor self-esteem supports the practice of unprotected sex. A sense of self-worth is part of what allows a man to feel a sense of some control in his life, to make choices about life, and to feel that he contributes to the course of his future. People take better care of things and selves that they value, feel connected to, and responsible for. Hopelessness breeds feelings of helplessness and passivity, and impulsive, self-destructive behavior.

It is perhaps in its impact on gay sexuality that the tragedy of AIDS having engaged these particular communities is seen most clearly. The warning that AIDS "does not discriminate" and the political hope that it is "everyone's issue" have no bearing on the special meanings it has had in the gay communities. It would be difficult to overestimate the destructiveness of the epidemic's entanglement with the psychological conflict that gay men have always borne simply because they were gay. Plain and sensible fear, as well as fear propelled by homophobia and hatred, threaten to steal our sexual lives from us and leave us void of an important part of who we are. Relatively early in the epidemic, Carl, a psychotherapy patient in his mid-sixties, spoke of his own life:

> I'm afraid this epidemic has really thrown ice water on my sex life. I never thought a little piece of rubber could do that, but condoms have created in me a real sense of grief, a sense of loss about what used to be. I can't mess around with those things and all the other problems involved with sex now, and I'm pretty sure now that I'm too old to ever outlive the need for all these precautions—my God, you go to the bedroom with an arsenal of pharmaceuticals with the hope you won't kill each other making love. The good part for me is that I'm old enough to take an early retirement on sex. But young people, I don't know what they're going to do about it. I'm glad I'm not in their position. Even at my age, I've begun to wonder who I am. I say I'm gay, but, you know, I don't have sex with men anymore. That leaves me wondering just what it is that constitutes my being gay these days. When people ask me now, I'm tempted to say, "Oh I used to be gay, but I'm retired now."

As with every aspect of the epidemic, each man must find and negotiate his own path out of communal trouble. The loss of our capacity for sexual, human intimacy is certainly one of the three great dangers of the epidemic, behind only physical suffering and loss of—relatively young—life. Many of us will find paths that conserve or restore our capacity for intimacy while allowing biological survival. But a question must be posited on behalf of those who harm no others and for whom sexual intimacy in its ordinary, and now sometimes dangerous, forms is the path of choice. Why is it that we mourn the fated, ill, and dead because they fulfilled their human needs in an age when it appeared to cost nothing, but now only censure and ostracize those who do the same in a new age when it may cost them their very longevity on Earth?

Chapter 9
Being Here: Other Kinds
of Survival

I will go for a walk before
bed, a little stroll to settle
the day's upsets. One thing always
follows another, but
discreetly—tree after telephone pole, for instance, or
this series of unlit houses. One moment follows
another,
helplessly, losing its
place instantly to the next. Each frame
fails, leaving behind
an impression of motion.

As for death, at the moment I
think it strangely overrated.
—Keith Waldrop, from Around the Block[1]

Erik Erikson, in his concept of the eight stages of man,[2] posited an immensely influential scheme of psychological and social development, which has come to permeate our thinking about human life and development in the United States. He speaks of central developmental tasks, tasks that weave an inner sense of self and an outer world of people, cultural values, and social realities into a life that provides an experience of self-respected and other-respected identity, a capacity for intimacy, the realization of productivity, and a final sense of integrity in the waning years of life. This modern vision has actually been realized largely within privileged American and Western European societies, for it carries an assumption of *assurances about life* that is unavailable to many, including many who have grown up into the gay communities. Many black gay men, for example, have grown up in circumstances that do not allow a young man's survival to adulthood to be taken for granted, even without HIV. But where Erikson's vision is unrealized or unrealizable because of economic and social disadvantage, it remains an aspiration for many, and an important description of at least one set of possibilities for productive, satisfying human life within a humane and equitable society.[3]

Erikson wrote, however, in an American age before the uncertainty about life returned equitably to all—at least within gay communities— this time through the prospect of HIV infection. Because it is precisely Erikson's point that human development is a weaving of the inner experience of self with the outer realities of culture and society, one must wonder how his vision could account for the reality of the AIDS epidemic—for the deaths of so many men in their twenties, thirties, and forties; for the suffering, for the profound isolation of the gay communities (and now other minorities) in their "private" epidemics; and for those who are left surviving. The cultural values and social realities of the gay man in America are now quite extraordinary and not at all what Erikson—indeed, any of us—had in mind for human life.

What can we say about the developmental tasks facing the gay adolescent, who must integrate an inner sense of homosexual identity with a homophobic and self-hating culture that has added the horror of HIV to its arsenal of reasons the homosexual man is contemptuous? How is the gay adolescent to live with a social reality that sometimes places the uninfected man in the disenfranchised minority within his community?

How do we describe the developmental tasks of the young man in his twenties who, seeking a capacity for trust and for intimacy with others, fears that sexual intimacy may kill him? How do we address his fears that, should he fall in love, that connection may be limited to a handful of years before one or both dies a grueling death by AIDS?

What can we say about the developmental tasks of the man, still alive in his thirties or forties, who must believe in the possibility and importance of a future while death and loss stretch ten or twenty years into his past, and to the horizons of his future? How is he to feel that his life's work will be a meaningful contribution?

Finally, what can we make of the developmental tasks of the man who survives to old—or *older*—age, and looking back on a life disrupted and derailed by physical horror, indigestible losses, and painful isolation, must find within himself a sense of integration, rather than feelings of disgust and despair?

Some possible answers to these questions lie within the suppositions of Erikson, himself: The gay American must find hope for life that does not deny the cultural and social realities of life, but acknowledges them. These are not normal times or normal lives as many of us have come to expect them in late-twentieth-century America. But the realities of our lives must be included in any paths we find to travel. False paths, paths that deny reality, ultimately lead nowhere. They will lead us from our true selves, from the ability to connect with others, and from an inner capacity to love and be loved. If paths rooted in reality lead through deep sand, or are more treacherous than we expected, then we will not travel as far in a day. If they lead to destinations other than those we expected, we must rethink our plans and our purposes in life.

Ron, a psychotherapy patient and anesthesiologist in his late thirties, had a dream about this subject. Ron had been living in San Francisco for fifteen years, but had remained uninfected. He had been talking often about moving from the city, for his life had changed profoundly over the first decade of the epidemic. Many friends had died, and he had a new lover, after eight years with his last. He found the city changed: "There seems almost nothing left of what it was in 1980." We talked often about these subjects in the two years I had been seeing him, and in the weeks before the following sessions, about his sadness in the changes he had witnessed.

"I had a dream a few nights ago that, amazingly, was very comforting—because we had been shipwrecked on an island and we couldn't get off. It was like *Lord of the Flies*—the landscape had that sort of look, and the people didn't look like they belonged there, living on an island. And come to think of it, it was all men. There were a lot of us, like maybe fifteen or twenty, and there was this sort of college dormitory quality to the relationships, but of course we were older. Will [the patient's current lover] was there, and Michael [the patient's former lover, who was now ill with HIV] was there too, and they were talking to each other, but they seemed to get along and I didn't feel uncomfortable in the dream about their being together."

"You said you were *comforted* by the shipwreck—or perhaps despite it," I commented.

"Well, yes. The dream started after the shipwreck, or I don't remember that part. We were just *there* and that was, you know, the assumption of how we got there. I knew that in the dream, I think, though this may be something I made up afterwards. But there was no ship, nothing left of it that ever came up in the dream that I can remember."

"It is interesting though, that something that normally provides you with such pleasure and escape [Ron had an ocean-going sailboat on which he did long excursions] ended up so badly in the dream."

"Well, I hadn't thought of that. But I felt no distress about having had a wreck. And, it wasn't the wreck that was comforting, it was— believe it or not—the realization that we would have to stay there, and that we *could* do that. It hadn't occurred to us. We thought we were going to be leaving, and we were always waiting to get rescued, but when we realized we weren't going to be, it seemed as if there were this tremendous opportunity—that we were going to stay there and, I guess, make our own society. We started working together for each other rather than for the rescue, and this brought us much closer. We had a society again, but it was just a different one than we'd had before we got stranded."

"How were you a society?" I asked.

"At the beginning of the dream there was this contraption with a fire in it on the cliff up above the beach, and we spent all our time gathering sticks—driftwood, I suppose—and things to burn in it. There was also something like that in *Lord of the Flies,* something to signal planes or ships. Whatever it was—you know, it was how we were going to get out of there. Everything revolved around keeping it filled and, I guess, smoking. It's funny, but I can't remember exactly what it *did,* because I think it was just my assumption that it *smoked.* Maybe if you kept it filled with sticks, it just sent out SOS signals—quite a radio—but in any case it was how we were going to get out of there. That was the point. It was sort of a barrel hanging on stilts and there were pipes and things coming out of the bottom of it, and there were valves that had to be turned on and off in various sequences. It was very demanding. I had to get it all *right*—the sequencing of the valves and so on—and I had a lot of anxiety about it. In some way I had become the person who was in charge of it. I had to manage it, and it was my responsibility to see that it kept working and to coordinate people about bringing wood up the hill. And being so anxious, I was sort of barking orders to everyone else, telling them to go here and there and get this and that. We would put the wood in the top. It changed some during the dream, I think, but it was always some sort of tall contraption. And very complicated."

"A barrel hanging on stilts?" I questioned.

"Something like that. As a matter of fact, it would swing around in the wind and I had to grab it and keep it from swinging around too much. For some reason that was very important. That was part of my job."

I thought about the image for a minute. "When you talk about a barrel on stilts with valves coming out of the bottom, it sounds like an IV pole with a drip bag hanging from it [a device used to drip intravenous solutions into a patient's bloodstream]."

Ron suddenly started crying when I said this.

"What came up?" I asked.

"I don't know."

"I was also thinking of your having to keep it from *swinging around too much*. It's like keeping an anesthetized patient's vital signs from swinging around too much."

"I started crying because I realized that you were there too," Ron said, still crying.

"I was where?"

"On the island with us. You were with us. I guess I had forgotten that."

"And do you know why you remembered my being there at that moment, just after I suggested that this might be an IV pole and you started to cry?"

"When you said 'an IV pole,' then I thought, 'Well, this is another dream about AIDS.'"

"You do tend to discount the connection of AIDS to a lot of feelings—and dreams."

"It's amazing how much sense it makes. I'm in charge of the IV, and this is going to save us from the island. And you're sitting here now helping me interpret this. In the dream you did the same thing, because you said to me, in that way you ask questions that makes me think a bomb is about to drop, 'Well, Ron, why is it that you want to leave the island?' and that made me think about it. This is what I was talking about before—it is our coming to terms with living on the island, staying there, and I think that is about coming to terms with AIDS. Not necessarily having it, but living in that world, accepting it. The contraption, the IV, was our fighting being there, it was how we were going to get out, our trying to get away, and when we accepted it, it was very comforting.

"At first, when I talked about staying on the island, everyone was very upset. There was a lot of conflict about this. No one had the idea of staying there, and I don't know why—it was your idea about staying there, but I was the one who broke it to the group—but when I said, 'We'd better start thinking about *living* here rather than spending all our energy trying to get out of here,' everyone was very upset and they acted as if I was sabotaging the whole effort to get out of there. But we weren't going to get out—we couldn't—and I knew I had to convince them that was true. I said, 'You know, we're going to use up all the wood and have none left if we keep this up.' And I remember feeling so much relief at not having to take care of the contraption—the IV pole—and just trying to get back to life. The other people came around on this, and there was also this feeling that we were a community again, that we were working for a real life as a community because we weren't constantly running up and down the hill fetching sticks."

Over the next few weeks we talked about Ron's realization that for the entire first decade of the epidemic he had lived as if the epidemic were a diversion from his intended course in life, and that he would, indeed, soon return to the life he had expected. For Ron, an anesthesiologist providing pain control for HIV patients, the IV equipment represented, in the dream, his nonacceptance of the epidemic. Ron usually worked with patients in terminal stages of AIDS who had severe pain, uncontrolled by normal medication. His ability to help control pain might improve their quality of life, and allow them to remain alive slightly longer. That clarification helped him begin to consider the possibility that, although life in an epidemic was not what he had expected life would be about, he did not realistically think it would be over during his lifetime. He held little hope, in 1991, for a vaccination or curative treatment, and yet he continued living as if the epidemic were something he anticipated escaping from.

When he was able to acknowledge—in the dream—that he would be staying on the island, his approach to living was quite different. The difference changed the ultimate experience dramatically. During the therapy sessions following Ron's relation of the dream, we discussed some of the differences this realization made within the dream, and within his life in the epidemic. He had begun to take the metaphor of the dream quite seriously as a metaphor and guide for his life in San Francisco.

After weeks of these discussions, Ron said to me, "I see that we have a whole island here, that the whole island is a possibility, not just a limitation, and that we have to find a way to make a life here instead of just taking refuge while we wait for a rescue."

"You make it sound like an opportunity."

"Well, no. But it's the one we got. I mean, this isn't even in question at this point in the epidemic."

It seemed clear to Ron that the hope for gay communities, earlier in the epidemic, lay in a cure for HIV disease—in a rescue. He now thought this an unrealistic expectation, and even if it were to occur, it would be unrealistic to expect the end of the epidemic to mean that everyone would revert to being who he used to be and the gay communities to what they were.

"We are all profoundly changed by what has happened," he said to me, "and survival must now mean being who we are and can be, given what we're living through."

Ron's dream metaphor for the AIDS epidemic involved life in the forces of nature, life unbenefited by the assurances of civilization many of us have come to assume in twentieth-century America. Ron's solution evolved into a reevaluation of expectations and assumptions, and an adaptation to a new and often difficult life.

Schemes and Visions: Denial, Hope, and Survival

Genji was still haunted by the impermanence of worldly things, and now that the Emperor was beginning to reach years of discretion he often thought quite seriously of embracing a monastic life. It seemed to him that in history one so often reads of men who at an immature age rose to high position and became conspicuous figures in the world only to fall, after a very short time, into disaster and ignominy. . . . But so many questions arose concerning the education of his children and their future at Court that there could be no question of his actually taking his vows, at any rate for some considerable time; and what exactly he had in mind when he began building this hermitage it would be hard to say.—Lady Murasaki, from The Tale of Genji [4]

Ron's contraption on the island, and the idea that it would lead to rescue, was a *scheme*. The scheme occupied the time and attention of the men on the island, allowed them to cope with—and deny—their feelings about being stranded, and thus provided a sense of a *certain kind* of hope. But Ron's realization that rescue was unrealistic, and that he and the others could and must make a life for themselves on the island was a *vision* (that, interestingly, he attributed to his psychotherapist in the dream). This vision provided access to connections among the men, to feelings, and to the development of a real and fuller life, instead of a life in temporary refuge. Most importantly, it provided a substantial sense of hope, for it was based not on the denial of feelings and reality but on a clarification of the truth.

In the first decade of the AIDS epidemic we mostly mustered schemes to deal with the reality of the situation and our feelings about it. Schemes may be useful for temporary refuge. They often serve us, but largely by detaching us from our feelings, ourselves, and thus, ultimately from others. Our AIDS education—such an important cultural force in many gay communities—typically has encouraged the proliferation of schemes for addressing feelings about the epidemic. One spectacularly uninsightful encouragement to schemes is seen in the manic prescription of the San Francisco AIDS Foundation in its 1994 "Outliving Forecasts of Doom" postcard campaign:

> Got Places to go. Single Gay Man with plans to make. A few years ago, I couldn't think ahead to the next week. Now, I'm organizing the first Queer Space Shuttle Voyage. 10 . . . 9 . . . 8 . . . 7! More than one way to get to heaven!

In this climate of publicly promoted schemes, gay men have adopted a variety of their own: substance abuse, twelve-step programs, workaholism (especially in AIDS services), depressive isolation, exercise, meticulous diet, gluttony, avoidance of sexual intimacy, partying, ritualized sex, safer sex, dangerous sex, and religious devotion. Many of these schemes, when part of a substantial approach to life's problems, are of genuine value. But taken alone, and used to avoid a realistic appraisal of one's situation, such schemes can only get us through an afternoon, a week, or, if particularly apt, a few years. Used as schemes, and rooted in denial, they provide respite from the epidemic and our feelings about it at immense cost: the impoverishment of our humanity.

It is so often said in the epidemic that denial provides hope, and without hope, all will be lost in a sea of indifference, resignation, and despair. Such feelings are surely among those of the author of the first Queer

Space Shuttle program. During moments of overwhelming reality, denial provides protected space in which to live until we are able to begin to assimilate, digest, and accommodate or change the reality. But denial does not even allow us to recognize that there are problems, and it absolutely prohibits our appraising and addressing them. For that reason, denial—and the schemes that it breeds—cannot serve as a foundation for *life* solutions. In all but temporary refuge, denial is a hopeless—not a hopeful—posture, and provides only a pretense of hope, which inhibits the understandings needed to develop substantive hope. Substantive hope comes only out of the contemplation of hopelessness itself, and it is only from such contemplation that alternatives to hopelessness are born. Woody Castrodale wrote me about his thoughts on denial and hope.

> What is "hope"? Is it an intra-psychic event only, or can it be shared between several persons? Do HIV-negative men hope for some kind of "miracle" to happen in order to ward off their own very real fears of what may happen to them?
>
> Could it be that hoping for some way out of our own confusion and fear is actually a manifestation of a real and undeniable "split" in the gay community? HIV-negative men can realistically hope for something, although it is not exactly clear what this *something* is. However, does it make sense to project this hoping onto men who already have AIDS? Maybe, by doing so, we are not allowing HIV-positive men to feel the full range of their own emotions. Or maybe it doesn't have anything to do with emotions per se, but rather that, once a gay man is HIV-positive, he has a different destiny to live out from the one we [negatives] do.
>
> Is the question of hope related directly, in some way, to the psychological denial of death? That is to say, perhaps hope is essential and perfectly healthy for anyone who is not "immediately dying." And perhaps to talk about hope is an existential absurdity for people who feel they have death bearing down on them so close at hand.
>
> Does hoping for something remove us from the immediacy of our own lives; the pain, the joy, the moment-by-moment pleasure?
>
> Is hope a basic, necessary confusion about the ultimate nature of human life in death?[5]

In his conjecture, Castrodale raises another important reason that we maintain denial and impede the development of substantial hope—survivor guilt. Survivor guilt may be partly ameliorated by denial, because denial enables the survivor to deny the event that is the basis of his guilt. If the epidemic is not, after all, so bad—"we're outliving forecasts of doom"—then one has less to be guilty about, because survivors and nonsurvivors differ about something not so important. Castrodale implicitly raises the issue of guilt when he speaks of hope as a manifestation of a "split" within gay communities, and subsequently expresses the thought that perhaps "hope is essential and perfectly healthy for anyone who is not 'immediately dying.'" An uninfected man's substantial hope about his own life often aggravates his guilt about survival, because he feels that his hopefulness represents an accusation of hopelessness about the lives of positive men. Indeed, many men—positive and negative—experience a negative man's explicitly stated hope that he remain uninfected, as an invalidation of the lives of positive men. For the uninfected man who acutely experiences such guilt, a self-limited condition of emptiness and hopelessness *or the mustering of false hope* is often the guilt-ameliorating solution. Both possibilities allow the uninfected man to share the hopelessness of many positive men. In the San Francisco AIDS Foundation's version of false hope, it is the "Single Gay Man"— HIV status unstated and irrelevant—who is on his way to outer space. Thus survivor guilt, as well as the simple emotional pain of experiencing the epidemic, are both sources of the denial and false hope to which so many of us have clung.

The AIDS epidemic is now a form of life that promises to endure in most gay communities. When it seemed possible that HIV transmission might be controlled through behavioral change—or, more likely, that we would be able to prevent and treat it medically—schemes and other kinds of false hope made sense. They offered to sustain us until we were rescued. But advancing unabated into a new century, the epidemic now demands real vision about the lives we lead, for only vision will provide sustaining meaning and lives that express that meaning. Hope rooted in vision—substantive hope—lacks the absoluteness of denial, and it will not protect us from all pain. Living in an epidemic, we will know pain if we know life in any real sense. Substantive hope, because it allows us to know the world, to know ourselves, and to know others, is in many ways the most we can ask of life: it is all here, it is all there is, and it is our only opportunity.

Other Ideas of Survival and Visions of
Life in the Epidemic

It happened that Osan and Moemon also made the pilgrimage together. They and the
flowers they saw seemed to share a common fate: no one could tell when they might
fall. Nor could anyone tell whether the lovers again might see this bay and the hills
around Lake Biwa, so Moemon and Osan wanted to make it a day to remember.—Ihara
Saikaku, *from* Five Women Who Loved Love[6]

What form might genuine hope and an authentic life take in the AIDS
epidemic? Could a gay man answer this question as he might have before
1982? Matt, a 31-year-old who first encountered AIDS at the age of 25
with the death of his boyfriend David, began examining this issue during a psychotherapy session in a rainy and cold December, on the first
anniversary of David's death. Through the remainder of San Francisco's
rainy season, Matt and I met twice weekly and explored his adjustment
to life as a gay man in the epidemic.

> I have really lived so deeply in sadness my whole life that it is
> only now that I have even known what it was—and of course, this
> has a lot to do with being here [in therapy] and starting to come
> out of it. It was transparent to me. I always thought it was just *life*.
> My loneliness as a child, the problems with my family, and all the
> years I've spent trying to be straight—it's just all made me very sad.
> But as I understand a lot of this, I really feel as if I'm emerging out
> from under a rug that I've always lived under, a rug that was just
> my personal sadness.
> But now I'm wondering what I'm going to *do*—I mean, there's
> so much sadness *in the world* with AIDS, and I'm afraid that this is
> going to just linger with me and take off where my personal sadness
> left off—I am thinking about David and wondering if I will ever
> be able to get over his dying. I used to really get into Christmas
> carols—they lifted my spirit when I was a kid—and I'm finding
> this year, for the first time, that I have no reaction to them. People
> start singing and I just have no reaction. I relied on that, and I'm
> really left wondering, with the state of things for the gay world,
> what I'm going to do. It's not just Christmas carols, it's all the little
> things I've used to not have bad feelings. I thought just a minute
> ago as I was talking, "Well, I can escape to Disneyland," and then I
> thought, "Well no, I can't do that because there are no real people

there—no real relationships there." I was thinking about going home tonight—alone—and I don't think I can do it. I'm going to call Tim and ask him to come spend the night with me.

Matt and I talked that session about his effort at "coping" with the epidemic, in the sense of schemes, and about their limitations, and we also talked about something more substantive. Matt felt that in current circumstances he would have to live differently than in what he called "nonplague times," and that this would entail concentrating on his capacity to live, to live intensely, and to experience himself and others. In a session three days later, he told me:

"When I left here Monday night, I stopped at the hospital to see Jeremy, Jim's lover. When I got there, his bed was empty, and I went out and asked a nurse where they'd moved him. She said, 'Oh, the patient in 4012A? He died this morning around nine o'clock.' That was it. No explanations, nothing. Just one more dead. I didn't know Jeremy that well, but it was—well, it left me feeling completely empty, desolated, as if he'd been my best friend. I was just spinning. I thought to myself, I've just got to get over my sadness—not get *over* it, because I know now that it's important to have it. But I've got to get out *from under* it, because it keeps me from living. At the same time I felt this shock about Jeremy, I also felt this tremendous urge to go out and *live* when the nurse told me he was dead—to really go out and make the best of it, because *I* had the opportunity, and I could do something for Jeremy who didn't—and for myself."

"What did you do?"

"Well, actually, I just went out and had dinner by myself instead of going home. Being in public gave me a sense of normality, of people being able to do normal things, even while Jeremy and all the others are dead, and I really needed that right then. Tim did come and spend the night, and we were sitting in bed having tea and pears, and I was telling him about Jeremy and also what *we'd* been talking about [here in therapy]. We talked about that for a long time, because I know Tim feels a lot of sadness about things too. But after I turned out the light, he just fell asleep, and I watched him for a long time. And it dawned on me what an amazing thing it was . . ."

Matt trailed off at this point, and I finally said, "You said, 'What an amazing thing,' and then you seemed to drift inside."

"Well I was thinking about it, and I was also thinking that I was kind of embarrassed talking about the two of us being in bed together."

"Why would that be embarrassing?" I wondered.

"Well, it was partly just about being in bed with a man, and this voice in my head saying, 'You know, two men, with their four hairy legs, aren't supposed to be in bed together. You're supposed to be in bed with a woman—that's what's normal, and this looks pretty funny.' But it was amazing . . . it was. Just having him there, and watching him sleep. I would think about his having his own body, and it being different from mine—not different exactly, but *his own*—how we each had lungs and a heart, just that this whole complicated person—thing—separate from me in some ways and very connected in others, lying there *sleeping*. This seemed so incredible at the time. I felt how much it meant to me, and how much company he was for me, even when he was sleeping. It was very primitive. When he breathed out, I could smell the pear and tea, and also the smell of his breath, which I like. I could also just make out his skin in the light from the hallway, his arm, and ear and face in the dark, and he seemed incredibly beautiful and powerful. It was the *intensity* of things we were talking about on Monday. But just the smell of his breath with the pears made me think, 'This is wonderful, this is amazing—that people can eat things, that we move around in our sleep, and are existing in our minds when we do that. That we kiss, that we breathe.' Especially that his smell could be so good and mean so much to me. I know it sounds corny, but there's nothing else you could want from life but this. It seemed perfect, and it seemed like a reason all in itself to be alive. Tim and I have had so much trouble in our relationship, and in both our lives with AIDS [although both are uninfected], and I thought, 'Just this minute is worth everything, and it doesn't matter what we do tomorrow, just having Tim in my bed for this minute makes up for anything. I'll just have to deal with tomorrow when it comes up, and right now it means nothing to me.'"

"How do you think this experience answers the concerns you were talking about on Monday?" I asked.

"The concerns?"

"I'm thinking of the sadness that the epidemic has brought to your life, and the sadness that existed before the epidemic. And

I'm wondering if you find a solution to the sadness in the kind of experience you're describing with Tim."

"I'm not sure," Matt answered after a moment of hesitation.

"Can you say why?"

"Well, I have the idea that you think I'm just sidestepping it, that this is a way of avoiding it, of denying my sadness and AIDS, rather than answering it."

"That sounds to me like it might be your reservation. I don't think I said anything like that."

"No, I said that. I do have that idea. For one thing, I've never expected life to be about things like that. I've expected it to be about big things, about who I am in terms of my career, and about having a family—now that I've come out, I'd say just having a lover and a *lifestyle,* whatever the fuck that could mean. I think of all the times people say about other people, 'Oh, all he's got in his life is his flower garden,' or something like that. It's belittling."

"And yet you found having Tim in bed quite transforming—or so it seems from the way you told the story."

"I did. That's true. But I also have trouble letting go of all the assumptions I've always had about what was *supposed* to be important, how I was *supposed* to live, what I was *supposed* to do with my time. I was thinking about my Dad calling up if he were alive, and he'd say, 'So, Matt, what's going on? What are you doing with your life?' What would I say? 'Who me? Oh, I'm smelling Tim.' But my Dad's expectations just don't apply anymore. I feel very clear about that, because I know going back and forth about this, that when I try to live a normal life . . ."

"Normal?"

"Hmm. Yeah, a *normal* life. A life that you'd have if everyone wasn't dying or dead. This reminds me of the first line of [the novel] *Afterlife,* and it fits to a T: 'If they hadn't all died at once, none of this would have happened,' or something like that.[7] That's how I feel about my life, and I feel more that way as I come to understand how I've got to change—and definitely change my assumptions— in order to live with this and not go crazy. What I'd started to say was that as I go back and forth from a normal life to a life where I appreciate all these little things, and see that they are a purpose in themselves, or that right now, this minute, is a purpose in itself, then, I see that I can only have a "normal" life by denying what's going on all around me. When I don't deny it, then none of the old stuff makes sense. It looks ridiculous. When I was having dinner after going to see Jeremy, these two guys—very well-dressed, high-maintenance types—were walking out talking to each other, and just as they passed my table, one of them said, 'People have to understand that deficits are not always liabilities. Take Disney for example . . .' and then they were out of earshot. And I thought, '*Wow,* these two guys have *no idea* what's going on. They have no idea what life is about,' and I started to laugh out loud because it seemed to me that they were just delusional—that seemed very, very clear."

"And yet there is some part of you that is tempted back into that—that denies the epidemic and your feelings about it, and gets back into a so-called normal—even delusional—life?"

"Definitely. Because I *forget.* Because I don't *want* things to be the way they are, and if I actually *act* as if they're not, maybe they won't be. Because I'm afraid to let go. Because I'm afraid that I'm just using it as an excuse."

"Tell me what you mean by using *it* as an excuse," I asked Matt.

"That I am just using the epidemic as an excuse for my depression. That I've always been depressed, and I'm using the epidemic so I don't have to get over it."

"But you've been talking about the epidemic as a basis for getting out of your depression—*out from under it,* you said."

"Hmm. Yes, I've gotten confused here," Matt responded after a moment's thought.

"What about the epidemic as an excuse? What about that feeling?"

"Well, I have often had that idea. I guess at one point, when I was committed to being depressed, so to speak, I had the feeling a lot that I was using it. The epidemic was my rationalization for why I was depressed. It was a way of not having to change, of saying, 'Leave me alone, because now I have a good reason to be depressed and there's no hope of doing anything about it.'"

"What was the rationalization? That the whole epidemic just had you down?"

"Well, I would think, Jeff is dead, Bruce is dead, Dylan is dead, and lots of my other friends have HIV. So, why shouldn't I be depressed?"

"And it seemed that you were exploiting that to justify being depressed?" I asked.

"Yes, that it was an excuse. But right now, I'm thinking, 'Well, shit, what would it take to get you depressed? Isn't that enough?' Are we supposed to *not* get depressed by that?"

"It is understandable to me, although you seem to doubt it."

"Right now it's understandable to me too. I'm thinking that the idea—that I wouldn't be depressed by this, that it was just an excuse—was really a way of denying how much it has all meant to me, denying the effect that it really has had on me. That it *is* having on me. And a lot of it comes from my family, from this idea that you're not supposed to have feelings—this whole thing we've talked about. That it's just not OK to have feelings about anything, including everyone dropping dead."

We sat for a few moments, and I responded. "Yes, I'm sure your family's approach is involved, and that you're wanting to deny the impact of the epidemic is involved too, because that's just an internalization of your family's feelings about feelings. It's also about not wanting to feel the pain of the whole thing. But I doubt that you can just dispense with the epidemic because you don't want to have feelings about it."

Four days later Matt sat down and immediately picked up where we had left off:

"There is something else—about the feeling that the epidemic is an excuse for being depressed—that is related to what we were talking about last week. The idea that it's an excuse, you said, is the desire not to have the feelings, or something like that. And I'm also thinking that it's about this nagging feeling I have—not that AIDS isn't that bad—but that my feelings about it don't have to be that bad, that there *must* be something for me to do about it. There must be a solution, there must be a way out, and I'm just not looking for it so I don't blow my excuse. I sometimes think you know what this is, and you're waiting for me to figure it out on my own."

"Do you?"

"Actually, I think that you don't know. I don't either, and neither does anyone else. But I have this assumption that there is always a solution for everything. You just have to find the right specialist or whatever. When my Dad got sick [when Matt was 16] is when it first struck me that we couldn't have a solution for everything, and that he was actually going to die, and that there wasn't anything to do about it. It was going to happen, and that was that, and no one could do anything about it. It was amazing to me. Before that I thought, well, this is the modern world, and we live in a democracy, and my parents are very smart and rich, and there's always something to do about any problem that comes along. But AIDS—you know, it's finally made it *completely* clear to me that we can't be safe in life, that it's all very tenuous. My Dad dying only started that, but AIDS has finished it off. Remembering that is one of the big things that helps me remember that you have to live your *own* life, that you can't live out other people's expectations."

In a session later that week, we returned to the idea that the epidemic not only served as an excuse to be depressed, but—in apparent contradiction—that it served as an excuse to live fully.

"When I was talking about getting out from under my depression, of really learning how to live, the idea that the epidemic was an excuse for that, too, is clear to me now. It's as if I'm using the epidemic to throw off all the assumptions I was talking about—thinking about my career and a future, and so on. I'm saying, 'Well I'm living this irresponsible and reckless life because the epidemic is making me do that. Under the circumstances it's OK, and you can't criticize me for that.'"

"Who can't?"

"I can't. And my Mom can't. Mostly I can't. And I guess my Dad can't. But I have this nagging doubt that I could have a normal life, that I could save money and make plans for the future, and do things other people do, but I'm not, because I have this excuse."

I commented on Matt's insight: "This is very much related to the idea that you shouldn't be depressed about the epidemic. I say this because the idea that you shouldn't be depressed or that you shouldn't be living your life in a special way are both denials of how really significant the epidemic has been for you. There's no need to feel depressed or to feel that you have to change your assumptions and values, because you're just skating through this thing. Both feelings deny what the epidemic has meant to you."

"Well, when I look at my solutions—I was at my friends Mark and Lenny's house the other night, and Lenny, who *has* HIV, said,

'The worst thing I can think of is dying with money in the bank.' And I asked why, and he said, 'Well it would mean that I wasn't having a good enough time while I had the opportunity.' I thought, 'Well, I feel that way too.' What we're taught, really, is to *hoard* in life, to not spend money or whatever it is we have to spend, to hold on to everything, to keep it for the future. The epidemic makes me feel like that just doesn't make any sense at all. I can't see it anymore. But then suddenly I think, 'Yeah, well, Lenny *has* HIV and you don't, and you're just using this as an excuse to be irresponsible.'"

"You mentioned the idea of irresponsibility before—and living recklessly."

"Yes, well, that's my idea about it, particularly when I'm in 'the epidemic is an excuse' mode."

"And what makes a particular form of life irresponsible? Or reckless? For that matter, where do you draw the line between recklessness and hoarding, as you put it."

"I don't know," Matt answered, "but I know that it's changed because of the epidemic. I don't know if I live recklessly or not."

"What do you do that might be reckless?"

"I guess I'm talking about not planning—not holding onto things for the future. Also, I'm just not willing to give up anything today that's important to me with the idea that I might regret it later. I feel like I have to use everything *now*. And I would say that I especially include in that my *life*. It's not really dangerous stuff—I don't mean that. But I wouldn't call it prudent either. My mother is terrified that I'd have *safe* sex with someone who's positive, and the only thing I could say to her is 'Mom, you have no idea who I am anymore. You have no idea how I live, what the reality of my life is.' She's never seen a dead person, and I think of how familiar I am with death now. When Dylan died, I lay on the bed with him—with his body—and I held onto him for a long time. It was amazing, and I know how close we all are to being dead, that it is just a little step over a line that we walk around pretending isn't there. It's there for all of us, and holding onto Dylan like that made me feel very close to it, that I accepted it. It was very *reassuring* to me."

Matt sat silently for several minutes and then continued.

"My mother doesn't know what that's about and she's 64. She doesn't know what my life is about anymore—she's just too far from it. What it's about makes me value different things, and lots of them are things that seem reckless to her. To me, this is a line I have to walk now. I know that *really* living is not as safe as hoarding, and I know, more or less, how I got to this. But I couldn't tell her, or anyone else, how to understand this. It's something that *happens* to you. You don't do it."

I thought for a moment about what Matt had said, and about his willingness to tread close to the line and accept the consequences. "I accept your conviction about that."

"Yeah, it seems to me that you do understand that. I hardly know anything about you, but I think you know about this."

"But I should also say," I continued, "that I think it's worth keeping an eye on despair, because it can make recklessness look like living fully—like passion. Recklessness and passion—I think there are some differences between them."

"Oh, I'm sure there are. But I would just say that one of the changes in me is that I'm going to err on the side of using things up, not hoarding—except when I get frightened, and I'm trying to feel that less. The truth of what's going on—the epidemic and all the people it's taking—well, that just keeps sinking in deeper and deeper for me, and the further it goes, the more I know that my feelings about life are right, and the less I get frightened. I have so many friends who have just hit the *hold button*—I mean, they're on hold and they're just using their lives up waiting on hold, and I couldn't even tell you what for. A cure, I suppose. Which is not impossible. But we have no idea if this will ever end. Sometimes I think to myself, you are going to feel like an idiot if suddenly there's a cure and this whole thing is over. I think that fear—and in some ways I'm really not clear on it, but the idea of a cure is a fear for me, as well as a hope—comes up in my most hoarding times: 'You're shooting the wad and on Tuesday the epidemic is going to be over, and you won't have anything left.'"

Matt sat silently for several minutes, and then seemed to arrive at a new insight.

"What I'm really sitting here thinking—it's about shooting the wad. What I'm really feeling when I think that is: If you shoot the wad and then you *don't die*—and by that I mean if I *never* die. That's really what we all think walking around in our lives—that we're *never* going to die, because if we didn't believe that, if we believed that *someday* we were going to die, we wouldn't put up with all the bullshit—and we wouldn't hoard. We just don't believe we're ever going to die, and that's how we're *supposed* to feel."

"Whose expectation is that?"

"That's *everyone's*. My idiot boss—if the people who worked for him really believed that one day they were going to die, no one would listen to him. We'd all be saying, 'Oh there's something better than this. See you later, Jack.' "

"So there's freedom in the knowledge you're going to die."

"Exactly. Because if you believe you're going to die, if you really believe that, then it makes life unnecessary. And that's so liberating, because the minute you know life is unnecessary, you're freed to live it any way you want. Oh, it's so slippery, but it's so important, and I hate to think it's taken all this suffering for me to understand it. But *that's* what I understood when I held Dylan: I thought, 'Oh thank God, life can all be over with too, because that makes it so much more worthwhile.' I *will* end up like this—I mean, it doesn't matter *when*. I *will* end up like Dylan, but in the meantime I have to do whatever I want, whatever is important, whatever I can be proud of. And I think to myself, how many of my friends will I have to see dead before I know this is the truth? How many people will I have to see dead before I stop forgetting this?

Other Kinds of Survival

The entire modern deification of survival per se, survival returning to itself, survival naked and abstract, with the denial of any substantive excellence in what survives, except the capacity for more survival still, is surely the strangest intellectual stopping-place ever proposed by one man to another.—William James[8]

Imminent—or, as Matt argues, simply inevitable—death is our most important and only authentic teacher about the value of human life. For Matt, one important human question raised by this insight is precisely the question raised by William James's observation: why do we understand survival as being about longevity, rather than about the richness and fullness of life? Has the 80-year-old man, unrealized, disheartened, and disappointed with his life, survived in any important way? Has the 30-year-old who has contributed much to family, friends, lover, and society, but is now dying of AIDS, failed to survive in a human sense?

This far into the AIDS epidemic, many find it self-evident that merely surviving the epidemic biologically is not an adequate goal, but that we must insist on lives as human beings who, above all, develop or regain our capacities to live fully and passionately. If fear—and *it will be fear*—obscures this understanding, it will be, for those with HIV in their bodies and those without it, among the greatest losses exacted by the epidemic.

Ken, a heterosexual psychotherapist working with several gay men, spoke to me about his concerns for the psychological health of the gay male communities and, in particular, his troubled sense of two gay men in his practice who seemed to be suffering badly in the epidemic. As a man living largely within the heterosexual community, he said:

> I sometimes thank God I'm not personally within the gay community, that I have something else to retreat to. I think that the trauma of the epidemic has created such problems, such psychological restrictions among men, such a deficit of a capacity for intimacy, that I can't see how gay men are going to come out on the other side of this. I don't know how you personally deal with this in other gay men. I feel like Donald [a psychotherapy patient of Ken]—and he's not the only one I've seen—is such a tiny part of the person that he must have been seven or eight years ago, that there is so little of him left as a human being after all his losses, that there is just no one home. He's very, very closed off, very inaccessible to any kind of real intimacy.

During this conversation, Ken also discussed Dan, a psychotherapy patient in his late twenties. Ken expressed concern that although Dan was not closed off like Donald, he seemed at special risk for contracting HIV.

> "He spends most of his time with HIV-positive friends, and talks a lot about his experience with them—that their lives are so much richer and more intense than those of his negative friends, and about feeling so connected to this. It's with them and their sensibilities that he feels at home. And I wonder if he wouldn't feel more at home *having* HIV."
>
> "Is it your fear that he will contract HIV because of this identification?" I asked Ken.
>
> "Yes. I think he's at great risk for that. These are the only people who mean anything to him. I can't see what else he has. And if

the people who mean so much to him—I should say, who mean *everything* to him—have HIV, why shouldn't he?"

"Is contracting HIV the worst thing you think might happen to him?" Ken hesitated at my question.

"I know there are all *sorts* of issues here. Is it OK to say *no?*"

"It's OK with me. But, as you know, you can't say that to just anyone."

"I think his greatest risk is to end up like Donald. Here are two guys very much alike, trying to live through the same epidemic, and one is so out in the ozone, so unconnected to other people, and the other so intensely involved. I think the greatest danger for Dan would be to end up out there and disconnected like Donald. If Donald lived to be a hundred and if he were to remain that disconnected, I'd have to say that would be worse than getting HIV. He suffers terribly because of his inability to connect with other men."

I was trying to sort out the issues at this point. I asked Ken, "Does Dan have to get HIV to be connected? No—that's not the question. That's what people ask when they're trying to dismiss the possibility that HIV transmission and intimacy are related in any way at all. I should ask, is Dan going to get HIV *because* he's connected? That seems to me the real question. It's intimacy, and living fully, and HIV that we're talking about—and whether the first two lead to the latter, and how."

"I just keep thinking that within a very intimate relationship it must finally be hard to avoid HIV. Denial of one's own and the other's feelings—I mean denial of longing, of sexual desire, of fear, of all sorts of feelings—seems to be necessary for a lot of gay men to keep them completely safe. I'm thinking of fear, distance, denial of feelings, of all of these being used by Donald to protect himself from HIV—and it's that they 'protect' him from so much else—like *a life* that he can be reasonably happy in. I suppose some people can make the distinction, but some people can't. Some people just can't exercise whatever is necessary to steer clear of HIV and still have substantial relationships."

I asked Ken if he thought Dan had a realistic appraisal of the risks of HIV and was willing to take them anyway, or if, perhaps, he was exercising some denial about the risks.

"I'm not sure about that. He works with people with HIV all the time, so he *knows* what it is, though I know that doesn't completely answer your question. I would have to say that he has the attitude that it doesn't matter if he gets it, and that there is mixed up in that a strange combination of optimism and discouragement. I remember a session when we were specifically talking about unsafe sex, about 'fucking,' and Dan made a comment about condoms and how they really interfered with his sexual intimacy in a very important way. I could see that he was talking about the way that physical connections serve to represent emotional ones—I mean, we're all into that, and it's the very basis of the connection between physical and emotional intimacy. For the first time I understood the importance of condoms—how it is that they come between people and disrupt intimacy in many senses. I don't know how gay men haven't appreciated that as obvious. It's one thing for me, as a heterosexual who hasn't used condoms since high school, to not quite understand that. But gay men failing to understand that suggests some denial is involved. I've had a lot of patients who talk about condoms as if they were the best thing since sliced bread—until you get into it just a little bit. Then mostly I see that they're angry and frightened about AIDS, and that the condom represents the whole thing to them."

I commented at this point: "The sense of separation, of emotional intimacy disrupted by a breach in physical intimacy—I know that is extremely important for many people. And, of course, fumbling around with condoms can really put a dent in the flow of things. But something else that may not be obvious to you is that the very presence of a condom is a constant reminder that you might be killing each other at that very moment. These feelings are more easily repressed or denied if there are no condoms around. How does fear of killing and being killed fit into your ideas of physical intimacy and their representations of emotional intimacy?"

Ken looked startled.

"It's a horrible thought. I have to say it again—I just don't know how you're all living with this. At the very time Dan was making a case for not using condoms—that is the *optimistic* part, the attempt at intimacy—he then suddenly started talking about multiple losses of friends, really family to him since his biological family has disowned him, and I don't remember exactly what he said—it was sort of, 'You know, so *what* if I get HIV? I don't want it, but that's not the most important thing either.' That comment left me with the feeling that this discouragement about losses made him care less about getting HIV, but also made him care more about intimacy."

"Instead of less . . . ," I interjected.

"Yes, that if he was going to lose those he loved, he was also going to have intimacy, and if that had to cost him having HIV—well, that's how it goes." Ken paused for a moment.

"The stakes just get higher and higher when you're living in an epidemic. That's the sense I had from Dan. I know that it's not what we tell patients, but it seemed to me to be courageous and to be the product of some very positive values, psychologically speaking. You can see in Donald and Dan that, again, they are going in opposite directions. Loss and depression can seem to lessen the value of intimacy or to increase it. We so often talk about loss and depression, and about its destructiveness, but, of course, people who are depressed maintain a connection to their emotional lives and sometimes to those of others. Donald doesn't have that, and in not having the depression, you might say that he doesn't seek the ecstasy that Dan does. Donald has abandoned the entire arena of feelings, and valuing them, and living in them."

Ken was again silent for a moment, and then asked, "But what of the self-destructive aspect of Dan? This is what people focus on when they hear this: 'This man doesn't care if he gets HIV or not.' I never know quite how to answer this."

I pondered this, for I think we had come to a crucial issue. "Do you think that Dan, in his intensity of feeling is any more self-destructive than Donald in his inability to feel?"

"Is it OK to say *no?*" We laughed at coming up on this question again, and I tried to respond:

"It's a matter of values, isn't it? It's really about the purpose of human life, and people are all over the place on this. There are people who think that making money is a reasonable purpose in life, and one doesn't have to live in the epidemic very long for that to look awfully empty. There are others who think that the purpose of human life is to make it as long as possible, and I suppose Donald, and a lot of other people who live physically, if not quite emotionally, in the epidemic, would be among these. Dan is following a different path, and it isn't one that's going to be easily intelligible to people leading lives outside the epidemic—or to many leading their lives *within* the epidemic, for that matter."

Ken looked as if he were pondering this idea, and I continued.

"There's so much pressure in the gay community to 'survive' this thing—it's human, it's political, it's from everywhere, and it's understandable. But the epidemic has to be an opportunity for people to follow their own values—otherwise we're just saying, 'Everything is going to be taken away from you, and we're also going to tell you how to feel about that, and what to do about it.' This epidemic so frightens us that we feel we have to dictate responses to it. But it's precisely the epidemic that makes it so important for people to live their own lives."

Ken seemed very sobered by this description.

"I particularly see what you're talking about in the disapproval leveled at 'late' seroconverters [those who become HIV positive later in the epidemic, with knowledge of how HIV is transmitted]. It is such a simplification of human life, and such an imposition of values. I'm thinking of it from a human point of view. I know that Dan's direction isn't for everyone, but I find him incredible and courageous in many ways. I find such humanity in him. There has to be some way that at least our psychotherapy acknowledges his insight."

My conversation with Ken tread along the edges of a delicate issue, for it called into question the very "deification" of survival, without regard for "the excellence in *what* survives," which James refers to. It is, on the whole, a question the gay communities have not been able to openly acknowledge, especially against the denial of mainstream society and forces within the gay communities that would have us believe that gay men "are doing well in the epidemic." Both conspire to "normalize" the epidemic by denying the radical form of life it has created for many gay men. Against this substantial denial, an awareness that the epidemic raises questions about fundamental values is increasingly apparent as the epidemic endures. Shortly after my conversation with Ken, I received a phone call from Woody Castrodale. He told me of a recent session of the HIV-negative men's group he facilitates in San Francisco:

We realized that night in the group that we'd spent virtually the entire last year talking about our psychological issues, about addressing them so that we could survive the epidemic, and that right now this seemed to all of us archaic, anachronistic, from another age—and I don't know if it's just the people in the group or just across the board. At this point I told the group that I had been walking down Castro Street several nights before, and I saw one of my lovers, Edward, whom I still know very well and with whom I have sex occasionally. I guess we met in about 1977, and he was sitting this night in Marcello's Pizza and I went in to talk to him, of course. After about a half hour, he said to me, in this strange way, "Woody, I'm no longer negative." Edward is the last thread in my life back to the time—the time before all this happened. I didn't say a thing. I sat there stunned, and leaned against the wall, and he kept talking, and it was like an earthquake in my life, because he's the last one left. I felt a million thoughts—I felt bereft, I felt completely shaken, I felt suddenly, my God, I'm having a million thoughts which I've never let myself think.

Richard is a mover and shaker in the group, and when I told this story, he said, "Well, Woody, are you going to get yourself tested? When you were sitting there in Marcello's you must have been terrified about your health." And I thought, "No, that is not what I was thinking at all," and being told what I was thinking made me realize what I really thought. I said to Richard, "No, none of what you're saying actually happened," and then I just had to honestly blurt it out, and I said, "When Edward told me he was no longer negative, my immediate thought was 'My God, I hope I'm not still negative, because that way I'll be able to go on with Edward just as we have for the past fourteen years, and everything will be fine.' I won't have to go through this horrible thing of thinking, weighing, and deciding." Another man suddenly burst out, "But Woody, that's it—having to think, and weigh, and decide all the time. If I made the choice to be positive, then I wouldn't have to worry about it." And then someone else said, "Yes, but it's a horrible death. In the middle of the night you might think that, but when the sun came up . . ." And we all realized suddenly that it is a choice, and we've only denied that because it isn't *rational*.

For the first time the group spontaneously came to the realization together that, in fact, there are issues in life, other than surviving, that are extremely important, and the group rejected the notion, for the first time, that survival is everything. A friend had talked about this several months ago over dinner, and it stunned me, because not many people talk about it, about how the culture pushes the idea that survival is the foremost value. The group has never been comfortable with the idea that that might not be true—but last night there was a consensus that there are issues that are pushing against this idea of surviving.

Ted, another man in the group that night, suddenly said, "I find I'm always making the wrong decision." I asked him what that meant, and he said, "I'm making decisions, meeting people, and deciding not to get involved with them, and I'm afraid this is the wrong decision." This really stunned the group into silence again. "I'm afraid this is the wrong decision," he said again. Suddenly we could all admit that maybe it's better to get involved with people and live fully and richly. Am I going to *engineer* myself so that I can live on and survive, or am I going to let my life be rich and complicated, and not consciously, logically engineer it? I've thought of that, but never brought it up because it was too unclear to me. But last night everyone could suddenly resonate on this, that we could allow ourselves to become involved with people, that we could just live our lives, and not restrict ourselves—that we had this *choice*.[9]

How modern society, including most men living in the epidemic, has come to so transparently experience longevity, rather than happiness, as the essential purpose of life, is a question worth pondering. We are taught that there is a *survival instinct* inborn in humans and other animals. Although there is some truth in this idea, it is also an exaggeration and distortion of Darwinian evolutionary theory. Darwin merely proposed that the natural selection process favors those whose constitution and behavior is most conducive to survival. But this is essentially a tautology. Darwinian theory does not propose, as the popular conception imagines, that those who survive do so because they are *motivated* to survive, or *intend* to survive, or even that traits that favor survival exist in order to create survival. Survival simply happens or it does not. Those who survive merely survive, and the evidence for that is the consequence that survivors have survived. Motivation and intent seem to be exclusively an experience of the human cortex, and, indeed, many humans are both motivated to survive and intend to do so. But such feelings are not instinctual, they are the product of acculturation, socialization, and education. The human infant who crawls from a fire does so to avoid pain, an instinctual behavior that has contributed to the consequence that many humans survive fires. The more acculturated adult who runs from a fire also avoids pain, but he also often runs with the intent of surviving.

The distinction between instinct and intent is important. It is social-ization that instills intent to survive. The purposes of society are clear: Society, as the machinery that promulgates collective values that pro-vide the individual with meaning (another cortical event), is motivated to survive. Dead people do not further the mechanisms, values, mean-ing, productivity, or security of a society, nor do they assuage the grief of those left behind. The individual easily takes on these community purposes as his own. Longevity—and sobriety, which is about everyone staying in the same world of *consciousness*—contribute importantly to "community" purposes such as filing documents accurately, purchasing consumer goods, and speeding financial instruments on their way to the banks of "successful" people. At this—admittedly the most impov-erished end of the spectrum of social motivation—we see most clearly that what is good for society is not always good for the individual. In many cases, survival per se may have nothing whatsoever to do with the subjective value of an individual human life.

"It has suddenly occurred to me," Woody Castrodale virtually shouted to me over the phone several days after our previous conversation, "that science has somehow become *survivalist*."

> I have just realized that Western science is at odds with *erotic* life, in the broad sense. And I mean by that, life that is about *life* rather than about survival. Life against death: You can't have your cake and eat it too, you can't live your life if it's all tangled up in avoid-ing death. But the average person doesn't buy it. Eros, love, hate, survival—at this point in the group, we just go round and round this. It's all that the group is about anymore.[10]

The capacity to live erotically, in this broad sense of the term, is an elusive one. It has been the subject of much Indian and Asian religious tradition, but in the West all but the fringes of society have ignored or shunned it. In India, China, and Japan, the structure and needs of society have always indomitably overshadowed the individual and his needs. Buddhism, Chan, and Zen thus served as necessary antagonists on be-half of individual, human life. They are literally traditions of "turning on, tuning in, and *dropping out*."

In the West, Judeo-Christian traditions have on the whole been the instruments of society, not its antagonists. These traditions, especially since the sixteenth century, have largely concerned themselves with conformity, social contribution, and thus with survival per se. Though

Jeffersonian democracy has been an attempt to simultaneously address both social needs and individual life, it has not adequately served as a source of insight for the gay man of late-twentieth-century America. Now one relatively small participant in a terrible world pandemic, we in the West have so little native wisdom to draw upon in spiritual support of subjective life. As children of our spiritual traditions, we continue to instinctively distrust the erotic life that is about everything but survival. As Jeffersonian democrats—and as Puritans—we envision erotic life as misinformed, selfish, or pathological. Despite the life-affirming meanings of eroticism, it brings to most of us, who have in the name of society destroyed so much on Earth, nothing but a vision of beastliness and social annihilation.

Closing Words

Kevin's life taught me many important lessons—to be generous, to find the humor in everything, always to be as sexy as possible, and to savor every moment.—A 26-year-old college mate of Kevin [11]

Other kinds of survival is about different kinds of survivors, as well as different visions of survival. The juggernaut of HIV—the fear, illness, death, and loss—has frightened us all. It has made us afraid of ourselves and of each other, and it has made us afraid to love and to be in love. It has taught many of us to be not only afraid to die but afraid to live, and it is teaching many of us to settle for lives that mean too little. In this epidemic—and perhaps always in life—there are so many ways to lose lives of passion. We can lose them to the manic denial of feelings, or we can lose them to overwhelming depression, grief, and guilt. Other kinds of survival must include our reaching for lives that mean as much as possible.

Everything in life does not have an answer, and not everything is recoverable. But some efforts and some solutions promise more than others. In the gay communities, neither new decades of mania to disguise our grief from ourselves nor decades of depression and isolation are acceptable or necessary. Both are roads that can only help realize the horrible and perceptive vision of a 23-year-old with HIV: "Sometimes," he said to me matter-of-factly, "I'm glad to think that in ten years I'll be dead. By then, the only gay people left will be the *stingy* ones and the *lonely* ones whose lives were ruined by watching the rest of us die."

Such stingy, lonely, ruined lives will be hatched out of the fear that now tempts many of us to circle guard, in unconscious hopes of immortality, around our own living corpses—ferociously protecting lives not worth living, because they are lives sacrificed to nothing but their own extension. Each man, in his own way, must find a different, more human path, one that cuts down the middle between numbing fear and immobilizing depression, and that allows him to live with passion, irony, honesty, personal and sexual intimacy, and a sense that every moment, in itself, is life.

There are ways in which the epidemic has been a uniting force for gay communities. Politically, many have never been stronger, although this truth is often limited to AIDS matters. In *gay* matters—which is to say, human matters and matters of the heart—HIV has struck terror and grief into too many lives. This has divided our communities, many of which had been on roads to social unity and personal integration. We now find ourselves divided between positives and negatives, between those who can risk intimacy and those who cannot, between those who can imagine other kinds of survival and those who cannot, and, for many of us, divided within ourselves. We all live with HIV in one sense of the idea or another, and it cannot be otherwise. But the solution to our divisions is not that we all have HIV within our own bodies, that we suspend intimacy in hopes of better times ahead, that we hang tenaciously to empty lives, or that we accept lives divided within ourselves. All these divisions become less compelling if we understand that HIV is not the final divider, because survival is not the final criterion. Life lived fully, however long or short, must be our most important criterion, and if that is understood, HIV cannot divide us from each other or from ourselves.

There are many reasons we have clung to ideas about survival in and for itself: because we have been blinded by the denial needed to protect us from the awful, nearly unimaginable experience of the AIDS epidemic; because that denial has been supported by a society that has acted as if it is substantially concerned with HIV only when it thrives in the bodies of heterosexual celebrities; and, importantly, *because we have been unable to mourn our lives as we expected them to be*. Our lives can no longer assume or expect what they would have, had none of this happened. The worst *has* happened. We must begin the painful task of mourning and rethinking our old visions of our lives, for they are no longer possible, and they can no longer serve our needs or purposes.

We in the gay communities have some important advantages in dealing with mourning old lives. Many of us have already been through it in coming out as gay. For a man to publicly declare and integrate internally his homosexuality requires a rethinking of all the assumptions and expectations about life he grew up with, and a mourning of the life they might have provided. In its final moment of courage, coming out requires an abandonment of the life that was expected of us and we expected of ourselves, for a life that seems unknown and dangerous—but inevitable. With as much courage and understanding as we can muster, we must do this again in the age of AIDS if we are to have full, human lives. We must come out as a people who refuse to live in denial or fear, who refuse to be separated from each other in life by the prospect of death, and who value life too much to spend it on nothing but its own preservation. Rand Schrader, a man dying of AIDS spoke the following words, and they are for all of us, whether we are now dying of HIV in our own bodies or of HIV in the bodies of those we love and have loved:

> Now I am getting ready to be sad and I am sad and it is setting me free, at last . . . free to be alive to enjoy what *is* instead of what I wanted there to be, and free to be alive to enjoy who I am instead of who I needed myself to be. . . . Stripping away the illusions we have used to hide the present from the moment we're in, we can choose to appreciate and savor what is left. The friendship in our lives, the love in our homes, the satisfaction in our work, and the amusement in life around us will make us happy, if we allow it.[12]

A closing observation about other kinds of survival: No one can do it alone. Coming out in pursuit of the fullest possible life, like coming out as gay, requires a community to come out into. Both are ways of redefining how one thinks of oneself, lives, relates to others, and experiences the meanings of human and sexual intimacy. I hope that enough of us are able to come out into other kinds of survival to provide communities that can continue to support human life by welcoming those who have had the insight and courage to try to do the same.

Courage is requisite for this new coming out, not only because as gay men we must abandon our lives as we expected them to be. We also now need courage because we find ourselves face-to-face with an old, destructive—and revitalized—enemy that many of us thought we had long ago subdued or defeated: homophobia. It is homophobia, not AIDS, that has thrived most dangerously in the confusing turmoil of the epidemic. It is homophobia that motivates us—negative and positive alike—to relinquish our lives to those who would tell us what to do and how to feel; and it is homophobia that motivates these authoritarians—many of them gay men—to dictate to the rest of us. For too many of us who are uninfected, it is homophobia that obliges us to test for HIV antibodies every six months in terror that our homosexuality has finally reaped its just reward. For too many of us who are HIV-positive, it is homophobia that motivates us to accept medical treatment that ruins what lives we have left and extends them by months. For all of us, it is homophobia that drives us into retreat from intimacy and sexuality that once gave our lives meaning, leaving us with lives of fear and loneliness. HIV tests and medication, presented as the "responsible" choices, are often nothing more than a way to pay penance for being homosexual. We have now lived through the epidemic quite literally being told what and what not to swallow—depending on antibody status—and have thus allowed our lives to once again slip from our grasp into the hands of those who too often believe, if quietly, that we should not even be what we are.

A new coming out into other kinds of survival for those living—or dying—in the age of AIDS is about the same thing as the old coming out. It is about not relinquishing our lives to others who, in their own homophobia, would tell us who to be and how to do it. It is about excising the homophobia of mainstream society and the homophobia within ourselves, both empowered by their ride on this ruthless epidemic. Each of us must decide who he is, what is important to him, and how he *wants* to live his life, however long or short. Other kinds of survival must be about taking back our lives for what we each want them to be, and mustering the courage to do this even—no, *especially*—in the fearsome eye of a plague.

Epilogue

The Idea of Bearing Witness

If I end this book without discussing Primo Levi, my friend and cohort in the investigation of the meaning of human life, Linda Zaretsky, will never speak to me again. In 1989, shortly after San Francisco's second "big" earthquake and the downtown construction crane accident,[2] I related to Linda the following dream about myself and Dan, who was then my lover:

> "Dan and I were walking down the street and there was a very beautiful, old-fashioned truck with a crane on it. Just as we came along, some men were demonstrating it, and it quickly extended itself for miles through the city, weaving around buildings and other obstructions. But, just as it was completely extended, the tip—now several miles away and into the Marina [district of San Francisco]— began to quiver, and then swing more and more wildly side-to-side. As it did this, it began to destroy building after building with a terrible rumbling noise, and shortly the city was engulfed in fire, a cloud of smoke and dust billowing higher and higher above it.
>
> "Dan and I were suddenly sitting in wooden bleachers next to a playing field in Napa [north across the San Francisco Bay from the city] watching a football game, which is something neither of us has ever done. The playing field was located in a huge, absolutely flat plain that ran down to the edge of the bay. The wife of one

football player scurried along behind him as he executed each of the plays, an infant strapped to her back in a carrier. The others in the bleachers, eating and drinking from picnic coolers, were very involved in the game, and cheered and carried on wildly as each play was made."

"Sounds like a very heterosexual, sports-minded, suburban crowd," commented Linda.

"Absolutely. And in the dream that was very comforting, because these were ordinary people who were completely untroubled by the disaster going on in San Francisco. But we also felt peculiar about being there. The most amazing part was that right behind the game you could see San Francisco in the distance and, though the destruction was absolutely silent, this incredible cloud of smoke rose above the city for miles, and flames flickered up above the tallest buildings. No one noticed this except me. Dan and I, sitting in the bleachers, felt very safe in this ordinary, heterosexual environment, but I said to him, 'Dan, look over there, because you can see the city burning. It looks like it's burning right to the ground.' We were feeling very ambivalent about whether we should stay at the game and be safe, or go back to town. It was very disturbing to be watching the city burn while sitting among those who neither knew of the disaster, nor cared."

Primo Levi was an Italian Jew imprisoned by the Nazis during the war, and he wrote about the importance of bearing witness.[3] Bearing witness to what happened, he said, was the only way the event of the Holocaust might be kept real. It would only be in a continuing affirmation of its reality that it could remain meaningful, and thus bearable. Denied or forgotten, said Levi, the Holocaust would be unbearable. Indeed, in the faded memories of April 1987, Levi finally found his life after the Holocaust unbearable, and he killed himself.

I find Levi's thought—and his final act—intelligible, though I think Linda understands him better than I. Having talked recently about Levi with Linda, and sitting by a pool, I finally understood more completely the idea of bearing witness. A small boy standing at the edge of the water shouted repeatedly to his father.

"Daddy, watch me! Watch me! I'm going to jump in the water." His father waved back at him. The boy jumped, and the act accomplished, he climbed out of the pool and ran to his father and demanded, "Did you see me? Did you see me jump!?" His father, talking with another adult, nodded distractedly in the affirmative, and the boy seemed immensely pleased: "I have jumped in the water!" he shouted, and, dancing off toward the pool for more fun, he finally seemed satisfied. The reality of the jump—affirmed by his father's recognition—was established, and it was thus also meaningful.

Watching this exchange, I thought about how many ways we bear witness to each other's lives in adulthood too, and how important that is. As with the boy at the pool, events become real and meaningful at the moment they are acknowledged and understood by others who are important to us. Bearing witness is not only an acknowledgment of the event, it is an acknowledgment and understanding of the *experience* of those who have lived it. In my dream of escape from the huge phallus destroying San Francisco, it was not enough for Dan and me to merely *watch* the event, sitting in the bleachers among those who knew nothing about it. The experience of those still in the city was one of being watched—not witnessed—and *our* experience was not being witnessed by those around us. Although Dan and I might have borne witness to each other's experience, the shared witness of only two is usually not enough for big, enduring social events. It is broad social recognition—particularly of painful, isolating, and seemingly meaningless experience—that transforms the subjective experience from a personal delusion or *folie à deux* into a witnessed, real, meaningful, and therefore bearable one.

It is a remarkable fact of life in the cerebral cortex that simply sharing an experience makes it meaningful. Apparently we never get over the infantile shock of finding out that we are not our mothers. Perhaps it is because of this early, painful discovery that human life seems so often about being trapped in separate bodies, which is also to say in separate minds that never actually know another's experience. We thus devote our adolescent and post-adolescent lives to trying to feel that we have separated, are autonomous, and have our own identities—and the remainder of our lives trying to bridge the seemingly inescapable, painful experience of essential isolation. The effort to share consciousness—of social events, literary ideas, or simultaneous orgasm—is a universal pursuit of the human cortex, if not always a successful one.

The importance of the meaning derived from shared consciousness is demonstrated in the significance we attach to social rituals, which are partly a conventionalized expression of shared consciousness. That the convention does not always induce similar consciousness in all participants is another matter, and one confirmed by the number of family Thanksgiving dinners that have ended in conflict, accusation, and despair. When social ritual is not too conventionalized—which is to say that it remains connected in some way to the subjective experience of participants—it can be immensely important in helping to confirm individual happiness, or assisting survival of what might otherwise be unendurable, private misery.

In the epidemic, attending a memorial service for a dead friend and viewing the Names Project quilt not only create tangible events in remembrance of the dead, they allow us to assemble, to experience feelings about the losses, to see that others experience apparently similar feelings, and (perhaps) to understand our own. In such shared events, the losses become real and important, instead of simply remaining disturbing figments of subjective experience. It is in this sense that bearing witness is most powerful and important: that we recognize and share each other's internal experience of the public event, and thus supply the event with public meaning that can be reinternalized by the grieving individual. Thus shared and formed by social recognition, the subjective grief somehow becomes more bearable.

Psychotherapists bear witness to the feelings and insights of patients, and this is one reason that so much good psychotherapy is conducted with the therapist's silence, or with his or her spare reflections or clarifications, which the patient can reinternalize. In bearing silent, or nearly silent, witness to our patients, we allow them to exist in a way that they have not previously found possible or allowed themselves; and we validate the reality and importance of that subjective existence with—sometimes only implicit—recognition and understanding. I am always surprised by how much psychotherapy is accomplished by simply allowing patients to exist *as themselves* in front of me.

The importance of bearing witness to the AIDS epidemic, as experienced by the psychotherapy patient or the friend, cannot be overestimated. With HIV medically uncontrolled and spreading rapidly, it often seems that bearing witness is all we can do to keep the epidemic bearable. This is apparent in the complex feelings that are often evoked by the thought of the epidemic *ending*. In fleeting moments of fantasy about a cure for AIDS, many gay men experience an explosion of grief about what would seem a joyous event. Woody Castrodale spoke to me about this subject on the phone.

> Last night in group, Tom said, "I'm beginning to be aware that if there were a cure, I would feel an enormous amount of resentment."

Well, there was a stunned silence in the group, and I realized that I felt that—way, way down—but I had never been able to verbalize it. Others said they had the same feelings too. Tom is one of those people who has lost two lovers, and this puts him in a certain place, like me. He said, "I have lived through all this, and I recognize that I have suffered through all this *stuff* in my center, that I have taken a stance toward it, that it's been my destiny to live with this, that my two lovers have died and I have suffered through all of that. It has *meaning*. If a cure came along, the whole balance would be changed. All of this meaning would be gone, because suddenly people would be living on, and the whole thing would be old history. My God, when there's a cure, I'm going to have an enormous problem."[4]

When it is over, Tom's apprehension predicts, the epidemic will vanish into meaninglessness, and with it, all of the feelings that have become part of who we now are. It is thus *we* who will vanish into meaninglessness. At the moment of a cure, we fear, the deaths will be trivialized, seemingly a twist of timing and fate. The enemy will no longer seem indomitable, but petty and unworthy of those it took from us. The environment of emergency and intensity, of comaraderie and shared experience that now makes *some* sense of our adrenalin-driven lives, will be gone. We will be left, the morning after, with nothing but loss and grief pounding in our heads and hearts. Our denial, no longer needed to make the fight seem possible, will suddenly be gone too, and in its place, an indelible emptiness that will haunt us from the shadows for the rest of our lives.

Ways We Can Bear Witness

After the epidemic, should there be such an age for us, life will be difficult regardless of how we conduct ourselves. The worst possibilities, however, will be realized by meaninglessness rooted in our inability to adequately bear witness to the epidemic *now,* while it is conducting its fiendish work. There is so much going against the effort to bear witness and sustain meaning in our lives: a profound predisposition of denial within the gay communities, enlisted to protect us from what often seem unmanageable feelings, and to contain shame and guilt that we so often harbor within ourselves for being homosexual and having AIDS; and the extraordinary denial of a profoundly homophobic society troubled by seemingly more important problems, and acknowledging the epidemic only sporadically and with cynical, covert hopes that HIV and AIDS will remain within excommunicated populations.

Bearing witness arises from a state of mind—a willingness and capacity to acknowledge and understand the truth. But it is also an act that can be facilitated by community and society rather than hindered, and we have within gay communities at least the rudiments of means to do that. I have, within the main body of this work, implicitly offered some social forms that may help us bear witness, but I would like to offer a more pragmatic inventory of some other possibilities to help us both as whole communities and as HIV-negative communities. These include our writing, our AIDS education, and, importantly, psychological groups.

My writing and the writing of many others are acts of bearing witness. The AIDS epidemic that has spawned so much horror and loss has also spawned some writing of insight, eloquence, and truth. To name only a few, the works of George Whitmore, Robert Ferro, George Stambolian, David B. Feinberg, Paul Monette, Andrew Holleran, and J. W. Money have contributed immensely to our capacity to bear witness to the epidemic.[5] This writing describes our experience and feelings, understands them, and bears witness to their truth and importance. I conceive of the Names Project quilt as being among these works of fiction and nonfiction, for it is both of those—as well as a monument that is at once so personal and so public, so particular and so universal, and conveys, unlike anything else, the *enormity* of the epidemic.

AIDS education, because it is such a pervasive, prominent cultural force and public reminder of the epidemic within gay communities, might help us bear witness, despite its primary pragmatic mission of reducing HIV transmission. In fact, helping provide gay men a sense of meaning about the epidemic—the very foundation of lives worth living and therefore worth protecting—would contribute to that primary mission. AIDS educators, on the whole, do not perceive this obvious truth, for they are heirs to an approach to public health education that is as narrowly conceived as that which purports to teach children an appreciation of human culture by having them memorize the dates of important events. In the United States, at least, AIDS education has so rarely been informed by psychological insight or the truth of gay men's experience in the epidemic that it has been unable to either help bear witness *or* more directly motivate changes in sexual behavior. Educational approaches that enlist and assist denial and that promote half-truths and untruths cannot change the way a person experiences and thinks about his life, and therefore cannot ultimately change important behavior. While such approaches may enforce short-term behavioral compliance by exploiting endogenous fear, social compliance, shame, or guilt, the internal sources of behavior remain untouched, and the individual finally, perhaps in secrecy, returns to the dictates of his feelings. The internal sources of truth remain untouched and unsupported by the public voice.

To be effective in *any* sense, our education is going to have to really acknowledge the broad human realities of life in the epidemic. This means *affirming* gay men's complex and difficult experience rather than attempting to normalize life—or simply feign normality—in these most abnormal of circumstances. In the San Francisco AIDS Foundation's "Outliving Forecasts of Doom" campaign, the advice offered for living in the epidemic is to "play it safe, make a plan, see it through." The validating *truth* is that the epidemic is far from being merely a *forecast*. It has already exceeded our wildest and cruelest imaginations. The campaign's glib advice to "make a plan and see it through" is a ridiculous prescription for a *lifetime,* is unvalidating of real experience, and is an effort to enlist denial against the substantial difficulty of creating a viable life in the circumstances in which many gay men find themselves. AIDS Foundation educators apparently would like to simply wish away the realities of life in the epidemic. This is an encouragement to not know the truth, tell the truth, or bear witness—and like *all* buried truths, the epidemic thus misrepresented will surely become unendurable. Helping to bear witness—and thus doing good prevention work in the bargain—will require that our education realistically acknowledge the complexity and depth of feeling of many men, even when that acknowledgment does not appear to immediately support the goal of reduced HIV transmission. Our education must account for the nature of life in one of the longest-enduring disasters in twentieth-century history, and the fact that HIV is communicable by ordinary, desirable, and necessary human behaviors. AIDS education—a pervasive and potentially potent and constructive force in gay communities—is truly in need of a *renaissance*.

Psychological interventions are another important means to bearing witness to AIDS, finding meaning in it, and perhaps surviving it. Much of the material in this book is taken from individual and group psychotherapy work, and those processes allow complex feelings to be clarified and understood, and are thus supportive of both the perception of human truths and survival. But individual psychotherapy is a costly, resource-limited, and time-consuming process, and is unavailable to the majority of those in the gay communities. Psychological *groups,* however, have much broader potential, and it is thus important to pragmatically discuss their possibilities and workings.

The idea of "groups" has become something of a cliché. They are now widely available to address problems spanning the spectrum from overeating to death. They are organized in any number of ways, and "facilitated" or led by people of every range of insight, training, and experience. Initially within the province of psychology, groups were born in their modern form after World War II, and gained appeal at that time for many reasons. They offered economy, requiring the services of only one or two psychotherapists for eight to ten therapy patients; they helped accommodate the huge population of returning veterans and others who appeared to require psychological help after their experiences with the global disaster of war and racial annihilation; and they were something psychiatrists did not mind letting clinical psychologists do, since there were not enough of the former to do all the work, and the latter seemed intent on clinical work from which they had theretofore been largely excluded. In more recent times, groups have come to be led or facilitated by mental health professionals other than psychiatrists and psychologists, by nonprofessional *peer group* leaders, and by no one—which is to say, *self-facilitated.*

Today we also generally make a distinction between *therapy* groups per se, *support* groups, *drop-in* groups, and *one-time group workshops.* The single most critical issue with any group is the quality of the facilitation, regardless of the credentials of the facilitator. Although groups professionally conducted as therapy groups seem to me to offer the most potential for profound change, other forms of groups, depending on the quality of facilitation, can and have been extremely useful. *Therapy* groups are directed at the clarification of psychological conflict and its resolution in the group—which is to say, interpersonal—setting. *Support* groups, properly speaking, are concerned with "emotional support," which involves the development or strengthening of existing psychological defenses against conflict, rather than clarification and resolution of the conflict. This more limited objective is sometimes appropriate because of the nature of the problem being addressed, the unavailability of experienced facilitation for a true therapy group, or because of the objectives and goals of group members. *Drop-in* groups are generally conducted as support groups rather than therapy groups. Finally, *one-time group workshops,* which offer a very wide range of forms and approaches, may function as limited therapy or support groups, depending on the aims of the group and the availability of facilitation that would allow true therapeutic exploration.

With regard to professionally facilitated therapy groups, we have come to recognize in the last two or three decades that they offer much more than economy and efficiency, and that in many ways they are neither substitutes for, nor substituted for by, individual psychotherapy. Groups offer a unique milieu in which the interpersonal consequences of intrapsychic conflict are expressed and worked through. Just as the *transference relationship* (between therapist and patient, in both "directions") of individual psychotherapy is the vehicle for resolution in that modality, the social environment of the group—really, a "society" of eight or ten— is a vehicle of a different sort, which can provide insight and resolution that is not as available in an individual psychotherapy. The experience of meaning achieved through bearing witness cannot, by its very nature, be an individual matter. The process requires a social and cultural context out of which meaning is created by the act of mutual recognition and understanding. Therefore, just as groups for HIV-positive men allow bearing witness to the experience of having HIV, groups for HIV-negative men are a natural choice for problems about potential survival these people are experiencing. A group for HIV-negative men allows a man to come out to his peers and consolidate an identity as an uninfected gay man within a community of shared experience.

In San Francisco we now have at least some experience with all kinds of groups for HIV-negative gay men, and they have proved immensely productive. Regardless of how they are conceived and conducted, all these groups have had to meet certain requirements to usefully assist negative men in meeting their psychological objectives and to provide an environment that allows bearing witness to their experience of the epidemic. The fundamental requirement of all groups is that they provide a "safe" venue in which HIV-negative issues may be discussed openly, honestly, and confidentially without fear of neglecting, offending, or hurting HIV-positive men or incurring their resentment or anger. That venue must not, *in itself,* support the guilt of HIV-negative men. Thus these groups must be limited, in their initial selection, to those who believe themselves to be uninfected. Feelings about neglect, offense, hurt, resentment, anger, and guilt *will be* an important part of what many negative men have to deal with in the group. But the group is not the place to have those things actually occur or be repeated, any more than an individual therapy is the place to have conflict with parents reenacted by a careless therapist. The group, like the individual therapy, is the place to *explore the feelings* about the problems.

This fundamental, uncompromisable requirement is, of course, precisely the one that makes groups for HIV-negative men so personally and politically controversial within gay communities, and so difficult to fund. In fact, in most gay communities, the idea of groups for HIV-negative men is still *unspeakable*. In addition to the discussion of the complex relations of positives and negatives in chapters 7 and 8, a simple statement about the purposes of groups should be added here. The idea that HIV-positive men might need groups for themselves is self-evident to anyone, because it is obvious that they have important, common issues that can be shared and discussed only among themselves. Feelings that HIV-negative groups are more about excluding positive men than about including *only* the issues of HIV-negative men are rooted in the failure to perceive the special problems of being uninfected in many gay communities. If some positive men, having acknowledged that there are special issues for HIV-negative men, still feel there is an exclusionary or isolationist intent to HIV-negative groups that is not implicit in positive groups, then they must look at their own feelings about being positive. To some extent, positive men who are unable to experience HIV-negative issues as something other than "viral apartheid" are projecting onto uninfected men their feelings about themselves—feelings that make them feel undesirable or excludable.

While the idea of *safety* in any kind of psychological intervention is of paramount importance, it is also among the most abused and misused concepts in the conduct of groups, especially support or drop-in groups. In *any* well-run group, safety can mean only one thing: any honest expression of feelings or thoughts will be received and tolerated by the group, and an attempt will be made to honestly respond to it. This will be done without physical violence or undue emotional hurt to other members, and without abandonment of the group. This essential objective is most easily accomplished in a professionally facilitated therapy group, because the group leader will have the necessary skills to mediate and limit conflict to a safe and constructive level. When the idea of safety comes to mean, as it often does in poorly conducted therapy groups and many support groups, that members be polite and "nonjudgmental" toward each other, then the prime therapeutic objectives are undermined. Interpersonal interaction—as opposed to social form—necessarily involves feelings and judgments about others, and unless they can be expressed and discussed truthfully, the group can provide neither insight nor the meaning that comes of bearing witness. Unfortunately, this may be a limitation of many support groups by nature, although with talented facilitation this is not necessarily so. It is the quality of facilitation and psychological aptitude of members that will ultimately limit the group's accomplishment.

Denial is the opposite of both bearing witness and psychological insight. When therapy or support groups take the idea of "support" literally, little genuine work can be accomplished. The function of a group is not to make its members "feel better when they leave than when they came in," as one poorly supervised peer facilitator has routinely billed his weekly support group for San Francisco gay men. It is the function of a therapy group, like individual psychotherapy, to help people attain the insight that allows them to *make themselves* feel better. Although that is a more complex and difficult task than soothing hurts through mutual, collusive support and the bolstering of defenses, it is an effort that produces authentic and lasting results. The precarious situation of uninfected gay men demands that we aim for authentic results. At this point in the epidemic, we should accept merely supportive efforts as nothing more than stopgap efforts until we are able to muster appropriate services. Survivors of the epidemic are not going to be simply "supported" through it, and the attempt is an invalidating denial of the real difficulty many men are understandably having.

When the experience of group members includes life in a profoundly painful, enduring, and insoluble event like the AIDS epidemic, such cosmetic—if kindly—collusion in denial can be very tempting. A support group like that offered by the UCSF AIDS Health Project for HIV-negative gay men—*Negatives Being Positive*—implies by its very name that its purpose is a collusion with denial, in the hope that men will feel better in the most superficial sense of the idea. The group's name dictates how men are to feel while in attendance—*positive,* not to be confused with *HIV-positive*—and thus forecloses on all the other things that one might feel while living in a plague. Were the title instead *Uninfected Men Ultimately Feeling Better Pending an Exploration of Why We're Feeling So Bad that We Need a Group,* one might have more confidence in the purposes and productivity of the group, and in the agency's ability to assert the idea that it is all right for uninfected men to *not* feel positive, in either sense of the idea. On hearing about this group and its sister group, *Positives Being Positive,* Ed Wolf, longtime facilitator of San Francisco HIV-negative groups, summed up the confusions succinctly: "So let me get this straight. It's fine for positives to feel positive, and negatives to feel positive. But we don't want negatives feeling negative."

How group work is kept honest and productive, regardless of form, is a question with no simple answers. A talented and experienced group psychotherapist to lead the group is a good start. Therapy groups are most likely to offer such a leader, and this is the reason that I favor them above other forms of groups whenever resources can possibly allow them. Peer-facilitated groups are more easily and less expensively organized and may also be productive. The facilitator or cofacilitators should have regular supervision by a talented professional; and the use of cofacilitators for peer-led groups is especially recommended for important reasons too complicated to elaborate fully here. Briefly, cofacilitation may help to balance and stabilize the *structure* of the group, and to correct the deficiencies of understanding or interaction of any single facilitator. This is equally true of professionally led groups, though perhaps not as often a critical requirement. The San Francisco HIV-negative group cofacilitated by Woody Castrodale, who is so often cited in this book, is an example of a peer-facilitated group that has accomplished important work for its members, and may be fairly described as a therapy group, despite its nonprofessional facilitation. That Castrodale and some group members are men of exceptional intelligence and insight is no small part of this accomplishment. There is no formula or structure that can substitute for such qualities, regardless of the experience or inexperience of a group's facilitator.

Finally, there is the possibility of the "self-facilitated" group. Such a group can be useful, and many people have gotten together over the ages without even calling themselves groups and accomplished much. The obvious dangers are lack of experience, understanding, and insight on the part of group members; the impossibility of external, professional supervision (who would be supervised?); and the lack of a presence in the group that maintains an overview of the group *process* and keeps it on track. Such a group is highly dependent on the members' native capacity for insight. A self-facilitated group should be an effort of last resort for HIV-negative men, because of the potential destructiveness of the issues that now ensnare so many.

Member selection is a critical element of any group, and the careful screening and selection of members is one of the important benefits in a professionally led group. *Homogeneity* or *compatibility* in their ordinary senses are not the crucial issues so much as the potential for useful interaction between members. A single group member who is distinctly less psychologically developed than others in the group or distinctly less intelligent or capable of self-expression can seriously damage the structural integrity and process of the group. Such a member, especially when he engages in conflicted and hostile interpersonal relations, can be a shark in the water who keeps the other bathers too busy to attend to their original purposes for coming to the beach. As another example, an introverted and chronically withdrawn or profoundly depressed member may preoccupy the group and divert its efforts into guilt-motivated caretaking that will be unproductive for all. The structural and process problems resulting from such problematic member selection—and a host of others—will be much more difficult, or impossible, for the untrained leader to correct. Experienced and talented group leaders also sometimes make mistakes in selection, and when that happens, group survival can demand the removal of the mismatched individual. This is a difficult process for *any* group leader if the problematic individual and group are both to be respected, and the group is to remain productive. With an untrained and inexperienced facilitator, removal of a badly mismatched member will almost always be traumatic and destructive to the individual member, the facilitator, and the group as a whole.

I have already mentioned the basic requirement for all HIV-negative groups: that selection be limited to those who believe themselves to be uninfected. This is a largely straightforward matter of self-selection that usually poses no problems. In the unlikely—but not unknown—event of a member intentionally misrepresenting his serostatus, the leader's task is similar to that in working with any mismatched group member. One would hope for an experienced leader to deal with the situation. The presence of an HIV-positive member, particularly one who has intentionally misrepresented his HIV status, poses a serious danger for an HIV-negative group. Such misrepresentation on the part of a group member, whether about serostatus or other significant issues, sabotages the necessary environment of safety and trust in which the group must do its work. In the specific case of misrepresented serostatus, the issues of HIV-negative men, including guilt about positive men, cannot be honestly addressed because of the serodiscordant composition of the group.

A more subtle and difficult problem, and one most common in open-term groups (about which I shall say more shortly), occurs when an established group member seroconverts *during* the term of the group. Again, the problem almost surely demands the skill of an experienced, professional leader, although in this case the answer is very unlikely to be simple removal of the now positive member. The impact of a sero-conversion on the HIV-negative group may ultimately be productive—if traumatic—for the group as a whole, for it offers an important, not easily explored opportunity. If the ensuing process is properly handled, it is likely that the newly seroconverted member will ultimately leave the group for his own needs and reasons, and that this will be done with careful referrals by the group leader for both a new group and, perhaps, individual work. In a peer-facilitated or self-facilitated group, such an event may be *immensely* destructive to both the seroconverted individual and the remaining group. The man who has converted may feel abandoned by his former peers, and those remaining in the group may feel that they have, indeed, abandoned him. Such feelings, if they remain unexplored and unclarified, will only exacerbate the very issues, such as survivor guilt, that an HIV-negative group must address.

In general, groups are structured and conducted differently depending on their aims (therapy or support), expected duration, and attendance requirements. Open-ended or limited-term (generally eight to sixteen weeks) therapy groups almost invariably have a fixed membership that is expected to attend regularly. With such groups, the regularity of at-tendance and the extended time over which relationships may develop provide a maximally intimate and safe environment most conducive to psychological exploration. To the extent that membership varies session-to-session or the anticipated term of the group is limited, the environ-ment is less suitable for therapeutic aims. Thus drop-in support groups, in which attendance is optional and constantly changing, are generally limited in their psychological potential, and are usually not suitable for serious therapeutic approaches.

In general then, the longer the term of the group and the more stable the attendance, the better. But there is an exception to this rule: the *one-time workshop,* which can be a powerful intervention for address-ing HIV-negative issues. Typically running from one to three full days, a workshop possesses, by nature, stability of membership. But instead of time over which intimacy and a capacity for vulnerability are devel-oped, the workshop relies on two devices which, properly executed, can provide powerful and productive interactions between group members.

The first of these special "devices" is the extended, *concentrated* period of time. Spending an entire day together in a room partially suspends the consciousness of normal life, and thus many of the interpersonal and psychological defenses we employ there. This phenomenon is used by the "retreat" meeting, by training programs such as est (or The Forum), and is an influence in the kinds of relationships generically called "ship-board romances." The intensity of focus, capacity for vulnerability, and intimacy accomplished in such settings are often surprising, and often productive.

The second source of the power of the workshop is the use of a variety of programmatic devices, which may include education, struc-tured discussion, structured whole-group and small-group psychologi-cal interactions, or a variety of designed "exercises" aimed at uncovering and provoking feelings and thoughts that would otherwise be defended against. Such workshops are necessarily professionally conceived and conducted. In the case of San Francisco's Shanti Project, which has pio-neered such work for HIV-negative gay men in the United States, such workshops have proved immensely useful to participants. These work-shops have taken the form of one-day and three-day retreats, and have used a variety of educational, group therapy, discussion, and designed exercise approaches. Generally comprised of forty to fifty participants, and facilitated by three to six facilitators (among them psychologists and experienced group facilitators), these groups have been a revelatory and transforming experience for many uninfected men.

Bearing witness, in whatever form, is now a task of central importance for gay communities. There is so much conflict about what the epidemic *is* or *ought* to mean, but we cannot allow this understandable confusion or the huge inertia of internal and external denial to obscure our vision. Denial, in whatever form, is the opposite of bearing witness; it is the *lie*—about the epidemic, our lives in it, and our lives after it. Everyone, in his or her own way, must bear witness if we are to sustain or reinstate a sense of meaning in our lives by finding lives in other kinds of survival. If we fail to bear witness and live only in hopes of outliving the future, we shall all perish in seas of living despair or as zombies without the capacities to feel, love, or be loved, for fear that they will be perpetually taken from us by the meaningless or punitive conspiracies of microbes and time.

Notes

The quote on the dedication page is from Andrew Holleran, "A Place of His Own: How to Remember Robert Ferro," *Christopher Street,* Issue 26 (1989), p. 9. Holleran quotes a letter from Robert Ferro, who is talking about the imprisonment of Oscar Wilde.

1 Why We Need a Book about Being HIV-Negative

1   Ippy Gizzi, *Letters to Pauline* (Providence, R.I.: Burning Deck, 1975), p. 2.

2   The Honorable Art Agnos, introductory remarks at the Sixth International Conference on AIDS, San Francisco, 20 June 1990.

3   Ed Wolf, personal communication, 1990.

4   Gizzi, *Letters,* p. 11.

5   The San Francisco AIDS Foundation, *An Epidemic of Loss: AIDS in San Francisco's Gay Male Community, 1988–1993* (San Francisco: San Francisco AIDS Foundation, 1988), p. 24.

6   Woody Castrodale, personal communication, 1992.

7   James Dilley, Cheri Pies, and Michael Helquist, eds., *Face to Face: A Guide to AIDS Counseling* (San Francisco: AIDS Health Project, University of California, San Francisco, 1989); Mindy Thompson Fullilove, "Anxiety and Stigmatizing Aspects of HIV Infection," *Journal of Clinical Psychiatry* 50: 5–8; J. L. Martin, "Psychological Consequences of AIDS-Related Bereavement Among Gay Men," *Journal of Consulting and Clinical Psychology* 56: 856–862; Rachel Schochet, "Psychosocial Issues for Seronegative Gay Men in San Francisco," *Focus. A Guide to AIDS Research and Counseling* 4: 3.

8   Dilley et al., *Face to Face,* p. 132.

9   Fullilove, "Anxiety," p. 6.

10 Martin, "Psychological Consequences," p. 858.

11 Ibid., pp. 859–860.

12 James Dilley and Alicia Boccellari, "Neuropsychiatric Complications of HIV Infection," in Dilley et al., *Face to Face.*

13 Rachel Schochet, personal communication, 1991.

14 Woody Castrodale, personal communication, 1992.

2   *The Psychological Epidemic*

1   Keith Waldrop, *The Ruins of Providence* (Providence, R.I.: Copper Beach Press, 1983), p. 37.
2   Erik Erikson, *Childhood and Society,* 2d ed. (New York: W. W. Norton, 1963).
3   Linda Zaretsky, personal communication, 1990.
4   American Psychiatric Association, *Diagnostic and Statistical Manual of Mental Disorders,* 3d ed. rev. (hereafter *DSM-III-R*) (Washington, D.C.: American Psychiatric Association, 1987), p. 261.
5   Ibid., pp. 213–234.
6   The psychotherapist will recognize that I am referring here to men with "pre-oedipal" character styles, especially those with narcissistic or borderline kinds of development. Most of my discussion elsewhere assumes successful developmental transition to "post-oedipal" styles. It is among this latter group that we see the capacities for empathy, guilt, and ambivalence of feelings that make more complex psychological experience possible. Dysphoric depression and survivor guilt, as examples, demand these capacities. It is my general clinical impression that the developmental pressures and distortions experienced as a result of growing up gay may make the incidence of pre-oedipal character styles more prevalent in the gay community than in the population at large, and the pressures of the epidemic are clearly exacerbating this problem.
7   American Psychiatric Association, *DSM-III-R,* pp. 235–254.
8   Dilley and Boccellari, "Neuropsychiatric Complications," p. 142.
9   The ELISA test (Enzyme-linked Immunosorbent Assay), which is used alone in single administration to provide an "HIV-negative" result, has had an uneven reputation, and virtually everyone working in HIV health and mental health care services now knows anecdotally of cases of surprise seroconversions—the sudden conversion to HIV-positive status after repeated negative ELISA results without any known (or reported) intervening exposure. It is not clear whether the epidemiologic data are erroneous, the ELISA is technically flawed under certain circumstances, or the formation of antibodies is significantly delayed in some individuals. Gay men should understand that the accuracy and cost-effectiveness of the ELISA satisfies public health officials, who are responsible for the health of the entire U.S. population. But the use of such a test is not only a medical decision; it is an economic and public policy decision as well. It is not generally acknowledged that the "reliability" of any test—in the common meaning of the word—depends on the population to which it is administered. True *reliability* (as opposed to the common meaning of the word) refers only to the technical nature of the test (its ability to produce repeatable results with the *same* population), but this is not in question when someone asks his physician if the ELISA is "reliable." What the patient wants to know is, "How reliably can the ELISA determine whether or not I have HIV antibodies," and the question is correctly one about the *predictive validity* of the test (or, in the language of laboratory medicine, *predictive value*). It is the predictive value of the test that varies with the population being tested. When used to screen a population with a high incidence of the tested-for property, a test will show a higher incidence of false negatives (negative test results in people who are actually positive) than it would in the general

population, which has, in reality, a higher percentage of *true* negatives. Thus, the ELISA will have less predictive validity in "high-risk" groups like gay communities than in the general population. It is important to note that the Western Blot test is routinely used only to confirm *positive* ELISAs, and therefore does not address or monitor the ELISA's return of false negatives.

Because many are confused by the relationship of *reliability* and *validity* in testing, it is a subject worth reviewing briefly. The reliability and validity of a test are different but related issues. Reliability refers to the ability of a test to produce repeatable results (with the same population) and is an internal characteristic of the test, entirely unrelated to its usefulness. A test may be completely reliable and produce no useful information. Validity is about the usefulness or meaningfulness of the results, and may provide diagnostic, predictive, or comparative utility. Reliability, however, is fundamental, because a test with no reliability cannot have validity. A test such as the ELISA must be reasonably reliable, and it must be valid in different senses, depending on its intended use (diagnosis, prediction, or comparison). Predictive validity is one useful form of validity for the ELISA, for it would provide a reasonable level of prediction of the future development of clinical AIDS. The ELISA may also be used for its *concurrent* (comparative) validity, providing a reasonable level of detection of HIV when compared to other methods for detecting HIV, such as the polymerase chain reaction (PCR) now used to detect the DNA of HIV in the blood stream. If the true reliability (as opposed to popular "reliability") of the ELISA is limited, all forms of its validity would be limited by the limits of reliability: validity can be no greater than the square of the reliability. Thus a test with an 80 percent reliability could have a *maximum* predictive validity of 64 percent. True unreliability thus reduces all types of validity. Reliability does not assure validity, it only places a maximum ceiling on validity. The validity of the test has to do with the relationship of the test to the population, and the validity of the conceptualization underlying the test. If, for example, HIV were not the primary causative agent in clinical AIDS, the ELISA might have virtually no predictive validity in relation to the development of clinical AIDS, regardless of its reliability. At the 1992 Amsterdam International Conference on AIDS, I was informed by a UCSF immunologist that he believed that "the new ELISA introduced in April [1992] is substantially more reliable [in the technical sense of the word] than the old one."

3   Survivor Guilt and Related Family Matters

1   Christine M. Fahrenbach, "AIDS-Related Loss in Uninfected Gay Men: An Exploratory Study of the Psychological Consequences of Loss and Change," (Ph.D. dissertation, California School of Professional Psychology, 1992), p. 86.
2   Charles R. Tartaglia, "AIDS Anxiety Syndromes," in Dilley et al., *Face to Face,* p. 171.
3   Scott Walton, personal communication, 1989.
4   Michael Friedman, "Toward a Reconceptualization of Guilt," *Contemporary Psychoanalysis* 21: 520.
5   Thomas Moon, "Survivor Guilt and HIV-Negative Gay Men: A Review of the Literature" (preparatory paper for a Ph.D. dissertation, The Professional School for Psychology, 1992), p. 7.

6   Friedman, "Toward a Reconceptualization," p. 532.

7   A. H. Modell, "The Origin of Certain Forms of Pre-oedipal Guilt and the Implications for a Psychoanalytic Theory of Affects," *International Journal of Psychoanalysis* 52: 337–346, cited in Moon, "Survivor Guilt," pp. 7–11.

8   Geraldine K. Piorkowski, "Survivor Guilt in the University Setting," *Personnel and Guidance Journal* 61: 620–622, cited by Moon, "Survivor Guilt," p. 17.

9   Friedman, "Toward a Reconceptualization," cited in Moon, "Survivor Guilt," p. 12.

10   Michael Friedman, "Survivor Guilt in the Pathogenesis of Anorexia Nervosa," *Psychiatry* 48: 25–39.

11   Tim Teeter, personal communication, 1990.

12   The psychotherapeutic approach to men suffering with survivor guilt is straightforward, and, indeed, much "ordinary" psychotherapy is about survivor guilt in the broadest sense of the idea. All psychotherapists work with problems about separation from family, ambivalence about success, and relationship difficulties. Such issues routinely involve survivor guilt, even when working with those not living in an epidemic.

The defenses against experiencing guilt about *current* issues and the guilt itself must be clarified, and the patient's pain in response to the clarifications (*resistance*) must be interpreted too. In my experience, few psychotherapy patients have much conscious experience of guilt per se in connection with the AIDS epidemic, and the more severe the unconscious guilt, the more powerful the resistance to having it described clearly. Typically, those suffering most seriously from guilt about survival will deny guilt, coming to therapy with some combination of anxiety, hypochondriasis, depression, and social or sexual dysfunction—problems, typically, that they would like "removed" without exposing or touching any underlying issues. They may acknowledge some question about why they are among the survivors—the "Why not me?" question—and they will often be found to be engaging in unconsidered unprotected sex, substance abuse, or other self-destructive behaviors.

Such survivors often identify strongly with particular HIV-infected men, perhaps partners or best friends, or with positive men in general. Men with significant guilt about survival are often found working in AIDS services, and at "burnout" levels. The sublimation of feelings of guilt and depression into such socially sanctioned forms of "acting out" is a common—and not entirely unuseful—process among those living in the epidemic. Many will feel that their seronegative status has created a violation of allegiance to the gay community and threatens their identity as gay men. This is an experience of abandoning the gay community, just as one might experience abandonment of the family: separation, success, and happiness are intrinsically acts of abandonment. Though such unconscious beliefs span a wide spectrum, an unusual and extreme version is expressed by a female-to-male transsexual who told his psychotherapist that his transformation to a gay man would be complete only when he had contracted HIV.

When signs and symptoms like depression, anxiety, and social or sexual dysfunction have been clarified as aspects of survivor guilt about current events, the psychotherapy may then begin to interpret more completely the older feelings connected to them. This process will ultimately involve the recognition of connections between the current guilt and much more long-standing developmental issues and conflicts where they exist. As in all therapies, this connection making, when supported by real insight, is powerful and may reduce the grip and power of self-destructive feelings. "To a degree not generally recognized, psychopathologies are pathologies of loyalty" (Friedman, "Toward a Reconceptualization," p. 530). But when it is understood that guilt about surviving those who are lost to HIV is irrational and unrealistic and that it is compelling because it connects so powerfully to earlier feelings of guilt, the psychotherapy patient may then begin to feel that he has a right to have the best life he can—at any rate a decent one—and that trying to do so is not violence against, betrayal of, or abandonment of those less fortunate.

I am frequently reminded that individual psychotherapy is not a resource available to all, and this is true. But the kind of process I am describing to deal with this most troubling and destructive phenomenon in gay communities is approachable in other ways. In my experience, groups can be useful in addressing these issues, and they have as an additional advantage the possibility of offering the individual a new community or "family" of allegiance, and one that shares some important issues. Groups are discussed in some detail in the epilogue.

In contrast, public educational programs directed at gay communities cannot engage in such analysis. But they can assist in important ways that they are not now, by and large, doing. The recognition that such complex feelings exist, that they affect people's behaviors, including sexual behaviors, and that they are an acceptable and normal response to the epidemic would be an immense contribution to a social climate that permitted men to acknowledge and explore the issues. Public education is discussed further in chapters 7 and 8 and in the epilogue, but the point should be made here that most public education, particularly in the U.S., now simply colludes with the individual's denial of complex and conflicting feelings about AIDS, sex, and survival. The social climate generated by this education encourages denial and precludes an exploration of the problems. It creates precisely the kind of "conspiracy of silence" with which so many gay men have grown up in their families and in a society that has tried for centuries to ignore the existence of homosexuality itself.

13   Ed Wolf, personal communication, 1990.

4   Life in the Shadow: Loss and Mourning

1   Keith Waldrop, *Potential Random* (Providence, R.I.: Paradigm Press, 1992), p. 26.
2   Gizzi, *Letters,* p. 11.
3   Erik Erikson, *Identity and the Life Cycle* (New York: W. W. Norton, 1980), pp. 57–67.
4   Ibid., pp. 62–63.
5   Ibid., p. 61.
6   Gizzi, *Letters,* p. 16.
7   Erikson, himself, would be the first to acknowledge that the accomplishment of basic trust in infancy is no assurance that the adult will not experience depression and a sense of loss as a result of conflict or regression in response to trauma later in life, and that the "accomplishment" of a developmental task is by no means absolute or permanent. Early developmental accomplishments, however, establish a foundation

that is likely to provide the adult with more psychological resilience in the face of trauma.

8   Waldrop, *Ruins,* p. 38.

9   Gizzi, *Letters,* p. 22.

10 Fahrenbach, "AIDS-Related Loss," p. 254.

11 Keith Waldrop, *A Windmill Near Calvary* (Ann Arbor: University of Michigan Press, 1968), p. 5.

12 Sigmund Freud, "Mourning and Melancholia," in *The Standard Edition of the Complete Psychological Works of Sigmund Freud* (London: Hogarth Press, 1953–1966).

13 As with all such psychological description, it should be clear that the "stages" I am describing are not to be understood too rigidly. The psychological transitions between stages are often characterized by a gradualness and a waxing and waning of "progress" that make the transitions sustained experiences, rather than discrete events. The overall process of grieving is also characterized by moments of precocity and of regression. In total review, however, the stages of the grieving process, or inhibitions to the process, are more or less recognizable in virtually all who have suffered losses.

14 The experiences of multiple losses and of survivor guilt both also contribute to denial and repression. Both multiple losses and survivor guilt make the experience of an individual death more ominous and more painful, and both denial and repression may be brought to bear on the experience. In addition, multiple losses and survivor guilt interact with the process of mourning in specific ways that are the subject of the remainder of this chapter.

15 Waldrop, *Windmill,* p. 5.

16 Keith Waldrop, *The Quest For Mount Misery and Other Studies* (Isla Vista, Calif.: Turkey Press, 1983), p. 6.

17 With reference to the model of grief outlined in chapter 4, the first critical point in the grieving process is the transition between what I called an acute state of powerful, perhaps overwhelming, feelings and the initiation of the grieving process per se. This transition, which is generally preceded by an unconscious assimilation of the reality of loss, places certain requirements on the individual's internal life. He must have the *ego strength* (strength and organization of personality, and a subjective sense of relative wholeness) to tolerate conscious acknowledgment of the loss, and to undertake the process of grieving. Grieving requires some capacity to begin emotional separation (*decathexis*) from the dead person, to be alone, and to tolerate sadness and feelings of depression. Most importantly, grieving requires the capacity to experience loss, for the experience of loss both instigates grieving and occurs as a result of engagement in the grieving process (as a result of decathexis itself). Grieving allows the experience of loss to surface to consciousness more or less as the individual can tolerate the experience and begin to assimilate a new sense of himself and the world.

The ego strength necessary for grieving may not be available to many living in the AIDS epidemic because of the amount of accumulated loss—and anticipated loss. The individual may remain in an acute, post-death phase of numbness or manic defense—which I have likened to physical shock—in order to remain intact and functional. We are now finding that men living in the epidemic may remain in these psychological conditions for many years.

For those who, because of constitution or relatively fortunate circumstances, are able to make a foray into grieving, an accumulation of losses over time may create a grieving process of immense, perhaps unmanageable complexity. The fundamental grieving processes of decathexis and recathexis are in many senses global, and it is improbable that an individual might successfully experience initial decathexis about a more recent loss, while recathecting in connection with an older one. If still newer losses are repeatedly thrown into this delicate and complex process, it is likely that a retreat to the acute, pre-grief stage of experience would finally result. Furthermore, the later stages of grieving require more than the capacity to experience loss, depression, and being alone. A capacity for recathexis to new people is needed. The introduction of new losses during this recathexis can only inhibit or reverse the process. The ego strengths necessary for grieving, and the special requirements of recathexis—a capacity for vulnerability and trust—cannot be sustained by a man constantly reshocked with new losses. Finally, one cannot be in acute shock about a new loss while still grieving older ones. Shock is a global condition that eclipses the kinds of fragile psychological operations necessary for grieving.

18 I am indebted to Charles Dithrich for his insight on this issue, conveyed to me in a personal communication, 1992.

19 Fahrenbach, "AIDS-Related Loss," p. 192.

20 Waldrop, *Quest,* p. 8.

21 In talking with a colleague about this session, I wondered how he might have handled the "self-disclosure."

He said, "Oh, I would have told him eventually, but I think I might have spent two or three weeks working through some of the issues connected to his question."

"But this is a man who has been traumatized by living with an incredible amount of loss and death," I responded. "Could I send him home for three days wondering if his therapist has HIV too?"

"No, I see your point. Given his circumstances, it might be just a sadistic exploitation of the [transference] relationship. But I'm also thinking that the unknown of HIV status is a tension that must pervade the treatment, because that's what gay men are living with in the world. You have to maintain the neutrality that allows the patient to create what he needs to create."

I thought for several moments about this comment, then said, "I see your point, and, of course, I agree with it generally. I haven't thought about the HIV issue in quite that way. But I still think it's too destructive. Sometimes it's more destructive to the therapy to not reveal information than to reveal it— and it seems to me that would usually be the case here. In any case, all I said to Jerry was, 'I *believe* I'm HIV-negative.' That leaves some room for the ambiguity you're talking about, and it expresses my belief that these things are not completely clear-cut, that the ELISA is not a completely reliable instrument. But it is not so frightening that he might withdraw from the work."

As a final note, I would like to say that we, as therapists—which is to say as human beings—living in the AIDS epidemic, have suffered a tremendous amount of loss, and feelings about this are inevitably brought to our work with gay men, especially those with HIV. I think we must be very careful in examining how our feelings about loss affect our therapy patients. I have already spoken of the guilty therapist's entanglement by virtue of trying to repair parents or siblings in the person of the patient. In contrast, a "professional" expression of anticipatory grief is altogether too easy in a subtle decathexis from patients who are ill or dying. Such decathexis may be dismissed or rationalized as a proper maintenance of boundaries, but the differences should be apparent to any psychotherapist examining his own feelings. Neither such withdrawal, nor an entanglement in the issues and conflicts of the patient, can well serve a therapy.

22   Ron Henderson, personal communication, 1991.

5   Being Outsiders: The "HIV-Negative" Identity

1   Waldrop, *Potential Random*, p. 24.

2   It was Ed Wolf (personal communication, 1994) who pointed out to me the significance of the term "HIV-negative": "Why do we refer to men without HIV as HIV-negative? Don't we really mean that they're just *uninfected?* But of course, this implies that positive men are *infected,* and this is offensive to many of them."

3   Woody Castrodale, personal communication, 1992.

4   Linda Zaretsky, personal communication, 1990. Zaretsky discussed not only the feelings of defectiveness and otherness that are experienced about people with chronic illness, but also the feelings of vulnerability, through identification, that they arouse in others.

5   Susan Sontag, *AIDS as Metaphor* (New York: Farrar, Straus and Giroux, 1988).

6   Darrell Yates Rist, "The Deadly Costs of an Obsession," *The Nation,* Vol. 248, 13 February 1989.

7   Robert Ferro, *Second Son* (New York: New American Library, 1988), p. 107.

8   Albert Innaurato, "Solidarity," in George Stambolian, ed., *Men on Men 2* (New York: New American Library, 1988), pp. 116–117.

9   Woody Castrodale, personal communication, 1992.

10   Ben Schatz, personal communication, 1992.

6   Being Alone

1   American Psychiatric Association, *DSM-III-R,* pp. 335–358. The term *personality disorder,* in its implication of a disease process, is the kind of misrepresentation that psychology often makes in imitation of a medical model. Nevertheless, the term often usefully indicates familiar constellations of character traits that help clarify the psychological development and personality organization of an individual.

2   The *schizoid trend*—or character development, in more serious instances—that may result from these developmental pressures (as well as from issues not pertinent to the discussion here) are familiar in gay communities. Most importantly, there is a denial of internal life (mental and emotional experience), resulting in a restricted range of

emotional experience and expression, including an incapacity for empathy, and for guilt, which relies on empathy for others. Such an individual lacks a capacity for ambivalence, especially ambivalence of feelings, and there is a *splitting* (dissociation) both within the self and in relation to others. For example, homosexual feelings may be "split off" from other aspects of self, so that a man may love his overtly homophobic parents, feel homosexual, and deny that there is conflict in his relations with his parents. Likewise, the homophobic aspects of the parents may be split off from the warm, familial couple for whom the man buys an anniversary gift. Through such splitting, contradictory feelings need not be experienced as conflict because they are not experienced as existing in the same person.

Splitting also fosters *part-object relationships,* relationships that do not account for the other as a whole human being. (Other people, unfortunately, are *objects* in psychological parlance.) One may relate, for example, to another person as only a sexual object, with no sense of his total life, his internal experience, or his needs and feelings as a person. In engaging in such part-object relationships, one's sexuality is isolated from one's other thoughts and feelings, and from those of the sexual partner. The isolation allows the forbidden and conflicted activity to be kept separate from one's "normal" life, and one is spared the experience in normal daily activity of feeling conflict and pain about being homosexual. Other features of a schizoid trend or personality are the use of *projective* and *obsessive-compulsive* defenses. Projective defenses attribute to and "project into" others the things that one would like to get rid of in one's self. Obsessive-compulsive defenses, discussed in chapter 7, rely on obsessive mental processes or compulsive behaviors to bind internal anxiety, often arising out of unconscious conflict.

3 Ed Wolf, personal communication, 1990.
4 Waldrop, *Windmill,* p. 46.
5 Walt Odets, "The Secret Epidemic: The Impact of AIDS on Uninfected Men," *Out/ Look,* Fall 1991, pp. 45–49.
6 *Out/Look,* Winter 1991, p. 6.
7 Whether the psychological difficulties of the two men presented here could or should have been explored and clarified had there been no epidemic is not the point. The opportunity would have existed, and their own painful feelings about their lives may well have motivated them to do so. The opportunity in the context of the epidemic is much narrower, because the psychological conflicts are obscured and supported by the existence of so much plausible reality. When the problem is less one of fixation, as it seems to be in these two instances, but more one of regression, it is even clearer that the epidemic is not only erecting serious impediments to the psychological growth of gay men, but is in many cases reversing it.

The epidemic is such an unfamiliar and extreme situation that the psychotherapist often comes up against difficult judgments in working with gay men about how to interpret feelings and behaviors. I will concentrate on the issue of anxiety because it is the focus of these examples, but the question I am raising is pertinent to most feelings explored in psychotherapy. In the case of anxiety, the question is how much is realistically focused on HIV transmission (which is a real-world issue of importance) and how much is a displacement of anxiety from other psychological conflict.

The answer—so often the case—is that useful interpretation may need to acknowledge both issues. The patient's experience of realistic anxiety does not preclude the anxiety having other *meanings*.

In the case at hand it became clear during therapy that Michael's anxiety about HIV was realistic, but that the anxiety also included the meaning that Michael feared being touched by another gay man because he feared his own homosexuality and physical contact would confirm it. This was often experienced by Michael as a (projected self-) disgust of other gay men and disgust at being touched by them or touching them. He came to see that such disgust was not about HIV, but had other meanings. HIV not only brought up fears for Michael about the realistic possibility of being infected with a dangerous virus, it also represented disgust of, and fears about, being homosexual, and fears that HIV would be the retribution he received if he and another gay man were intimate, physically or emotionally. In Michael's unconscious meanings, he would become contaminated and defective through homosexual contact.

Another way of stating the problem would be to say that *resistances* to interpretations also often have validity in a realistic sense. The realistic concern must always be acknowledged before interpretation of the meanings, or the resistance becomes entrenched in fact and logic: "Yes, contracting HIV is certainly a real concern, but I wonder what *other* meanings touching might *also* have." Having done that, the question then becomes one of how one refocuses on the psychological meanings. Staying with the examples at hand, it is my experience that men who exhibit unusually strong anxiety about HIV transmission also invariably include among their realistic arguments concerns that are patently unrealistic. Their *feelings* do not distinguish between the realistic and the unrealistic. Like Michael, who initially felt "disgust" for HIV, another of my psychotherapy patients asserted that he did not kiss because of the fear of HIV transmission. But pursuit of this "realistic" concern revealed that he really did not have much belief in that possibility, and this allowed the suggestion that perhaps he was also experiencing some anxiety about something other than HIV transmission. Such inconsistencies between a patient's feelings and his thoughts (or between conflicting feelings or conflicting thoughts) are often the opening for psychological interpretation.

Living in the age of AIDS, we are dealing, as I have often acknowledged, with an immensely complex phenomenon. What is realistic and what is not often are not clear. But the clinician working with gay men must have as much sound knowledge as possible about AIDS in order to open avenues of interpretation that otherwise remain obscured by realistic argument. This knowledge must include not only known facts about HIV transmission, but also information about the clinical progression of AIDS, treatment possibilities and side effects (including psychoactive properties of primary AIDS treatments), and the implications of the numerous and complex medical situations in which people with AIDS, and the partners of people with AIDS, find themselves. This is a substantial responsibility for the clinician, and is one especially difficult for the average heterosexual clinician, for whom AIDS may not be a part of nonprofessional life.

The consequences of lacking such knowledge are apparent in a conversation I had with Norah, a heterosexual psychotherapist to whom I had referred a client, Les, in 1986. He was a gay man in his early thirties, was uninfected, just out of a four-year relationship, and starting to date again. Though Norah had little more than minimal experience with gay men, I knew her to be extremely competent, as well as familiar with gay issues from a psychological viewpoint. After seeing Les for almost a year, Norah called me to consult. She was concerned about Les and about the progress of the therapy, and reported that he was becoming more and more isolated and was increasingly suffering from both impotence and generalized anxiety. She was having great difficulty making sense of these developments, and we got together for lunch to discuss her concern.

"What are his feelings about AIDS?" I asked her.

"Well, he's HIV-negative and we haven't really talked much more about it than that. He hasn't really brought it up."

I could already sense her discomfort with the conversation. "But this man was in a relationship when the epidemic began," I said. "Now he's out dating, and I'm sure he's got a lot of complex feelings about AIDS—about the whole thing."

"You know, Les hasn't brought up the issue of AIDS *once,* and I'm just suddenly realizing that I have been colluding with him in this big silence about something that must be very important to what's going on. I'm stunned to realize this all of a sudden."

"Yes, I'm sure," I commented. "But I'm not sure it's the kind of thing you could have known about."

"I once asked him if he was having safe sex, and he said yes. I guess I just kind of left it at that. He's HIV-negative, he knows about safe sex: end of problem."

"That's really the beginning of the problem," I said. "For example, what kind of sex does he have, or does he want to have? *How* safe does he think it is, and how safe, as nearly as we know, *is* it?"

"*How* safe?" asked Norah.

In further conversation it became clear that Norah was unfamiliar with the complexity of safer sex, and the conflicted feelings that might surround it. Well informed by the general media, she held the popular view of "safe" sex as unequivocally safe, but also expressed alarm at my suggestion that Les was in all likelihood having sex with positive men or men of unknown antibody status. She also lacked the specific knowledge that might allow her to begin to tease the psychological issues out of the realistic ones. Such natural limitations may make it difficult for any but the most informed in the heterosexual psychotherapeutic community to now work with gay men, regardless of their grasp of the developmental and psychosocial issues generally affecting gay men. I have not made a referral of a gay man, regardless of HIV status, to a heterosexual therapist since my conversation with Norah.

8   Waldrop, *Windmill,* p. 43.

9   I do think that the new asceticism is now, in the early nineties, losing some of its hold on some segments of the gay community. Queer Nation, for example, is an organization devoted to "kiss-ins," an important statement about human life and one's right to be more than economically productive. The very use of the term *queer*

is unabashedly unapologetic for anything, including a natural, human sensuality and sexuality.

10   Although it is now common parlance, especially within twelve-step programs, to refer to "sexually addicted" people, sex cannot, properly speaking, be an addiction. Addictions, by definition, entail the use of substances (or, perhaps, habitual behaviors such as regular aerobic exercise) that produce tolerance (requiring progressively increasing amounts for a given subjective and physiological effect), create cellular changes in the body in accommodation of the substance (or behavior), and produce physiological (and often psychological) signs and symptoms when the substance is withdrawn (or behavior discontinued). Sex can, however, be engaged in *compulsively,* but this is a psychological process, not a physiological one. Compulsions are generally thought to help contain anxiety that arises when unconscious conflict threatens to become conscious. They are often a response to depression, loneliness, and other dysphoric feelings. These insights, and others, more usefully describe sexual compulsivity.

The importance of making a distinction between addictive and compulsive processes is that the labeling of something as an addiction too often forecloses on the effort to understand its meanings. An addiction is presumably something that one *has,* and the addiction per se has no more meaning than a virus cold. In contrast, a compulsion is something one *does,* and simply curtailing a compulsive behavior with behavioral solutions is likely to provide no insight into the meaning or psychological purposes of the behavior. Compulsive behaviors generally have developmental roots and psychological meaning.

The ideas that alcoholism is a disease and homosexuality a physiological (genetic, prenatal, or constitutional) condition are related to the idea of addictive behaviors. All three are efforts to relieve the individual of responsibility for his feelings and behaviors. But the need to relieve one of responsibility is based in the tacit equation of responsibility and blame, and blame is altogether something other than responsibility per se. Blame is about others' disapproval, and one's own shame. It is much more important to dissipate the destructive feelings of blame and shame, not by declaring certain behaviors the result of addiction, disease, or physiology, but by recognizing that people have complex feelings and often do not understand them or their expressions. Such an approach dissipates stigma by clarifying the meaning of our lives, including our self-destructive behaviors, rather than by declaring certain behaviors "out of our control." Control is an issue only when we are afraid of our feelings and would deny them.

Finally, it should be clarified that some behaviors, such as cigarette smoking, may entail both addiction and compulsion. In such a case, both the addictive process and the psychological one must be addressed. The compulsive use of a potentially addictive substance may hasten addiction, because the use will be frequent and repeated. Likewise, an addictive substance may come to be used compulsively in response to craving, which arises in an effort to maintain the physiological accommodations made by the organism to the substance.

7   *Being Together: The Relations of Positives and Negatives*

1   Ron Henderson, personal communication, 1991.

2   Chuck Frutchey, personal communication, 1992.

3   Woody Castrodale, personal communication, 1992.

4   I have written in much more detail on the subject of primary prevention, its neglect, and how it might be restored in "Why We Stopped Doing Primary Prevention for Gay Men in 1985," *AIDS & Public Policy Journal* 10 (1) (1995).

5   *Asians and AIDS: What's the Connection,* the Asian AIDS Project, San Francisco, 1988.

6   Tim Teeter, personal communication, 1989.

7   Gizzi, *Letters,* p. 8.

8   Woody Castrodale, personal communication, 1992.

9   The term *obsessive* refers to mental processes, and *compulsive* to behaviors. Both "activities" entail repetition and, often, a subjective sense of the obsession or compulsion being involuntary and unsatisfying. When part of a coherently developed character style, perfectionism, rigidity, indecisiveness, a restricted expression of feelings, and lack of generosity are often other elements.

10 Some description of this psychological operation is provided in chapter 5, but there are aspects of it specific to uninfected men avoiding positive men that are discussed here. The two major psychological objectives of such projection are in some sense the converse of each other. One allows the defended individual to avoid HIV and the other to avoid his conflicts about homosexuality, and both may operate simultaneously.

In the first case, the individual may have substantial fears about HIV (about the loss of others or about contracting HIV himself, for example), or he may have difficulty with preexisting anxiety that is displaced onto HIV. He may simultaneously consider the exclusion or rejection of those with HIV unacceptable for ethical reasons or by virtue of guilt, possibly including survivor guilt. The confusion of his internal homophobia with HIV and the projection of that hatred onto others can provide the psychological energy necessary to overcome the ethical or guilt-induced inhibitions. Such an individual may withdraw only from those he believes to be positive and may not consciously recognize (or may actively deny) the strength or consistency of his avoidance. Or he may more consciously withdraw from the gay community as a whole, attributing the withdrawal to a disillusionment with gay life or the gay community in general. This individual may even be consciously homophobic, but the underlying avoidance of HIV will remain unconscious, for it is precisely the purpose of the psychological operation to deny negative feelings about those with HIV.

In the converse case, there is no inhibition about avoiding people with HIV, but feelings about homosexuality and AIDS are still confused. Thus it is the feelings about sexuality that remain unconscious and that are protected by the more conscious feelings about HIV. The avoidance of those with HIV is surprisingly well accepted in many smaller gay communities (especially those with lower rates of infections than those of larger, urban communities), whether this acceptance is easily acknowledged or not. While we do not see it commonly in larger urban gay centers, in smaller gay communities, I know numerous gay men, including psychotherapists and physicians, who knowledgeably have no HIV-positive patients or social contacts. While in these communities the exclusion of positive men may be commonplace and acceptable, avoidance based on homosexuality alone would not be viewed with tacit acceptance. In these communities, the HIV-positive population provides a scapegoat, a designated segment of a self-despising community that absorbs the self-loathing and anger that others are unable to resolve within themselves.

11   Waldrop, *Windmill,* p. 14.
12   Waldrop, *Potential Random,* p. 3.
13   Waldrop, *Windmill,* p. 4.

8   *Being Sexual: The Politics and Humanity of Gay Sex in the Epidemic*

1   Woody Castrodale, personal communication, 1992.
2   The San Francisco AIDS Foundation, *Impetus,* February 1991, p. 3. The history of the resistance to publicly acknowledging unprotected sex in the gay community is a subject in itself. In an article titled "Risky Business" (*The Village Voice,* June 26, 1990, pp. 35–38), Robin Hardy traces the public revelations about unsafe sex back to a UCSF School of Medicine study in 1988 by Dr. Maria Ekstrand, in which 25 percent of responders (out of a total of 686 gay men) reported unprotected anal intercourse within the past twelve months. Hardy also cites an Associated Press story from 1989 that reported a 400 percent increase in anal gonorrhea in Seattle. While such information has been available for a long time, it is only recently that the gay community has begun to acknowledge it and attempted to respond to the problem. Hardy points out, importantly, that the term *recidivism,* widely used initially to indicate a return to unsafe sex, is one borrowed from criminology.

Interestingly, two days after the publication of Hardy's piece (28 June 1990), the *San Francisco Sentinel,* one of San Francisco's three popular gay papers, published a page 5 story titled "Study: Young Gays Returning to Unsafe Sex," by Charles Linebarger. This piece is much more limited in scope than Hardy's and, in contradiction to widely available statistics indicating that unsafe sex is practiced throughout the gay community, concludes with a quotation from Dr. George Rutherford, a San Francisco epidemiologist: "The younger population of gay men and the older population may not be as integrated as we had thought. And it seems this younger group has not been reached by the public health messages that have changed the behavior of older gays."

As late as 1994, an anonymous educator at San Francisco's STOP AIDS Project wrote that, among other things, gay men find it difficult

> to make reasoned choices about what kind of sex we have [because of] the obstinate insistence of some mental health experts, policymakers and even some AIDS prevention workers who are to ignore data [sic] and inspire hopelessness. . . . Let's stop denying men hope by citing the erroneous statistic that more than half of young gay men will seroconvert or die [presumably from Hoover et al., "Estimating the 1978–1990 and Future Spread of Human Immunodeficiency Virus Type 1 in Subgroups of Homosexual Men" *American Journal of*

Epidemiology 134 (10): 1190–1199 (1991), from the NIH Multicenter AIDS Co-hort Study, which forecast that the majority of uninfected, 20-year-old gay men would seroconvert in their lifetimes], or deriding all AIDS prevention as a fail-ure and nothing more than a bunch of "slick pamphlets." Instead, let's respect each other's expertise . . . (*San Francisco Sentinel,* 18 August 1994, p. 17)

The same STOP AIDS educator also cites Al Kielwasser of GLAAD, who insisted after a television broadcast stating that one-third of gay men report unprotected anal sex [an indisputable, widely confirmed figure] that AIDS educators had "made up the statistics." Furthermore, the educator reported, Kielwasser went on to declare that AIDS educators had endangered the gay community by citing these statistics. The educator concludes: "How will you decide [about what kind of sex you have]? It's your choice. And if you want to find out how other guys are making their choices, and help us live up to our name, call STOP AIDS." These assertions are characteristic of the kind of education that insists that the epidemic can be "stopped" with com-monsense, simple decisions, and a denial of truths. As the real human complexity of the epidemic has unfolded, they have, unfortunately, become ever more strident and entrenched.

3 Jeffrey Kelley et al., "Acquired Immunodeficiency Syndrome/Human Immunodefi-ciency Virus Risk Behavior Among Gay Men in Small Cities," *Archives of Internal Medicine 152:* 2293–2297 (1992); Dilley et al., *Face to Face,* also contains numerous citations of 30–35 percent of gay men self-reporting unprotected anal sex.

4 I have found the materials from the Canadian Government, AIDS Vancouver, AIDS Committee of Toronto, and the Victorian AIDS Council, of Victoria, Australia (VAC), to be much more psychological in their approach than most U.S.-produced ma-terial. The Canadian and Australian materials generally acknowledge the complexity of human feelings and motivations, and take them into account, and also seem to acknowledge the relationship of homophobia to HIV transmission. For example, in contrast to American efforts that simply discourage alcohol consumption and sex in combination, VAC educational materials recognize that people often *will* use substances while having sex. They caution about the psychoactive effects, and rec-ommend a level of use that does not seriously impair judgment or cognition. In addition, they seem to me much more unabashedly erotic than most American ma-terials of the first decade of the epidemic, and are thus more engaging and convincing in their messages. On the subject of homophobia, a Victorian AIDS Council poster campaign stands out: A young man, embracing his mother says, "When I first told her I was gay, she wanted to know what she did wrong. Now she wants to take all the credit." VAC has done a number of similar campaigns addressing the self-esteem of young gay men. The AIDS Committee of Toronto produced a brochure (*can you relate? safer sex in gay relationships, think about it, talk about it,* 1994) discussing the negotiation of unprotected sex within gay relationships, a first and extremely important step in acknowledging the realities of a lifelong epidemic by trying to help educate men in making decisions that they are already making on their own—but without the benefit of education that would deny or prohibit the possibility of ordinary sex for a lifetime. It says:

We've both tested HIV-negative. If you are both *truly* HIV−, and you both *never* do anything to put yourselves at risk outside the relationship, you can stop using condoms. But it often isn't that simple . . .

The brochure discusses many issues pertinent to the decision to have ordinary sex within a relationship, including how a relationship is defined, the idea that love protects one from HIV, how to test definitively for HIV, and the ways that communication facilitates a relationship and reduces HIV transmission: "If you don't think you, as a couple, are willing and able to deal with the many issues that are involved, then play it safe by always using a laytex condom." Unfortunately, many educators dismiss such an approach because they use the (often dangerous) results of men making decisions about unprotected sex *without the benefit of education* to predict the results were educators to "condone" unprotected sex and help men develop judgment about when it is and is not prudent.

I have also become aware of one American educational effort that seems unusual and praiseworthy. A full-page advertisement from AIDS Project Los Angeles (*The Bay Area Reporter,* 25 June 1992, p. 27) asks in a headline, "Why Not Me?" and in the body of the ad states:

> How many of my friends have died? I don't even know anymore. . . . And when I tested negative, I felt like I had betrayed my friends, like I was better or smarter than them. Maybe that's why I didn't "play safely" that night—that way the test wouldn't mean anything.

> So what am I trying to prove? That I belong? That it's got to happen some day, so why fight it? It's too much to deal with. And nobody I know even wants to talk about it.

The psychological thinking that informs this approach is an immense improvement over the merely informational educational efforts that have dominated in the United States. Unfortunately, *most* of the work of the major prevention agencies is still distilled into the simplistic idea that survival of the epidemic is a simple, commonsense problem best summed up with the prescription, "a condom every time." I hope that more psychologically informed approaches will become an increasingly larger part of the work of these agencies.

5   Gay Men's Health Crisis, *The Basics* (New York: G.M.H.C., 1991).

6   This subject was discussed in an oral presentation at the 1988 International Conference on AIDS (A. Prieur, A. Andersen, A. H. Frantzen, C. Hanssen, C. Hoigard, and A. Valberg, *Gay Men: Reasons for Continued Practice of Unsafe Sex,* Montreal), though it has received little attention from AIDS educators in the United States. I extend my appreciation to Catherine Maier formerly of the San Francisco AIDS Foundation for calling this piece to my attention.

7   Robin Hardy, "Risky Business," p. 36. Hardy is citing the 1988 research of Dr. Maria Ekstrand, researcher with the Department of Epidemiology and Biostatistics at the UCSF School of Medicine.

8   Dr. Ron Gold of Deakin University, Melbourne, a respected AIDS researcher who has conducted extremely well-conceived and well-constructed studies with the gay male population in Australia, reported in a personal communication (1992) that approximately 25 percent of unprotected anal intercourse occurs "with completely anonymous partners." This figure held virtually constant in his three separate studies,

which included older gay men in Melbourne and Sydney and younger gay men in Melbourne (25.6 percent, 26.7 percent, and 23.7 percent, respectively). To what extent these figures are extrapolatable to U.S. gays is not clear, but I cannot see why they should not be.

Dr. Gold also reported:

> As regards Chapter 8 [of this manuscript] a lot of the reasons for unsafe sex that you highlight also came out in my studies, but only in very small percentages of the samples. There may be differences here because you are working with clinical samples, while the great majority of the men in my studies are not in therapy (though how representative of all Australian gay men my samples really are is of course impossible to know). Further, the deep traumas you found as a result of men having almost their whole friendship networks wiped out, are probably more common in cities (San Francisco being the prime example) where it has been possible to construct an almost totally gay personal environment. In a city like Melbourne . . . gays probably have, out of necessity, much closer links to the heterosexual community than they do in San Francisco, and therefore, possibly more heterosexual friends. The impact of the epidemic has thus probably been less devastating in Melbourne.

Dr. Gold's observations are interesting and important. With regard to the difference in our samples, a "clinical" population is certainly more likely to *self-report* psychological motivations for behaviors. Contrary to the most common intuitive explanation—that this group demonstrates more psychopathology—men in psychotherapy are more likely to provide psychological explanations for their own behavior because they are a group that thinks more psychologically than the population as a whole. People who seek psychotherapy often do so precisely because they are more psychologically conscious than the average person, and that consciousness is only enhanced by good psychotherapy. As a psychotherapy patient stated it, "I used to think I was depressed because it was raining, but I know that you're thinking of something more psychological than that." On the whole, my psychotherapy population probably demonstrates *less* psychopathology than I perceive and personally experience in the San Francisco gay community in general, and the ability and willingness of psychotherapy patients to express themselves psychologically is one of the important reasons for that. People are not without psychological conflict or distress simply because they are unable to make it conscious or articulate it; and it is not reasonable to assume that men who seek psychotherapy for personal and developmental reasons are in some intrinsic way more pathological. For those men who are in crisis—for example, with overwhelming losses leading to clinical depression—Dr. Gold's comments seem more apt. But such men tend to use crisis services and to drop out of treatment when the crisis becomes more manageable through short-term approaches. I have few such psychotherapy patients in my practice, and when I do, they tend to drop out early in the treatment. Thus little insight is accomplished, and most of the material I have presented in this work comes from longer-term patients.

Dr. Gold's second point, about the relationship of the gay community to the community at large, is important. In locales where the gay community is more integrated into the heterosexual community, losses within the gay community seem less massive, and the identification of the gay man is less centrally rooted in the gay community that is suffering the losses. In areas where the gay community, because of mainstream values, is well integrated into society as a whole, one often finds gay men who have little specific identification with AIDS. Amsterdam, because of social values accepting of gays, is a city where AIDS is rarely described as a "gay issue," although a vast majority of people with AIDS *are* gay. Though much concern is directed to those with AIDS, the percentage of the *total* population affected (as in the U.S. and Western Europe generally) is relatively low, and thus the gay man often feels no special personal loss at an AIDS death of someone unknown to him. His identification is much more with the population as a whole rather than with a "community" specifically and severely afflicted. I was told by a psychologist in Amsterdam, "Here we don't have these troubling conflicts between the gay identity and an 'AIDS identity,' mostly because we don't really have a gay community. Here, being gay is not much of a thing."

In a later personal correspondence of 23 December 1992, Dr. Gold reported somewhat different figures concerning unprotected anal intercourse among Australian gay men:

> I've just spent a week in Sydney trying to recruit gay men who have "slipped up" (by fucking without a condom in the last half year) into an intervention study I'm attempting. . . . I talked to about 300 guys in all. . . . As far as I can see, there are still a lot of slip-ups occurring: gay men seem to divide about evenly into (a) those who cannot believe that anyone could still be practicing unsafe sex and (b) those who believe that anyone who says he never practices unsafe sex is lying!

9 The best discussion of condoms that I have seen is *The Condom Educator's Guide,* a 38-page presentation available from FOG Press (c/o Men's Support Center, P.O. Box 30564, Oakland, CA 94604) for $10.00 plus postage, as of May 1992). Also available from FOG Press is *Captain Condom's Original Party Pack,* which includes a witty and informative 16-page condensation of the *Educator's Guide,* and a large, eclectic sample of condoms and compatible lubricants. At $4.00 as of this writing, the Party Pack's guided "voyage into the amazing world of condoms" is not only a good practical buy, it is an entertainment bargain.

10 Waldrop, *Windmill,* p. 11.

11 Waldrop, *Potential Random,* p. 27.

12 Waldrop, *Quest,* p. 8.

13 Hardy, "Risky Business," p. 37.

14 Rachel Schochet, personal communication, 1991.

15 Friedman, "Toward a Reconceptualization," p. 532.

16 Hoover et al., "Estimating the 1978–1990 and Future Spread of Human Immunodeficiency Virus Type 1 in Subgroups of Homosexual Men," *American Journal of Epidemiology 134* (10): 1190–1199 (1991).

17 William Hayes, "Boys," *Mother Jones,* July/August 1990, p. 69.

18 Hal Rubenstein, "Pedro Zamora's Real World," *POZ 1*(3): 41 (August/September 1994).

19 Ibid., p. 41.

20   Hayes, "Boys," p. 70.
21   AIDS Project Los Angeles, *EROS* 1(1): 5.

9   *Being Here: Other Kinds of Survival*

1   Waldrop, *Ruins,* p. 11.
2   Erikson, *Identity.*
3   In her review of the manuscript of this book, Eve Kosofsky Sedgwick made several interesting and useful observations that I have tried—despite my relatively enfeebled historical and political grasp—to acknowledge in the text. Her observations are important, and following is a portion of her comments.

It is not *at all* to diminish one's sense of the trauma of AIDS to acknowledge that the people for whom Erikson's Eight Stages represented *normal experience* have probably never been a majority of the human species. The claimed "normality" of this developmental path may mean various things (that access to these stages is *desirable,* say, even perhaps transhistorically desirable; or that it was, or was meant to become, common among people of European descent in the mid-20th century); but it doesn't suffice as a historical or contemporaneous backdrop for the present emergency. To achieve mature age has, in many non-war and non-Holocaust contexts, been relatively rare even for men (as it now is even in the U.S., for African-American men), and it was well into the present century that *a majority* of the women in the world died in childbirth, thus short-circuiting any supposed "life cycle." Perhaps similarly, it is exclusively for men (or postmenopausal women) that unprotected sex was ever undangerous in the many centuries before the Pill. (Even for men, until the advent of antibiotics, venereal disease created a context of danger for unprotected sex.)

Unless one is into "ranking oppression"—and isn't the appropriate thing to do with oppressions instead to expose and oppose the gravity of each of them?—these observations aren't about making the AIDS epidemic appear less devastatingly tragic or less appropriately an occasion for rage as well as reflection. Rather they're about why the points of relevance between AIDS and other mass experiences are so many and go so deep. If the meaning of AIDS in urban gay communities takes shape in a gestalt of what had been relative privilege—the *expectation* of good health and a long lifespan, say; the *expectation* of access to unprotected sex—the foil of those expectations doesn't diminish that meaning but in many ways enriches it.

In these comments, Eve elucidates the source of important and conflicted feelings that exist in much narrower focus in and between the various gay communities. Middle-class gay communities—or those men in gay communities with middle-class roots—are now lamenting the loss of *assurances* in and about life that many socially and economically disadvantaged gay communities—or men with other than middle-class roots—have *never* had, albeit for other reasons before the epidemic. This is a conflict that informs most of the public policy interactions of white gay men with gay men of color, and it is an important topic in its own right.

4   Lady Murasaki, *The Tale of Genji,* trans. Arthur Waley (New York: The Modern Library, 1960), p. 342.
5   Woody Castrodale, personal communication, 1992.
6   Ihara Saikaku, *Five Women Who Loved Love,* trans. Wm. Theodore De Bary (Rutland, Vt.: Charles E. Tuttle, 1956), p. 136.
7   Paul Monette, *Afterlife* (New York: Crown Publishers, 1990), p. 1. The actual quotation is: "If everyone hadn't died at the same time, none of this would have happened."
8   William James, *The Writings of William James,* ed. John J. McDermott (Chicago: University of Chicago Press, 1977), p. 651.
9   Woody Castrodale, personal communication, 1992.
10 Woody Castrodale, personal communication, 1992.
11 Wesleyan University, "A Death in the Family," *The Cardinal,* Winter 1991, p. 29.
12 The Honorable Rand Schrader in an address at the Shanti Project Los Angeles annual dinner, May 1992.

Epilogue

1   Waldrop, *Quest,* p. 13.
2   In 1989, shortly after the earthquake, a construction crane working on the roof of a downtown San Francisco skyscraper, tumbled onto the street below, killing several pedestrians and crushing cars.
3   Primo Levi, *The Drowned and the Saved,* trans. Raymond Rosenthal (New York: Vintage Books, 1989).
4   Woody Castrodale, personal communication, 1992.
5   Though there are many important pieces of writing unacknowledged here, among the works about the epidemic that I have found most moving are: David B. Feinberg, *Spontaneous Combustion* (New York: Viking, 1991); Robert Ferro, *Second Son* (New York: Crown, 1988); Andrew Holleran, *Nights on Aruba* (New York: William Morrow and Company, 1985) and "A Place of His Own: How to Remember Robert Ferro," *Christopher Street,* Issue 126; J. W. Money, *All the Girls I've Loved Before* (Boston: Alyson Publications, 1987); Paul Monette, *Borrowed Time* (New York: Avon Books, 1988); George Stambolian, "Resurrection," *The James White Review* 8: 3; and George Whitmore, *Someone Was Here: Profiles in the AIDS Epidemic* (New York: New American Library, 1988).

Index

Dr. Odets is a clinical psychologist in private practice in Berkeley, California. He is an editor and contributor for the series *AIDS Management: The Role of the Mental Health Community* (Hatherleigh Publishing, New York); author of two pieces for *AIDS & Public Policy Journal,* "AIDS Education and Harm Reduction for Gay Men: Psychological Approaches for the 21st Century" and "Why We Stopped Doing Primary Prevention for Gay Men in 1985"; and contributing author to *Therapists on the Front Line: Psychotherapy with Gay Men in the Age of AIDS* (American Psychiatric Press, Washington, D.C.). A member of the AIDS Task Force of the Gay and Lesbian Medical Association, he has spoken frequently on the psychosocial issues of HIV-negative men and AIDS prevention for gay men, including two international conferences on AIDS, conferences of the American Psychological Association, American Psychiatric Association, the National Gay and Lesbian Task Force, the National AIDS Update, and the National Gay and Lesbian Health Conference.

Library of Congress Cataloging-in-Publication Data
Odets, Walt.
In the shadow of the epidemic : being HIV-negative in the age of AIDS / Walt Odets.
p.   cm. — (Series Q)
Includes index.
ISBN 0-8223-1626-9   ISBN 0-8223-1638-2 (pbk.)
1. Gay men—Mental health.   2. AIDS (Disease)—Psychological aspects.   3. AIDS phobia.   I. Title.
II. Series.
RC451.4.G39034   1995
155.9'16'08664—dc20   95-1311 CIP